COMMERCIAL BAIL BONDING

COMMERCIAL BAIL BONDING

A Comparison of Common Law Alternatives

F. E. Devine

PRAEGER

New York
Westport, Connecticut
London

Library of Congress Cataloging-in-Publication Data

Devine, F. E.
Commercial bail bonding : a comparison of common law alternatives /
F. E. Devine
p. cm.
Includes bibliographical references and index.
ISBN 0-275-93732-1 (alk. paper)
1. Bail. 2. Common law. I. Title.
K5454.D48 1991
345'.056—dc20 91-8605
[342.556]

British Library Cataloguing in Publication Data is available.

Library of Congress Catalog Card Number: 91-8605
ISBN: 0-275-93732-1

First published in 1991

Praeger Publishers, One Madison Avenue, New York, NY 10010
An imprint of Greenwood Publishing Group, Inc.

Printed in the United States of America

The paper used in this book complies with the Permanent Paper Standard issued by the National Information Standards Organization (Z39.48-1984).

10 9 8 7 6 5 4 3 2 1

Contents

Preface

Demands of time and space have forced certain limits upon this study. Its scope is limited to pretrial bail law in the lower courts, since this corresponds to the typical bail situation in the United States. Many of the countries covered, however, place great emphasis upon bail granted by police or the use of summons, both of which avoid any court appearance by accuseds. The study's coverage ends January 1, 1989 for all countries, except for a few instances where cases were decided well before that date but were reported after it. Selection of countries for extensive discussion rested upon three criteria: (1) the usefulness of a given bail system for expanding knowledge about potential varieties of bail types; (2) the extent of the available case law developing that bail system; and (3) the recentness of the body of case law available. For all countries given major treatment, case law runs up to the deadline set. For lesser coverage, it normally comes up to at least 1985. (In three instances—Liberia, Tanzania, and Zambia—because of the particular interest of the bail system, countries were given limited treatment even though available material fell well short of this standard.) Few jurisdictions publish or even collect bail statistics. To provide some impression of bail in practice I have supplemented these with comments based on the bail results in the cases I have collected. Obviously, these are likely to be biased toward the more difficult cases. They are offered only to present a rough idea of practice in the absence of any better indications and certainly pretend to no statistical exactitude.

Numerous thanks are deserved, but few can be explicit here. I should like to thank the Fulbright Foundation for its Senior Scholar Award to study Australian bail, and the Australian Institute of Criminology and its people for their assistance in hosting my research.

Among the many libraries that have kindly extended the use of their facilities I should like particularly to thank the Institute for Advanced Legal Studies: University of London, the Australian National Library, and the Attorney General of Australia's Library for the repeated or extended access to their collections.

COMMERCIAL BAIL BONDING

1

Introduction to an International Perspective on Commercial Bail

The commercial bail system prevailing in most jurisdictions in the United States has long been criticized. A 1922 study edited by Roscoe Pound and Felix Frankfurter urged its elimination. It referred to "the disreputable professional bondsmen who make a business of exploiting the misfortunes of the poor" and charged that commercial provision of bail "tends to prostitute the administration of justice in the inferior courts." Where it could not be eliminated completely the study compared the need to control it to that for controlling "loan sharks."[1]

Two recent articles from the *New Orleans Times-Picayune* illustrate the reason for this tradition of criticism. The first of these recounts the complaints of commercial bail bondsmen that, because of jail overcrowding, judges have been releasing detainees who pose a low escape risk on their own recognizance or on that of someone personally connected to them. Thus, the bondsmen complain, these "bread and butter clients" are getting out of jail without having to pay the bondsmen, to the great detriment of their profits. The irony of the implication that the release system exists to enrich bondsmen rather than to secure appearance seems lost on all. To make matters worse in the bondsmen's view, continuing competition for the remaining clients forces them to consider writing bonds for higher-risk detainees, which poses a serious dilemma. Those "who don't want to take the risk of having to track down bail jumpers are seeing their profits dwindle." The unasked question is why should bondsmen profit if they are unwilling to secure the accused's appearance? The bondsmen's view of the system implied here is that it exists to provide them with low-risk profits from individuals sufficiently reliable that they could otherwise convince a judge that they are likely to appear. Thus, the system fails them to the extent that they are forced to choose between reduced profits or performing an actual service.[2]

The second article illustrates the risks if commercial bail providers do act to protect their profits. They hire bounty hunters, who are not subject to many of the restraints imposed on police, for a percentage of the bond. The article details the five-hour ordeal of a victim of mistaken identity who was "handcuffed, shackled, dragged into a car and physically and mentally abused." The six bounty hunters were charged with kidnapping. A follow-up article reported similar episodes.[3]

In a 1983 case, the U.S. Court of Appeals for the Fifth Circuit upheld the extradition to Canada on kidnapping charges of a commercial bondsman. Unlike the case of mistaken identity and abuse depicted in the newspaper, this individual functioned in a way that would have been lawful within the United States, but that was unlawful in Canada. The court's unavoidable conclusion was that a case for extradition for kidnapping was established. As the court noted in its reasoning, one salient difference between the two countries is that in Canada the practice of bonding for compensation is not permitted. The Fifth Circuit's understated comment that the "Canadian authorities took a very jaundiced view of his behavior" could be generalized as an expression of the view of the entire commercial bail system, not only in Canada, but throughout the common law world.[4]

This volume discusses the steps other common law bail systems have taken to prevent commercialism, and the legal arrangements instituted to establish systems of pretrial release which avoid it. The concern in these kindred systems to obstruct the development of commercial bail is a more telling reflection of the view taken of it than strident criticism would be. Those involved in the other systems care little what is done in jurisdictions in the United States so long as they are spared from doing the same. On occasion, however, proposals for reform in these countries have led to studies of options. On these occasions the role of American commercial bail bonding as a worldwide object lesson in what to avoid is articulated. At the same time that these jurisdictions provide a source of disinterested evaluation of the commercial system, since they eschew it so systematically, they also provide a veritable catalogue of alternatives that can be observed in operation.

The dilemma of pretrial release is an almost universal problem, at least for regimes which value the liberty of their citizens. On one hand, an accused who is released can avoid trial by flight, jeopardize the course of justice by tampering with witnesses and evidence, and commit other crimes. On the other hand, one detained pending trial is subjected to confinement very similar to that imposed as a punishment for crime without having been proven guilty of any crime. The civil, or Roman, law and the common law traditions, however, confront this with substantially different conceptions and legal frameworks. Such factors as early prosecutorial and even judicial involvement, a different approach to evidence acquired prior to trial, and the absence of some procedural protections necessary in adversary systems create a different context in which the dilemma is confronted in civil law jurisdictions as compared to common law ones. This tends to make the lessons of one common law jurisdiction more immediately pertinent to the others.

Existing common law bail systems share roots in the English bail system of the seventeenth and eighteenth centuries. James Wilson's *Lectures on Law*, influential in the United States in the formative period following the adoption of the Constitution, illustrates this. Wilson explicitly bases his treatment of bail law on English common law commentaries by Blackstone, Hawkins, and Coke.[5] Similarly, most other systems that have branched out from the original English bail system have kept a common core, however much it may have been modified over time. Examining this original bail system highlights the commonality that makes the developments and experiments in one branch of common law bail pertinent to the others.

THE COMMON LAW BAIL SYSTEMS

The English bail system of the eighteenth century developed from two related but distinct procedures: bail and mainprize. Both of these practices resulted in the accused being delivered from prison by a judge upon offering sufficient surety for appearance at trial. This was done by presenting third parties (called sureties) who would undertake financial liabilities (also called sureties) guaranteeing the accused's appearance. Bail and mainprize had become so similar that by 1635 Coke remarked that the description of one would as easily fit the other. Nevertheless, he identified three differences. First, while bail involved presenting sureties for appearance to answer only to the particular matter for which one was detained, mainprize involved presenting them for appearance to answer all matters and causes raised. Second, those serving as sureties in bails took custody of detainees. Consequently, they could imprison the individuals as jailors; correspondingly, they were answerable for any escapes. Mainprize implied no such custody and created neither the right to imprison nor the responsibility (beyond loss of the financial surety or pledge) for escape. Finally, whereas in bail the detainee was delivered by the court into the hands of the sureties, in mainprize no such delivery took place.[6]

In the first half of the eighteenth century Hawkins and Hale agree that the words *bail* and *mainprize* had much the same meaning and were freely interchanged. Hawkins, writing in 1721, considered the chief and perhaps the only difference between them to be the power of sureties in bail to detain or imprison the accused to assure appearance, while the sureties in mainprize lacked this recourse.[7] Nearer the end of the century Blackstone exhibited no remaining interest in mainprize. Highmore remarked that it had fallen into general disuse; he speculated that it required the simple honesty of ancient times and was displaced by bail due to the necessity for the greater powers given sureties under that alternative.[8]

The contrast between bail and mainprize emphasizes two aspects of the developing concept of bail. First is the importance of the individual sureties in both approaches, but especially in bail. They, even more than the accused, bear the responsibility for appearance in court. In fact, scant attention is paid to the role of the accused by these commentators. Second is the importance of the sureties' custodial responsibilities and powers in causing bail to replace mainprize.

Blackstone, writing in the last decade of America's colonial period, explains the workings of the bail system known to the founders of the United States. A suspected offender who was arrested was brought before a justice of the peace. After examining the circumstances, unless the suspicion was completely unfounded, the justice could either commit the accused to prison or grant bail. A justice of the peace who refused or delayed bail in the case of a suspect who was legally eligible for it commited an offense. Requiring excessive bail was also prohibited by the common law. However, Blackstone explained, what constituted excessive bail was left to the court upon considering the circumstances. Granting bail consisted of a delivery of the suspect to sureties upon their giving sufficient security for appearance. The individual bailed merely substituted, Blackstone remarked, their friendly custody for jail. Only parenthetically did Blackstone mention the defendant personally giving any security in a criminal bail.[9] This, plus the general absence of discussion of the personal security alternative in the earlier commentaries of Hawkins and Hale, indicates the lesser emphasis placed upon the accused's own security. In contrast, although Blackstone discusses the point only in the context of civil bail, the other commentators emphasize the need for at least two sureties who are able to meet the amount of security demanded in all criminal bails.[10]

The procedure for establishing a surety's adequacy is presented by Blackstone. When exception was taken to sureties, they were required to "perfect" or "justify" themselves to the court. This was done by swearing to be a householder and to be worth after payment of debts the amount of the bail.[11] Blackstone further pointed out that a justice of the peace who granted bail with insufficient sureties could be punished by a fine if the suspect failed to appear for trial. Highmore compounds this by explaining that if justices of the peace granted bail where they should not have, or knowingly and voluntarily took insufficient bail, the Lord Chancellor could revoke their commission and they could be punished in addition for negligent escape. The picture is completed by Hale's contribution that the sureties could be fined as well as have their surety forfeited if the accused escaped. Their protection was to reseize the accused if they feared any attempt to flee. Once they brought the potential absconder before the court they could be discharged, and the accused would be committed to prison.[12]

The form of bail in criminal cases, all of the common law commentators agree, was by recognizance. Although the option of cash deposit was sometimes available for certain types of civil cases with the court's consent, it appears to have been viewed as an alternative to rather than as a form of bail.[13] Blackstone explains very precisely the nature of a recognizance such as was used for bail. Generally, it was a type of deed which was used to encumber and later to discharge property rather than to convey it. Specifically, a recognizance was an obligation to pay a specified sum entered into before an authorized magistrate. It was undertaken, however, subject to a condition of performing a specified act, and performance voided the obligation in force. It differed from a bond only in the technicality that a bond created a new debt while a recognizance merely acknowledged on the record an existing one.[14] When employed in bail the condition for voiding the obligation to pay was producing the accused for trial. Thus the bail sureties acknowledged on the record before a magistrate a debt in the required amount. The debt was subject to the condition that they make the accused available as specified. If they then produced the accused, the debt was voided. If not, it was declared forfeit by the magistrate and the sureties were obliged to pay their pre-existing debt.

The bail system in eighteenth-century England from which later common law systems developed can thus be seen to be one which placed the primary responsibility for an accused's appearance upon the sureties. They were viewed as actively exercising a friendly custody of the accused with the right and ultimate recourse of imprisoning him and delivering him to the court to discharge their liability. This liability in criminal cases took the form of a recognizance, a pledge to pay if they failed to present the accused as they undertook to do. From these roots have developed not only the American system of commercial bail bonding but also the variety of other types of bail systems in the world today. In fact, the most commonly occurring bail system remains the traditional recognizance system with only relatively minor and non-essential changes in the bail arrangements just described.

THE METAMORPHOSIS OF AMERICAN BAIL

A single nineteenth-century case before the U.S. Supreme Court—the 1873 case of *Taylor v. Taintor*—goes a considerable way toward explaining the transformation of the friendly sureties described by Blackstone into the commercial bail bondsmen described in the contemporary news articles. That case underpins the present system in two ways. The first of these gives the support, only slightly qualified, of the Court to permitting sureties to whom payments have been made. In this particular case the defendant was released upon a recognizance with multiple sureties. A third party then indemnified the sureties by paying to them the amount of their bail bond, and they consequently permitted the defendant to leave the state. Since he was arrested while away he could not return. The bail was forfeited and appeal leading to the Supreme Court commenced. The state treasurer argued in part that since the sureties had voluntarily let the accused leave the state because they had received the amount of the bail they should not be permitted to deprive the state of the penalty incurred by their own action. The Supreme Court held that the fact that these sureties had been indemnified could have no effect on the outcome of the case. Indemnification of the sureties cannot act to increase their legal liability. Therefore the question of indemnification was to be "laid out of view." The only qualification that the Supreme Court made limiting this was to concede that the fact that sureties were indemnified was properly considered in an application by sureties for additional time to produce the accused. With the indemnification issue removed the Court agreed with the lower courts on the other issues affecting the forfeiture.[15]

The vital importance of this aspect of the case for the possibility of commercial bail becomes clear only by contrast with legal developments in other countries. Ironically, during the same period (as will be elaborated in Chapter 2) courts in England, India, Ireland, and New Zealand had variously held agreements to indemnify bail sureties to constitute illegal contracts, and the likelihood of indemnification to be grounds to reject sureties and even to deny bail. They had also established that payment of any amount on behalf of the accused to a surety constituted partial indemnification. Thus any commercial development was effectively precluded. Agreement for any payment constituted an illegal contract, unenforceable in the courts, and suspicion of any payment was reason to reject the surety and sometimes to deny the bail. Eventually these become crimes. However, even short of this, the obstructions to commercial bail created by the early indemnification cases abroad contrast sharply with the benign attitudes taken to it in *Taylor v. Taintor*. The legal way was cleared for bail for payment in the United States.

When bail no longer depends on the friendship to which Blackstone refers but is purchased, the original motive for an accused to appear—the consequences for the friend standing surety—is lost. What then replaces it? The second aspect of *Taylor v. Taintor*, which is much better known having served as an introduction to a popular movie on bounty-hunting, provides the answer: extraordinary power. As the court described the bail sureties' powers regarding the accused:

> Whenever they choose to do so, they may seize him and deliver him up in their discharge, and if that cannot be done at once, they may imprison him until it can be done. . . . They may pursue him into another state; may arrest him on the Sabbath; and if necessary, may break and enter his house for that purpose. The seizure is not made by virtue of new process. None is needed.[16]

Not only do the bail sureties have this power, but they may also exercise these rights through agents—bounty hunters. Whether or not all aspects of the sureties' power as described remain good law,[17] *Taylor v. Taintor* opens the bail system to both commercial provision of bail and bounty hunting as its complement.

THE COMMERCIAL BAIL BONDING SYSTEM

In many respects the statutes underlying commercial bail bonding systems, although differing considerably among themselves, reflect their common law origins. As in traditional recognizance systems, they often provide for a bail format in which the accused and sureties bind themselves to pay a sum upon default of appearance. Procedures for arrest of the accused by sureties, and for a two-stage forfeiture with an opportunity to show cause as to why it should not be made, are also often similar in commercial and traditional systems. Reflecting other bail varieties within common law countries, cash deposit is generally authorized as an alternative. A supplementary criminal penalty for bail absconders may even be included, although this is usually of recent origin relative to other aspects of the statutes. Absence of authorization for nonfinancial conditions of conduct to be placed on the accused as term of bail is typically a notable difference between the commercial systems' statutes and the noncommercial common law alternatives.

The crucial difference, however, between the commercial systems and all other bail systems is provision for a bonding or surety insurance company to act as a bail surety. These may even be granted a privileged position such as exemption from examination and approval as surety by the court considering bail. Typically, provision is made for licensing of and posting of a bond by the potential bondsmen. The licensing statute sometimes explicitly authorizes not only the acceptance of a fee for, or premium on, a bond from accuseds, but also acceptance by the bondsman of collateral or indemnity. As discussed in the following chapters, other common law systems not only do not authorize such payments but affirmatively work to prevent them to thwart the development of commercial bail.

Provisions for the employment and licensing of corporate bail sureties in the form of bonding companies is the distinguishing characteristic of the commercial statutes. With the exception of the Philippines and an ambiguous provision in Liberia, which does not seem to result in any important commercialization of bail, these companies do not exist outside the United States. On the contrary, other common-law-based bail systems stress personal ties to the accused in suretyship. Some have explicit law against all corporate sureties based on the conviction that corporations by their nature cannot properly fulfill the role they envision for sureties.

In reality, commercial providers of bail come to dominate these American systems even when statutory wording is in many aspects similar to that found in non-commercial bail statutes. Since recognizance even with personal sureties is rarely accepted without additional security even when allowed by these statutes, three options remain: cash deposit, property bond, or a commercially provided bond. Use of cash deposit is precluded for most accuseds by the relatively high amounts at which bail is set. Property bond is often discouraged by a demand for property security in excess of the amount of bail, frequently by as much as a factor of two. Thus, the only practical recourse is the commercial bondsman.

The bail bondsman, however, need not accept any given defendant as a client. If he does, like any surety he provides the financial security required by the court for release. For this the accused is charged a nonrefundable fee, commonly 10–15 percent of the amount of bail. Collateral may be required as well to secure the bondsman's risk. Nevertheless, bondsmen are usually able to avoid any deposit of cash or property themselves. A surety bond purchased from an insurance company by the bondsman for about a third of the amount charged the accused is acceptable to the courts; indeed, statutes often require its acceptance. In that case, the insurance company, not the bondsman, bears the risk of forfeiture. Notoriously, though, forfeitures are frequently either not ordered, not made final, or simply go uncollected. Bondsmen and bounty hunters have extraordinary powers if they seek an absconder but, as the newsclipping intimates, many prefer not to undertake this burden. Thus the police typically bear the primary burden for arresting absconders. Statutes sometimes abet this by providing automatic relief for sureties if the accused is arrested within a set time (up to as much as a year) even if the surety contributes nothing to the arrest. Thus the transfer of burden to the police is legitimized.

In short, practice under commercial bail undermines the logic of a bail system as it is understood in non-commercial bail countries. Accuseds lose money to the bondsmen regardless of their conscientiousness about appearing. Their financial motive to appear is nonexistent. They have no reason to feel responsible to the bondsman as they might to a closely connected personal surety. Apart from any personal sense of responsibility, their only remaining motive to appear is fear of the bounty hunter. The bondsmen, in turn, as sureties who are indemnified—sometimes two or three times over—frequently have little incentive to secure the accused's presence in court, and there is some possibility that the police will arrest defaulters without their intervention. If, however, all else fails, they have a reservoir of powers unavailable to the police.

THE PHILIPPINES

Although the Philippines' system of justice has a mixture of common and civil law influences, its bail system is decidedly a product of the American branch of the common law tradition. The basic provision is for release on the accused's recognizance with sureties, although provision is also made for release on recognizance without sureties. Sureties are authorized, as elsewhere, to arrest the defendant and seek their discharge from suretyship. As an alternative, a cash deposit may be substituted. Nonfinancial conditions of conduct are not authorized. However, as in American jurisdictions, commercial sureties are permitted. The result, as in American jurisdictions allowing unrestricted functioning of commercial sureties, is that they dominate the system. For example, of eighteen cases used here for points of Philippine law in which the nature of the surety is clear, seventeen have a commercial surety company as the surety. In the other case, release was under a property bond.[18] The basic similarity of this to the American commercial bail jurisdictions is evident.

Despite this similar framework, however, Philippine law is notably less obligingly adaptable to the interest of the commercial surety than is that in many U.S. jurisdictions. One respect in which this is the case is in the area of bondsmen relying upon the police in default of their own responsibilities. In sustaining a forfeiture, the Philippine Supreme Court noted that "the reason why appellant *again* failed to produce the accused, is because it ignored its express undertaking as bondsman and left the fulfillment of its duty to the P.C. [Police Constabulary] authorities." The court went on to hold that the request of the surety company to the police to bring the accused before the court and even its offer to pay all expenses incurred in doing so "did not cure its failure to comply with its duty under terms of the bond."[19]

A further line of cases also illustrates a similar lack of accommodation by Filipino courts to the interests of commercial bail sureties. The rule giving rise to these cases provides that if sureties (commercial or personal) fail to produce a defendant, forfeiture is declared. They are then given thirty days to produce the accused or give the reason for not doing so, and they must satisfactorily explain their initial failure. Unless both requirements are met, a judgment against the sureties is required.[20] This rule in itself is much stricter than that of many American jurisdictions in preventing dilatory tactics on a final judgment for the benefit of the surety. The courts' interpretation makes it more so.

The Philippine Supreme Court views its policy with regard to forfeitures when the accused is produced tardily as liberal—as indeed objectively it is. However, as compared to some American jurisdictions it is one of strict rectitude. The policy is that the discretion to forfeit should be exercised with a view to liberally considering that the best interest of the state is served by motivating sureties to locate and apprehend defendants, and to hold down premiums making bail more attainable and less expensive.[21] Even applying this policy, however, sureties are held to their responsibilities by Philippine courts.

Even when the bondsmen, or sureties, produce the accused within the allotted thirty days, complete cancelation of the forfeiture is rarely granted. The reason for nonappearance is considered very seriously. The Supreme Court has said that a bondsman who occasions a delay in the trial and disposition of a criminal case by not producing the accused when required is not entitled to total exoneration. This would put defaulting and nondefaulting bondsmen on the same level. Even with appearance within thirty days, the breach of the bail obligation remains, and the most the defaulting surety, or bondsman, should be granted is a reduction in the amount of forfeiture. Thus, even in a case where an accused was hospitalized and the charge had meanwhile been greatly reduced, largely because this explanation was not given at the time set for appearance the most the Supreme Court could countenance was a reduction of the bondsman's liability to "a more or less nominal sum."[22] Likewise, in another case where the accused was produced and the explanation was found satisfactory, a forfeiture of 10 percent of the surety amount was nevertheless enforced. In instances where the explanation was not satisfactory, was not given, or was not proven, production of the accused received mitigation of half of the amount forfeited.[23]

Considerations of liberality do not equally apply where, instead of mere delay in appearance, failure to produce the accuseds results from their absconding and becoming fugitives from justice. Where the public injury is permanent rather than temporary the situation is clearly different. In view of this, however, when the accused is produced by the surety, even after the thirty days, under some circumstances the forfeiture will be mitigated but not canceled. Thus a showing of diligent, persistent effort by the surety to arrest an accused will be rewarded.[24]

In the context of arguing for mitigation of forfeiture the Philippine Supreme Court requires a significant level of active effort by the bail sureties, or bondsmen, to achieve the presence of the accused in court. Failure by bondsmen to notify defendants in advance of their required appearance, and to immediately notify the court at the specified time of any problem with that appearance, will make the sureties liable to a partial forfeiture even if the accuseds act innocently in not appearing and are produced within the thirty days. However, mere notification is not in itself sufficient to vindicate a bondsman. Sureties, or bondsmen, are obliged to keep in touch with accuseds, and to maintain proper supervision over them. They have an "inevitable obligation, not merely a right, to keep the accused at all times under . . . surveillance." This requires them to keep careful track of the accused's movements. Claims for mitigation of forfeiture depend upon successful—even if belated—efforts by the surety or surety's agent to locate and produce the defendant rather than upon the mere presence of the defendant in court.[25]

Reflecting the same attitude toward the responsibilities of the bail bondsman is the Supreme Court's repeated insistence that reasons employed to argue against final forfeiture orders should be established by "admissible and competent evidence." Thus, the capture of the defendant by the bondsman within the thirty days allotted must be duly established, not merely asserted. The reason justifying the initial failure to appear must likewise be demonstrated. Merely alleging the serious sickness of the defendant is not sufficient: it must be shown to the complete satisfaction of the court. At least where damaging evidence to the contrary exists, expert testimony should be offered to convince the court. Similarly, long and continuous efforts to locate the accused should not merely be alleged: the efforts exerted should be shown. In the same manner the death of a bailed accused cannot be deemed to be established by hearsay evidence: the witnesses should be examined under oath by the court.[26] Less adequate proof of an otherwise apparently good reason may produce a partial mitigation of forfeiture, or none at all, rather than cancelation.

One final case further exhibits the marked difference between the view of commercially arranged sureties in the Philippines from that in many jurisdictions in the United States. In this matter, when the accused failed to appear the court ordered forfeiture. Within the thirty days the bonding company arrested the accused. Upon appearance the defendant convinced the court that he was not at fault in failing to appear. Counsel for the company agreed to refund all premiums paid by the accused; in consideration of this the court indicated it would reconsider confiscation of the bail. The accused subsequently reported to the court the surety company's failure to make the refunds, and the court made a final forfeiture order on the company's bond since it had violated the condition upon which the court's willingness to reconsider forfeiture was postulated. It did mitigate the amount of forfeiture in view of the arrest. The company appealed in part upon the placing of the condition on the reconsideration of the forfeiture. The Supreme Court unanimously not only upheld the lower court's conditional reconsideration but insisted itself that the premium be repaid to the accused on the grounds that the company's undertaking to do so was a consideration in the lower court's mitigation of the amount forfeited.[27]

In view of the prevalence of commercial sureties in the Philippines, how much generalization this one case supports is unclear. It seems to suggest, nevertheless, at least a latent strain of sympathy in Philippine law for the view—which in Pakistan becomes an explicit principle—that sureties not acting for profit should receive more favorable consideration regarding mitigation of forfeiture than those who are.

In conclusion, the Philippines exhibits the only bail system outside the United States dominated by commercial provision of bail. However, despite its general similarity, the Philippine system demonstrates in several regards a less lenient attitude toward its corporate paid sureties. Philippine law is much less willing than that in American jurisdictions to tolerate abdication by corporations of the traditional surety functions. Specifically, that country is less likely than many American states to allow bail bondsmen to benefit from the activities of the police in arresting an absconder or to excuse their default of function because it was compounded by police error.

Likewise, both in the law itself and in its application, the Philippines is much less likely than American jurisdictions to allow its commercial sureties to benefit from a belated appearance in court of the accused. Finally, as the case cited illustrates, some reluctance exists within the Philippines' judiciary to allowing a surety company to profit from an accused while the court is considering leniency regarding forfeiture for the company.

CONCLUSION

The discussion of the Filipino bail system and comparison of it with the commercially provided bail system in the United States suggests the two topics of this study. First, why should only the Philippines, with its former commonwealth position in the United States, have developed a commercial system? Why have none of the other countries with a similar common law heritage regarding bail developed a commercialized system? What have the other countries with a similar common law heritage regarding bail done to obstruct the development of commercial bail and why have they done it? The answer to these questions are provided in the next two chapters where the laws in various countries obstructing commercial bail are explored. Second, what do these countries substitute for commercial providers in their bail arrangements? Here the answers can be categorized into four alternative types, each of which is treated in a separate chapter.

Since the focal point of bail in the United States is in the lower courts, these are retained as the principal focus of study here, although in many of the countries discussed bails granted by the police are numerically very important. Bail in the superior courts is considered only as necessary to illustrate lower court bail. Similarly, the focus here is upon bail prior to conviction and especially upon bail prior to trial. Since bail after conviction raises a separate set of issues, this is considered only when a principle of general application contributes to the understanding of pretrial bail. To facilitate reference, judges of these courts of limited jurisdiction are referred to generally as magistrates, although local usage in some countries may vary from this terminology.

NOTES

1. Roscoe Pound and Felix Frankfurter, eds., *Criminal Justice in Cleveland* (Cleveland: The Cleveland Foundation, 1922), pp. 290, 292.

2. Bill Walsh, "Full Jails Give Bondsmen a Tough Time," *New Orleans Times-Picayune*, 12 May 1990, Sec. B, p. 1.

3. Pamela Cytrynbaum, "6 Bounty Hunters Held in Kidnapping," *New Orleans Times-Picayune*, 5 May 1990, Sec. A, p. 1; Pamela Cytrynbaum, "Bounty Hunters Catching Attention From Officials," *New Orleans Times-Picayune*, 31 May 1990, Sec. A, p. 1.

4. *Kear v. Hilton*, 699 F. 2d 181 (C.A. 5, 1983), esp. at 182–183, 184.

5. James Wilson, *Lectures on Law*, in *Works* (1804; rpt. Cambridge: Harvard University Press, 1967), II, 685–686.

6. Edward Coke, *A Little Treatise of Baile and Maineprize* (1635; rpt. New York: Garland Publishing, 1978), pp. 1–3.

7. Mathew Hale, *The History of the Pleas of the Crown* (1736; rpt. London: Professional Books, 1971), p. 124; William Hawkins, *A Treatise of the Pleas of the Crown* (1721; rpt. London: Professional Books, 1973), p. 88.

8. Anthony Highmore, *A Digest of the Doctrine of Bail; In Civil and Criminal Cases* (1783; rpt. New York: Garland Publishing, 1978), p. x.

9. William Blackstone, *Commentaries on the Laws of England*, Chitty ed. (Philadelphia: J. P. Lippincott, 1857), pp. 291, 295–297.

10. Coke, pp. 22–23; Hale, p. 125; Hawkins, p. 88.

11. Blackstone, p. 291.

12. Blackstone, p. 297; Hale, p. 127; Highmore, p. 191.

13. Highmore, p. 11.

14. Blackstone, pp. 340–342.

15. *Taylor v. Taintor*, 83 US 366 (S.C., 1873), esp. at 367, 369.

16. Ibid., at 371.

17. For a discussion see *Kear v. Hilton*, at 182.

18. *Rules of Court*, Rule 114, esp. s. 1, s. 2, s. 9, s. 10, s. 14, s. 15, s. 16, s. 17; *Bandoy v. Judge of First Instance*, 14 Phil 620 (S.C., 1909), esp. at 626.

19. *People v. Celestino*, 12 SCRA 572 (S.C., 1964), esp. at 575.

20. *Rules of Court*, Rule 114, s. 15; *People v. Caderao*, 7 SCRA 634 (S.C., 1963), at 643.

21. *People v. Orlando*, 13 SCRA 133 (S.C., 1965), at 135.

22. *People v. Castillejos*, 23 SCRA 108 (S.C., 1968); *People v. Familiar*, 17 SCRA 466 (S.C., 1966), esp. at 469; *People v. Caderao*, at 643; *People v. Guevarra*, 14 SCRA 349 (S.C., 1965).

23. *People v. Segarino*, 12 SCRA 395 (S.C., 1964), at 398–399.

24. *Communications Insurance Co. Inc. v. Villaluz*, 99 SCRA 492 (S.C., 1980), at 498; *People v. Weber*, 7 SCRA 218 (S.C., 1963), at 223; *People v. Ignacio*, 8 SCRA 634 (S.C., 1963), esp. at 636; *People v. Ornales*, 13 SCRA 133 (S.C., 1965).

25. *People v. Cabanero*, 22 SCRA 52 (S.C., 1968); *People v. Pacomio*, 12 SCRA 139 (S.C., 1964), at 141; *People v. Cordero*, 9 SCRA 691 (S.C., 1963), at 694; *People v. Ignacio*, esp. at 637; *People v. Guevarra*, at 350, 351–352; *People v. Ornales*, at 336; *People v. Ignacio*, at 634–635, 637; *People v. Weber*, at 222; *People v. Segarino*, 12 SCRA 395 (S.C., 1964), at 398.

26. *People v. Ornales*, at 136; *People v. Segarino*, at 398; *People v. Kusain Saik*, 8 SCRA 87 (S.C., 1963), at 90; *People v. Weber*, at 222.

27. *People v. Familiar*, at 467–469.

2

The Illegality of Commercial Bail Bonding in Common Law

Viewed from an international perspective, the commercial bail bonding system has provoked an almost universally unfavorable reaction. It has been observed that only one country, the Philippines, has adopted a commercial bail bonding system similar to the American system. What remains to be understood is why many countries sharing with the United States the common law heritage have obstructed the development of compensated bail bonding by measures up to making it a criminal activity. Some of these have done so with the U.S. example quite explicitly in mind. The origin of the movement against compensated bail bonding can be traced well back into English common law. In addition, however, at the crucial stage of this legal development, courts in Ireland and India, acting on their own perceptions, instituted preventative steps in advance of those contemporarily in place in England. Many countries contributed subsequent refinements.

DEVELOPMENT OF THE COMMON LAW PROHIBITION

England

Not widely realized in the United States is that commercial bail bonding would have been illegal under English common law for well over a century before it was barred by Act of Parliament in 1976. The essence of such bail bonding, as previously discussed, is that for payment of a sum, normally a percentage of the bail required, the bondsman will provide the financial surety required by the court for release of the arrested individual. English bail, although for well over a century not relying principally upon a third party's standing surety in bail matters, has and does permit sureties to be required by a court as an extra security for the accused's appearance. Such suretyship was added where needed to the accused's own recognizance until 1976, and to the threatened exaction of criminal penalties for absconding since then. The individual standing surety in the English system, like the bail bondsman, provides the financial surety required by the court for release of the arrested (although differences exist in the modes of liability and payment). Under the pertinent common law provision any payment to, or even deposit with, an individual standing as surety for bail of the whole or part of the amount of the surety was viewed as an illegal indemnity. The reasoning behind this view highlights the illogic of the bail bonding system as well as the condemnatory view taken of it abroad.

An early indication of the attitude of English common law toward indemnification of a surety is given by Anthony Highmore in his 1783 work, *A Digest of the Doctrine of Bail*. In this, Highmore censoriously points to indemnification as a danger that will arise if insufficient bail is required. He condemns it, at least in conjunction with absconding, as a "heinous aggravation of the offense." In addition, an appendix to the work contains a copy of a contract to indemnify sureties in an assault and wrongful imprisonment case before the King's Bench. Unfortunately, Highmore offers no comment on the outcome of the contract.[1]

The early English cases on indemnifying a surety were civil cases dealing with the legal status of agreements involving such indemnification. Within seventy-five years of Highmore's treatise a series of cases in English courts, principally the Queen's Bench, held that any agreement to indemnify a person standing as a surety was an illegal contract and was therefore unenforceable. In the first of these cases, *Jones v. Orchard*, before the Court of Common Pleas in 1855, the suggestion is clear that an already established public policy against payments to sureties existed.[2] The only previously reported case, from 1851, provided some backhanded corroboration of the policy's existence.

In that earlier case, *R. v. Broome*, the Brighton magistrates had rejected the proposed sureties on the sole grounds that they had been indemnified. Further application for bail was then made to a single judge of the Queen's Bench sitting in chambers. The attorney for the prosecution argued that indemnified sureties were unacceptable. Since the object of bail was to secure the appearance of the accused for trial, the argument ran, the judge should be satisfied that the sureties fully intended that the defendant would be surrendered for that purpose. Sureties who at the moment of tendering bail felt no assurance that the accused would be forthcoming, but on the contrary knew that this was not very probable, were not the sort of security the law required. The fact that the sureties were indemnified might reasonably raise doubt in the magistrates' minds as to whether the sureties really intended that the defendant's appearance be secured for the purpose of the law. Such a doubt, the attorney submitted, was entertained by the magistrates in this case. Nevertheless, the judge accepted the sureties and granted bail. He was guided in part by bail practice in civil cases and in part by a holding that the financial sufficiency of the sureties was the only inquiry properly to be made.[3] Nevertheless, the position of the magistrates and the argument of the attorney for the prosecution indicates the existence of the tradition, however insecurely established.

In *Jones v. Orchard*, the issue was complicated by the fact that under certain circumstances pertinent to the case the liability of sureties had been extended by statute beyond the appearance of the accused for trial to include assuring payment of prosecution cost. Ultimately the judgment in the case was based on distinguishing these two aspects of suretyship. The point of importance for commercial bail bonding was the view expressed by the court on contracts to indemnify sureties in criminal cases against the consequences of a default on the accused's appearance for trial. The Lord Chief Justice, speaking for the court, termed well founded the argument that such a contract was contrary to public policy. This being so, the contract was illegal and hence one which the court would neither enforce nor presume by implication to exist. The contract was contrary to public policy because it in effect reduced the public's security for the accused's appearance from two persons to one.[4] Since the same objection did not apply to a surety for the payment of prosecution cost, the court permitted recovery by the surety on the facts in this case.

There was one final deviation before the principle that agreements to indemnify sureties in criminal bails constituted illegal contracts was permanently established in *Wilson v. Strugnell* (1881). This occurred in 1862 in *Cripps v. Hartnoll*,[5] in which the surety was not allowed to recover the forfeited recognizance. This was done, however, on statutory grounds pertaining to the adequacy of the contract. The illegality of the contract as being contrary to public policy was not considered, and any distinction between bail in criminal and civil cases was denied.[6]

Wilson v. Strugnell[7] was heard in Queen's Bench in 1881 by the eminent legal scholar Justice James Fitzjames Stephens. Strugnell had been paid one hundred pounds by an accused, Manners, as security for his standing surety for him in a recognizance of the same amount. Manners failed to appear but the recognizance was never forfeited because of a jurisdictional dispute between the justice who granted bail and the justices of the court before which the defendant was to appear. He never reappeared and was eventually adjudicated bankrupt. Wilson, the trustee of the bankruptcy, sued Strugnell to recover the hundred pounds. Justice Stephens held that such a contract to indemnify a surety for bail against his liability was illegal and void, it being a contract contrary to public policy. He held this in part for the reason that the effect of the contract was to deprive the public of the security of bail. The money Manners paid Strugnell, he ruled, was consequently paid on an illegal consideration. Where money has been paid for such an illegal purpose, he declared, if the purpose is fully carried out it cannot be recovered, but where it has not been carried out it can be. Therefore, on his perception of the facts he ordered the money repaid. The crucial legal development in the case relative to commercial bail bonding was the holding that contracts involving payment to a surety for bail are illegal as being contrary to the public interest. They infringe upon it by undermining the surety's interest in assuring the defendant's presence for trial. Thus they deprive the public of the security for the accused's attendance intended by the process of bail.

In *Herman v. Jeuchner*[8] (1885) the Court of Appeal overruled *Wilson v. Strugnell* on one point. This court held that since the consideration and the promise complete a contract, where the object of either of them is an illegal act the contract becomes illegal and unenforceable. Alternatively viewed, since the illegality lies in the contract itself, once the contract is complete the indemnity cannot be recovered by the person being bailed regardless of whether the surety is forfeited.

A secondary aspect of this case, which is significant only when one's perspective includes the practice of commercial bail bonding, was that the indemnification was for not quite the full amount of the recognizance, but rather for one pound less. Whether the parties were attempting to skirt the law by this device does not emerge; it is evident that the court was so little impressed by the less-than-full payment as to take no notice of it. Thus partial indemnification was established early in the development of the law to be adequate to constitute illegality.[9]

A situation generally similar to that in *Wilson v. Strugnell* pertained in an 1899 case before the Queen's Bench: *Consolidated Exploration and Finance Company v. Musgrave*.[10] The most significant difference between this case and the earlier one was that the indemnification was made not by the individual seeking bail but by a third party. The court refused to accept this distinction as altering the illegality of the contract, saying:

> It is essential that the person giving bail should be interested in looking after and if necessary exercising the legal powers he has

> to prevent the accused from disappearing. This is necessary for the protection of the public, and anything which tends to hinder or prevent him from doing so is illegal.[11]

The court held that any indemnification is illegal and void since, no matter whether the accused or someone else indemnifies bail, the person who risks loss if the accused fails to appear becomes someone other than the person who has the power of bail. The wording *anything which tends* would also cover the matter of partial indemnification at issue in bail bonding.

A new stage in the common law development of the illegality of surety indemnification was entered with the case of *R. v. Stockwell*[12] in 1902. This was the first reported case when the transaction was tried as a crime rather than as merely an illegal, unenforceable civil contract. A further point of interest for bail bonding was that in this case a premium above the amount of the recognizance was paid to each surety. Such a premium is comparable to the payment made for the bail bond in a commercial system. The fact of this additional payment was included in the evidence of indemnification. *R. v. Stockwell* has subsequently been misunderstood by some as holding that indemnifying of a surety was not a crime. In fact what was held was that it was a crime, but only if there was intent to pervert the course of justice in addition to the intent to indemnify. Since the jury found no such additional intent the particular defendants were acquitted. Nevertheless, a major legal development had occurred. The nature of the charge brought in the case was that, contriving and intending to pervert and obstruct the due course of law and justice, the defendants unlawfully conspired to indemnify the sureties for their appearance against liability on their recognizances. The Recorder of the City of London rejected both the view that the act was illegal but not criminally illegal and the view that the intent requirement was satisfied by the intent to perform acts which tended objectively to pervert or interfere with the course of justice. Instead, he held that there was a crime only if there was intent to pervert the course of justice in addition to the intent to indemnify. The charge failed in this instance for lack of a finding of the further intent required.

The common law as it existed until replaced by the statute in 1976 was formulated in its essentials in the case of *R. v. Porter* (1909).[13] Here, one George Clark was bailed upon a recognizance of fifty pounds being entered into by Porter and another friend. Upon Clark's release he paid each surety fifty pounds, and later absconded. The judge (unlike the one in Stockwell's trial) instructed the jury that Porter was guilty so long as there had been a prior agreement for indemnification even if he did not intend that justice should be defeated by allowing Clark to escape, and this was what the jury found. The judge then ruled that the finding amounted to a guilty verdict.

The case subsequently came before the Court of Criminal Appeal where the Lord Chief Justice rendered the opinion. His opinion begins from the premise that not all contracts which are void for offending against public policy are criminal. To be criminal, the act contracted for must be not only improper or immoral, but must also tend to the public mischief. However, people are responsible for the natural consequences of their acts, so no additional requirement exists that the defeat of the ends of justice be intended as well as the act itself. Specifically, intent to enter an agreement to indemnify a surety is sufficient to constitute a crime. Further intent that the individual bailed should escape is not required, because the public interest dictates that defendants be brought to trial, and the taking of sureties is the only security the public has that they will be. If the surety is indemnified he loses his interest in the defendant's appearance. Therefore, in every imaginable case an agreement to indemnify tends to produce a public mischief. Consequently, the court ruled, any agreement to indemnify a surety is not only an unenforceable contract, it is a crime.[14]

After the Porter case, no further cases on the offense are reported until 1972. Three considerations may help explain what appears from the American perspective to be an anomaly. First, once a point of law is settled in England it is much less likely than in the United States to be appealed. Second, even if it is appealed, unless the law is altered it is much less likely to be reported. Finally, the nature of the activity involved in these cases is such that frequently they may not come to light except where an ongoing business of bail bonding for payment is present.

The 1972 case reaffirming the offense was *R. v. Foy*.[15] The appeal was heard by the Court of Appeal Criminal Division, with the Lord Chief Justice rendering the opinion. The case was considered a straightforward instance of conspiracy to indemnify a surety. Indicative of the established status of the offense, two divergencies from the pattern of the earlier cases never became issues. First, no indemnity was ever paid; second, the arrangement was for the indemnity to be paid in the first instance to a company of which the surety was a director rather than to him directly. He was then to reimburse himself only if his recognizance was forfeited. The only issue to arise on appeal was whether the trial judge had erred in not leaving the jury to decide whether an indemnification of bail was a public mischief. The appellate court found no error. Where, as here, there is a straightforward case of an act previously held illegal, the judge has no choice but to direct the jury that, if they are satisfied on the questions of fact, a conspiracy to effect a public mischief exists.

Two subsequent cases dealt secondarily with the crime of indemnification of a bail surety. In *D.P.P. v. Withers*[16] (1974) the House of Lords struck down the crime of conspiracy to effect a public mischief as being an offense unknown to the law. This was done principally on the grounds that, whatever may have been the case, the courts did not now have authority to create new offenses. As *R. v. Foy* made explicit, the offense of indemnifying a surety had been lodged within this category of crime. However, in eliminating the crime of conspiracy to effect a public mischief, the court preserved certain established, narrower subcategories of conspiracy as crimes. Included among these was conspiracy to pervert the course of justice. The reasoning was that whereas new offenses could not be created under the ambiguous general notion of public mischief, well-established legal principles must be applied to new facts. The courts had no more power to abrogate old crimes than to create new ones. Provided that the word *pervert* was properly and seriously interpreted, this was a category of crime well recognized by a wide range of authorities. Thus the crime of indemnifying a surety survived and indeed was reaffirmed. Its conceptual underpinnings were, however, shifted from conspiracy to effect a public mischief to conspiracy to pervert the course of justice.

The other case secondarily bearing on the offense of indemnification came before the Court of Appeal (Civil Division) in 1975. This was the case of *R. v. Southampton Justices, ex parte Green*.[17] The primary issue in the case was magistrates' obligation to consider sureties' means when ordering forfeiture of their recognizances. This was complicated in this instance because the surety was the absconder's wife. Lord Denning, Master of the Rolls, held that because indemnifying of a surety is unlawful, no account can be taken of joint property in assessing the wife's means. As a result he cautioned that a wife should be accepted as a surety only if she has sufficient separate property to satisfy the recognizance. Thus, to accommodate the crime of indemnification, the potential use of a wife as surety was restricted. This indicates clearly the serious view taken of surety indemnification under English law even though in the case of joint property the indemnification might seem to be only partial.

The final English common law case on indemnification was heard by the Court of Appeal (Criminal Division) in December 1977 after the passage, but before the effective date, of the statutory provision which would replace it. In *R. v. Head and Head*[18] the two defendants were approached by a party other than the individual seeking bail and offered indemnification in the amount of the required recognizance plus one thousand pounds each if they would serve as sureties. They were charged (reflecting the Withers case) with conspiring to obstruct public justice in that they conspired to procure, indemnify, and reward sureties in order to obtain a release on bail. The trial judge held that this was not a creation of a new offense. He also held that the object of the conspiracy was the obstruction of public justice, leaving no question of intent for the jury to decide. On appeal, the defendants argued that *R. v. Porter* had been wrongly decided. The appellate court sustained *Porter* and upheld the conviction. In so holding, the Court commented that the essence of the decision to grant bail was that the persons standing surety are sufficiently confident they can ensure the defendant's answering bail that they are prepared to risk the amount of their recognizance. Hence this conspiracy did obstruct the course of public justice.

A leading authority, Archbold, points out an interesting nuance of the reconceptualized offense. Although traditionally the offense was one of conspiracy, obstructing the course of justice (unlike effecting a public mischief) was a common law crime regardless of the element of conspiracy. Speculatively, then, indemnifying a surety without an agreement might have become criminal under the concept of the offense developed in *Withers* and *Head and Head*, although this is not the case under the 1976 statute.[19]

A further point made in Archbold bears even more directly on the practice of bail bonding. The focus of the obstructing justice category of crime is the tendency of the act to pervert the course of justice, not the proximity of it to that result. This undercuts any defense of bail bonding on the grounds that a large percentage of the amount of bail may remain to motivate the bondsman to secure the defendant's presence in court. Any reduction in liability would have the tendency to lessen the motivation, and that is enough to constitute the offense.[20]

COMMON LAW IN OTHER COUNTRIES

The case of *Head and Head* represents the final development of the common law crime of conspiracy to indemnify a surety in England. For some time before this case, a movement to restructure English bail law and to place it on a statutory base had been in progress, and prior to the resolution of the case the Bail Act of 1976 was passed. This did not, however, end the significance of the common law development. Jurisdictions in countries as diverse as Australia, Bangladesh, Canada, India, Ireland, New Zealand, Nigeria, Pakistan, Papua New Guinea, South Africa, and Tanzania, which follow (or at that time followed) or are influenced by English common law, have applied aspects of the common law as it is expounded in these cases.[21] In many instances these jurisdictions made their own contributions to the common law on the topic.

Ireland

Contributions to the law against indemnifying sureties in the second half of the nineteenth century were not limited to England. Apart from Ireland's application of the United Kingdom's law, a separate approach to creating an alternative remedy for indemnification developed independently in Irish case law of the period. In the 1857 case of *R. v. Gallagher*, denial of bail by the magistrate was appealed to the Court of the Queen's Bench.[22] The case involved what was thought to be a widespread conspiracy involving a large number of people. The Queen's Bench sustained the denial of bail on the grounds that, given the numbers thought to be involved, any sureties for bail might be indemnified by a subscription of funds to defray their liability. The court therefore reasoned that no amount of bail could assure the appearance of the accused for trial. Granting bail under these circumstances of potential indemnification, therefore, "Far from being a due administration of justice . . . would be ancillary to defeating the ends of justice."[23] Thus the real threat that bail sureties could be indemnified emerged as grounds to deny bail in Irish law.

The Gallagher case was followed and its principle was made more explicit by the Queen's Bench in an 1881 case, *R. v. Butler*.[24] Here again the offense seemed to be the result of a widespread conspiracy. The court restated the law governing bail in such matters this way: Where, if the bail security given is forfeited, the indemnification of the sureties appears probable, security by the sureties should be regarded as unreliable, and therefore, the accused should not be admitted to bail.[25]

Thus, in the same year as the illegality of contracts to indemnify sureties was firmly established in England in *Wilson v. Strugnell*, in a parallel development Irish courts reiterated the principle of over twenty years standing that the threat of indemnification was grounds to deny bail. Once the English version of the prohibition was established, under the union of the two countries then prevailing, it was applicable in Ireland. Thus, today Irish law recognizes both the illegality of contracts to indemnify sureties and the crime of conspiracy to indemnify them.[26] Significantly, however, for over two decades previous to *Wilson v. Strugnell*, Irish courts had independently concluded that indemnified sureties rendered bail unsound and fashioned their own remedy by denying bail in such cases. The opposition to the surety indemnification, which is central to the prevention of commercial bail bonding, can thus be seen to have an independent basis in Irish law in the nineteenth century. Irish commentators today are well aware of the need for this prevention. To quote one such assessment of American commercial systems: "The big business element of bail has often led to bizarre consequences, accentuated undoubtedly by the fact that there is no longer any personal relationship based on trust between the accused and his surety."[27]

India

The most extensive series of cases developing the law against contracts indemnifying sureties occurred in India. As in Ireland, moreover, this Indian development began prior to the evolution of the common law's firm position on the subject in England which eventually shaped Indian law. In 1878, three years prior to *Wilson v. Strugnell*, the Allahabad High Court reached a like conclusion and for similar reasons in the case of *Fateh Singh v. Sanwal Singh*.[28] The High Court upheld the refusal of a lower appellate court to enforce terms of an agreement regarding the indemnification of a bail surety. The lower appellate court had stated its reasons for this conclusion in detail: A surety who has been indemnified lacks the same interest in controlling the actions of the accused as one who has not been. Indemnified sureties may be quite indifferent, in fact, to the interest of society. They have nothing to lose by doing the accused a good turn, allowing bail to be forfeited, and defeating the requirements of the law. However, the lower court reasoned, any act such as the indemnification that is itself opposed to the principles of law is incapable of obtaining relief or abetment by a civil remedy. The court therefore concluded that the act of advancing "a money inducement" to a surety to stand bail was illegal.[29] The High Court added two considerations to what was said. It extended the conclusion to cover not only deposits by the accused but also deposits on behalf of the accused. It further pointed out that no magistrate who knew that a surety had been indemnified would be justified in accepting that surety. To do so would defeat the object of the law: securing someone who undertakes responsibility for the bailed individual.[30]

The next case in the development of Indian law on the subject is particularly interesting from the perspective of commercial bail in two regards. The transaction accomplishing the indemnification was camouflaged in this instance by an elaborate arrangement. A conditional sales deed to the accused's house was used to cover the indemnification of the amount of bail, and a nominal rent note was created to cover additional interest-like payments to the surety. In commercial bail bonding terms, therefore, collateral in kind was provided, as is common in such a system, and a fee for the surety's services over and above the collateral was also paid in the guise of rent. The Bombay High Court upheld a lower appellate decision that both the rent note and sale deed were illegal and void, and that no relief could be granted based upon them.[31]

In holding this, the court considered the argument that the English case of *Herman v. Jeuchner* should not be regarded as law in India. The court's conclusion was telling not only against the surety in this case but against commercial sureties anywhere. The surety bound himself to answer for the defendant's appearance. By obtaining indemnity he sought to deprive the public of the security afforded by his recognizance. A definite principle of public policy, therefore, had been established in England against the civil enforcement of such arrangements. In considering the applicability of the principle in India, the court reasoned that the principle of public policy

> depends upon considerations affecting the administration of public justice, which have certainly not less force in India than they have in England. We think, therefore, that . . . we are bound to regard the consideration of this agreement as opposed to public policy and to hold that the agreement is in consequence void.[32]

Three cases followed, in two of which details of the previous reasonings were elaborated. In 1914 the Calcutta High Court applied the principle of the *Consolidated Exploration and Finance Company v. Musgrave* to an indemnification by a third party, commenting that it "must apply in every country where English criminal justice is administered." The court's restatement of that principle, of course, included the notion that anything that tends to prevent or hinder the surety's interest in preventing the accused disappearing is illegal. Thus, whether indemnity came from the accused or another was irrelevant to the evil to be prevented.[33] As mentioned apropos the *Musgrave* case, the "tendency to prevent" wording would make the principle applicable to partial as well as complete indemnification. Two ancillary practices common under the commercial system would also run afoul of both the English and Indian cases. Collateral is frequently provided to the bail bondsman by third party relatives or friends of the accused, and the bondsman is typically insured against any loss on forfeiture. Both practices would be in clear violation of the ban on the third party indemnifying bail sureties created by the cases. Four years after its first decision on surety indemnification, the Calcutta court confirmed the illegality of contracts to indemnify bail sureties in overturning a judgment for a surety's recovery of the bail amount from the absconder.[34] In 1925 the Nagpur High Court considered a surety's claim based on his retroactive assertion of an implied agreement to indemnify his loss. Naturally this implied agreement was held to be as void as an explicit one. That court provided a slightly different emphasis in its reasoning which complements nicely what the Calcutta High Court had said eleven years before. The Nagpur court reasoned that sureties were required on a bail in order that the failure of the principal to appear may be at the peril of others besides himself. Thus the whole object of sureties is defeated if defendants are allowed to relieve the peril of the sureties and confine the risk to themselves by an arrangement between them.[35] To appreciate the mechanism the court contemplated here, the personal nature of the relationship between principal and surety preferred by Indian courts must be interposed. Thus, assuming that the person at peril as surety is someone with personal ties whom the accused would be reluctant to jeopardize, the reason not to allow the accused to extricate himself from the dilemma by indemnification becomes evident. Commercial bail can then be seen to institutionalize a variety of this resolution of the accused's dilemma which the Indian court strove to prevent.

In most respects the culmination of Indian law on indemnification of bail sureties was reached in a 1935 case of the Patna High Court, *In the Matter of Surja Narain*.[36] The case arose out of an episode in which a legal practitioner was indemnified for a large part, but not all, of several bails by a third party who had previously been rejected as surety. The issue was whether the practitioner should be disciplined for professional misconduct. In deciding that the practitioner's conduct warranted three months' suspension, the court reiterated that the personal element of suretyship was primary, and the monetary element secondary.[37] Among the additional considerations broached for the first time in Indian law in this case was the question of partial rather than complete indemnification. The fact that the apparent surety in the case was in reality liable for only a part—in this instance a relatively small part—of the bail for which the court thought him to be responsible constituted a fraud upon the court. Therefore, that the agreement was for only partial indemnification could not change the result.[38] This, of course, relates directly to payments made in commercialized bail.

Equally importantly, this case contains the best available Indian discussion of the possible criminality of agreements to indemnify sureties. Consideration of this matter begins from the premise that contracts of indemnity are illegal. The case law on that point laid down in England has been accepted as being law in India also. However, the matter here goes beyond this. The court noted explicitly that the practitioner had been charged with a quasi-offense: an offense of professional misconduct rather than criminal misconduct. In this context the landmark *R. v. Porter* establishing such agreements as common law conspiracies is considered. The court does not adopt *Porter* as law in India, remarking that the question of conspiracy law is unnecessary to decide for purposes of the present case. However, the court does use the reasoning in *Porter* elucidating the nature, as opposed to the criminality, of such agreements. "[S]uch an agreement," the court concludes, "constitutes a public mischief, and public mischief in the sense that it is against public policy as it would tend towards obstructing the administration of justice by the criminal Courts." Citing particularly the *Laxmanlal* case, the Patna High Court expresses no doubt that agreements of this sort are properly classified under Indian law as constituting a public mischief and as being contrary to public policy. Thus the wrongdoing necessary to find this legal practitioner guilty of professional misconduct, which goes well beyond entering into an illegal contract, is established.[39]

Although this opinion stops short of declaring even partial agreements to indemnify sureties to be criminal, it agrees with *Porter* to the extent of castigating them as public mischiefs tending to the obstruction of criminal justice. Something of this description is hardly appropriate to include in a justice system as they are institutionalized in a commercial bail system.

In the Matter of Surja Narain presents most components of Indian law on surety indemnification as it exists to the present. Contracts to indemnify are illegal and unenforceable, whether explicit or implicit. Additionally, such arrangements constitute professional misconduct within the legal profession. They have not, however, been made crimes, although neither have they been positively affirmed as not criminal. An ongoing awareness is reflected in Indian commentary, moreover, that they are crimes under English common law.[40]

A final case contributing to the law against the development of commercial bail in India was decided by the Punjab High Court in 1967. This case decided that corporations could not serve as sureties for criminal bails in India. This in itself would render any potential commercial surety operation petty in nature. However, the court's reasoning in this case ties the holding even more closely to commercialized bail. Sureties, the court premises, must be able to be compelled to exercise sufficient vigilance to prevent absconding. This is ultimately achieved, all else failing, by the imprisonment of the surety. Corporations, however, cannot be imprisoned. Therefore, nothing interposes to prevent a wealthy accused from indemnifyng a corporate surety and then jumping bail.[41] At the foundation, then, of the banning of corporate sureties in India lies the perception—and well-placed fear—that corporate sureties would facilitate indemnified sureties who would be indifferent to absconding.

South Africa

A 1932 South African case offers some parallels to its near contemporary, the *Surja Narain* case in India, while in some other important respects going beyond it. Counsel in the South African instance was in the practice of standing as surety for clients' bail up to the amount that they had deposited with him against the payment of their fees. The South African court immediately went beyond the result of the Indian case by pointing out that any arrangement or contract by which a surety purports to become indemnfied either by deposit or contract, and either by the accused or another, is illegal under the *criminal* law. Thus not only is an indemnification agreement unenforceable, it is criminal. The court then analyzes the effect of the arrangement described for consideration by the Bar for potential professional misconduct.[42]

The court's analysis reflects the same reasons for opposing payments to sureties advanced in other countries. For the purpose of securing the attendance of the accused, the Cape Town court comments, placing them in the position that under any circumstances they lose the amount that was deposited with their counsel and surety is undesirable. If the accuseds abscond, all that is forfeited is that amount, but if they appear they also lose the amount because it is paid to counsel as fees. A system that presents defendants only with the choice of either paying counsel a sum as fees to defend them or paying the state the same sum as bail forfeiture is therefore very undesirable for the administration of justice. Attendance of accused persons is advanced, rather, by having someone who knows them, or at least knows something of them, being prepared to undertake responsibility for their presence. A complementary aspect of this arrangement is that at least in some cases the defendant may have enough sense of honor not to want to cause a friend the loss of money. The court, not wishing to dictate to the Bar Counsel in a matter of professional conduct, confined itself to sending that body its remarks.[43] The court's objection to this arrangement applies perfectly to commercial bail bonding where the fee of the accuseds will be lost to them whether or not they appear in court.

New Zealand

Adding to the nineteenth-century common law against surety indemnification from England, Ireland, and India is *Jones v. Kirby*, which was heard by the New Zealand Supreme Court in 1896.[44] In this case the defendant failed to appear to answer bail and the surety's recognizance was forfeited. The question stated for the opinion of the Court was whether the surety, now the plaintiff, could sue the absconder to recover the amount forfeited. The Court in answering felt itself bound by three of the English cases discussed above, *Cripps v. Hartnoll, Jones v. Orchard,* and *Herman v. Jeuchner.* Although concern about the conflict between *Cripps v. Hartnoll* and the other two cases emerges throughout this opinion, the surety was found to have no right to sue for recovery of the forfeited amount. The surety's argument that, unlike an indemnified surety, one who only had a right to sue an absconder retained an interest in not having his recognizance forfeited was rejected. Thus *Jones v. Kirby* adds uncertain potential indemnification of a surety in the form of a right to sue for recovery of the forfeiture to the varieties held to be contrary to public policy.

More recently, in a 1960 case, *Ware v. Attorney General,* the same court reiterated that any arrangement for indemnity between principal and surety is "illegal." The court proceeded to support this conclusion with the same reasoning used against indemnification throughout the common law world. It removed one of the primary objects in suretyship, namely to ensure that the surety has a strong motive to see that the accused appears at the time and place specified. It does so by negating for all practical purposes the normal sanctions and compulsions which underlie a recognizance for bail since the surety has nothing to lose by forfeiture.[45]

Australia

Like England, most Australian jurisdictions have superseded the common law crime of indemnification of a bail surety with statutory provisions outlawing it. However, Australian courts have contributed some important aspects to the body of case law on the offense. Australian contributions to the common law on indemnification of sureties have for the most part been relatively recent.

A case from New South Wales in 1935 set the tone of the Australian cases and resulted in a six-month suspension of the solicitor who arranged indemnification of the surety by his client. The similarity of this result to contemporary cases in India and South Africa is evident. More influential than the disciplining of the solicitor—the only issue in the case—was the view taken by the court of the indemnified bail. It stated that this bail was quite plainly a sham. In reasoning much like that employed by the Indian and South African courts, it explained that the magistrate, in requiring a surety, was trying to ensure that someone would have a substantial stake in seeing that the defendant answered bail. By arranging indemnification, the solicitor entirely frustrated the magistrate's purpose—in that the surety had been indemnified he had no interest in the accused's appearance, and if the accused was willing to forfeit the amount he could avoid trial. The conduct of the solicitor was described as extremely improper. The court found difficulty in conceiving of a more serious interference with the processes of the criminal law.[46] In these parallel cases from India, South Africa, and New South Wales, each court reasoned independently of the others in reaching their similar conclusions about such indemnification arrangements' detrimental effect on the criminal bail process.

More recently, in *R. v. Titterington* (1953), that individual had stood as surety for another who subsequently absconded. In the course of entering his suretyship he had made an affidavit in justification of bail in which he had sworn that he had not been indemnified.[47] The practice of requiring such an affidavit seems to have arisen as a means of implementing the common law.[48] The evidence presented showed that Titterington had been given part of the amount of his recognizance by a third party who had also promised the rest. He was charged with perjury with regard to his affidavit. The defense argued that, since he had not been paid the full amount and since the promise to pay the rest was illegal and could not be enforced, he had not been indemnified. The judge of the Queensland Supreme Court directed the jury that payment of part of the amount of bail, together with the promise to pay the rest, amounted to indemnification.[49] Australian sources thus concur that payment to a surety of only part of the amount of the recognizance is adequate to constitute indemnification of the surety. Moreover, that payment was made by a third party rather than by the accused does not alter its status as indemnification of the surety.

An unreported case from Western Australia points up another aspect of indemnification, even though as one of Australia's code states the common law crime of indemnifying a surety would not as such apply in that jurisdiction. In this instance it was evident at the time the recognizance was taken that the proposed surety did not have enough money to cover a forfeiture. The accused himself was aware of this. He responded to it by telling the surety in the presence of police witnesses that he would sign his Alfa Romeo car over to her, although he never did. The accused absconded. In the course of the forfeiture hearing the magistrate pointed out that this arrangement was not within the concept of an approved surety and that the bail recognizance was as a result tainted by illegality (though not necessarily criminality).[50] This case provides a comparatively uncommon illustration of the point that the promised indemnification constituting the illegality includes goods as well as cash. This understood, the common commercial bail bonding practice of requiring collateral from accuseds as well as fees would clearly be precluded.

In *R. v. Baba*[51] the Court of Criminal Appeals of New South Wales followed the authority of *D.P.P. v. Withers* and refound "conspiracy to interfere with the due administration of the process of obtaining a release on bail" within the category of conspiracy to pervert the course of justice. Such a categorization, according to the New South Wales court, identifies and classifies more correctly the form of criminal conspiracy involved in the facts of such cases. This removes it, the opinion notes, from the contentious field of law related to conspiracies to effect public mischiefs, and thus avoids the need to enter into some of the deeper matters raised in connection with conspiracies to achieve other purposes within that category. The *Baba* case deals in addition with the question of sentencing in such matters. The court explains that: "The crime is one for which there is no specified maximum sentence. It is a common law misdemeanor and the matter of sentence is to be approached accordingly."[52]

Re Doneihi (1986)[53] plunged the Supreme Court of Queensland back into issues argued in the late nineteenth century. Some aspects of the case are reminiscent of the New Zealand case *Smith v. Kirby*. In *Doneihi*, counsel for the Director of Public Prosecutions argued against a surety seeking a reduction of forfeiture that it should not be granted because granting it would indirectly confer a benefit on the absconded defendant. Rather, the surety should first be required to seek recompense from the absconder (presumably by way of a suit to recover her loss). Since counsel for the D.P.P. was making these suggestions, the court felt impelled to review "serious questions of law" regarding indemnification of sureties.

After an extensive review of the case law, the court in *Doneihi* indicated its full agreement with the preceding cases. It therefore determines that: "It is illegal for any third party, in particular the defendant, to indemnify a surety because that strikes at the very essence of the surety's obligations under the law."[54] Hence, upon this analysis, the contention that a surety should seek indemnity from the absconding defendant before seeking relief from the forfeiture is incorrect.[55] So strong, then, is the common law tradition against payment by the accused or another to a surety that remission of a forfeiture is viewed as a preferable alternative to it for meeting any claims of a surety.

Potentially the most important of the Australian indemnifications of surety decisions was handed down in 1985. In the case of *R. v. Freeman, Kron and Kron*[56] the Court of Criminal Appeal of New South Wales overturned a critical aspect of *R. v. Porter* and, in effect, reverted in the direction of the position of *R. v. Stockwell.* The aspect at issue in both cases was whether the offense is adequately constituted by the intent to agree to indemnify the surety itself, or whether some additional intent indicative of a guilty mind is required. The accused in the *Stockwell* case was acquitted on precisely the lack of additional intent. The accused in *Porter* was convicted because it was not required.

In *Freeman, Kron and Kron,* a solicitor, probably at the direction of her employer solicitor, arranged for a surety, using as a cash deposit mostly funds that had been placed in a trust account with her employer by the accused. The solicitor testified that she had no wrongful intent and that she had believed that what she was doing was not unlawful. The trial judge instructed the jury on the basis of *Porter* that this was not an excuse. Thus the question of whether an intent beyond the intent to indemnify the surety was required to constitute the offense was reopened.[57]

The New South Wales Court of Appeals reviewed the question of *mens rea* in criminal conspiracy law in both England and Australia subsequent to *Porter* and concluded that a guilty intention is a necessary element in proving a perversion of the course of justice charge. With regard to cases of obtaining bail by using the accused's money, the gravamen of the crime lies in the corrupting of the bail process. Therefore, it implies that the intent to do this must be proven. "Essentially that intention involves perversion or wrongful manipulation of the procedures for gaining release on bail," including obtaining it, complying with its conditions, and ultimately answering it. An intention to enable the accused to abscond would certainly meet this requirement, but it is by no means the only intention which would. Based on this view, the court finds the ruling in *Porter* erroneous as regards intent in the light of subsequent legal developments.[58]

Furthermore, the opinion continues, since the charge is conspiracy, this offense is complete upon the making of the agreement. That the unlawfulness of the arrangement might subsequently become apparent (for example, when reading the bail documents or listening to the bailing magistrate) could not furnish the necessary criminal intent. However, such a discovery would establish the necessary intent to impart criminality into any subsequent reaffirmation of the original agreement.[59]

Thus *Freeman, Kron and Kron* would place some unwittingly established agreements to indemnify a surety beyond the scope of the common law crime. It does not, however, provide any serious opening to commercial bail bonding because, upon the second occasion of standing surety, information provided on the first would defeat any claim that perversion of the process was not intended.

Two decisions by the Supreme Court of Victoria illustrating a tangential aspect of the approach taken by Australian courts to indemnified sureties, complete the view of Australian common law. Neither case involves a charge of conspiracy to indemnify since, in both, the indemnification is merely suspected based on circumstances rather than established as fact. The two matters involve roughly similar facts in the pertinent aspects. Both were armed robbery cases in which considerable unrecovered sums had been taken. In both, when the accused absconded, forfeiture of a surety's recognizance was ordered and in both the surety applied for rescission of the forfeiture.

The earlier of the two cases was *Re Condon* in 1972.[60] In the course of this opinion the court noted evidence giving rise to a strong and probable presumption of guilt, the large sum taken in the robbery which remained unrecovered and unaccounted for, and the reasonable inference that all the participants including the absconder shared in some proportion in the proceeds. Given these circumstances it was impossible for the court to resist the conclusion that there was at least a possibility that, if the forfeiture order went unrescinded, the surety might eventually be reimbursed by the defendant. The court commented that it was proper to take such a possibility into account as a relevant circumstance in refusing to rescind the forfeiture.[61]

Re Wilkinson (1981)[62] expanded upon this principle. Under very similar circumstances the court in this case also suspected that either the money for bail (in this case a security deposit) had been provided by the absconder perhaps out of the proceeds of the robbery, or the surety knew that the absconder still possessed the proceeds of the crime and would use these to reimburse her in event of a forfeiture upon his absconding. In refusing to rescind the forfeiture in this case, the court elaborated on its reasons in greater depth than in *Re Condon*.

Any argument justifying rescission of forfeiture depends upon the premise that the surety is a "genuine" surety. If the facts alleged by the surety were to be taken at face value the court concedes that they would have gone a long way to successfully making the case for rescinding the forfeiture. However, they must instead be judged in the context of the surety's being genuine. If, on the contrary,

> the surety herself had not provided the money or gone into debt in order to obtain it but was acting as a mere cipher, or had been given the money by the principal, particularly if that money were the proceeds of the commission of the offence for which the bail was granted, or if, to the surety's knowledge, the principal still

> possessed the proceeds of the crime and was prepared, if necessary, to use those proceeds to recompense the surety in the event of the loss of the security provided as surety upon the principal absconding, then, in those circumstances it is not possible to treat the so-called surety as a surety in the appropriate sense.[63]

The reason for this stems from the fundamental notion behind the requirement of a surety, which is that

> the surety is the owner of the asset put forward as security for the performance of the undertaking. It is the risk of its forfeiture with the concomitant penalty that such forfeiture involves that is meant to provide the incentive to the surety to perform his duty. Thus, if he who becomes a surety is not risking his own asset or is not involving himself in a genuine liability to repay a borrowed asset—the typical example of which is the provision by the principal himself of the money which may or may not be the proceeds of the alleged offence—that person is not to be regarded as a true surety. In such a case the surety has no incentive to endeavor to ensure the principal's attendance at trial and, in consequence, the surety will ordinarily have difficulty in having his contacts with the principal interpreted as efforts to deter the principal from breaking bail. Each case must be looked at in the light of its own facts. But if a surety is such in no more than form only, the inference that the surety's actions were not referable to any duty cast upon a surety would, I should think, normally be drawn.[64]

Based upon these considerations, the court in *Wilkinson* found that the apparent suretyship lacked the appropriate degree of genuineness. Therefore it held that the forfeiture should be allowed to stand unvaried.[65]

Thus, not only does Australian common law follow the main principles of English common law regarding the illegality and criminality of indemnifying sureties, but it treats substantial suspicion of it as a factor to be counted against rescinding or favorably varying a forfeiture of a surety. Since any partial payment to a surety is well established as adequate, the indemnification conclusions regarding commercial bail bonding emerge on two levels for Australia. On the more abstract level, commercial bail bonding would undermine the genuineness of the sureties provided under it. More concretely, even the suspicion of it would create a disadvantage in the matter of forfeitures.

Pakistan

Pakistan is not among those countries where the basic common law criminalization of agreements to compensate sureties has been applied. However, the prepartition Indian decisions on agreements to indemnify constituting illegal, unenforceable contracts do apply. Moreover, Pakistan has produced a line of cases on the topic which develop a point of interest much like the Australian cases of *Condon* and *Wilkinson* just discussed. The leading case of this group, *Dildar v. State*, came before the Pakistan Supreme Court in 1962.[66]

Dildar dealt broadly with the considerations that should be taken into account by a court in ordering the forfeiture of a surety's recognizance. The court began from two premises with regard to the portion of this issue relating to compensated sureties. The first was that preservation of the system of releasing accused persons on bail is important to administering justice and minimizing the loss of personal rights. The second was that generally sureties may be assumed not to gain by standing as surety. Therefore, when courts are dealing with forfeiture, they should balance undue leniency, which might lead to interference with the course of justice, against undue severity, "which might lead to unwillingness on the part of neighbours and friends to come forward and give bail for persons under accusation."[67]

Whether the "sureties have any direct interest through . . . financial connection with the accused" thus becomes a significant consideration in assessing the extent to which a surety's recognizance would be forfeited. If any such financial considerations are present, the side of the balance motivating against harshness is eliminated or reduced. Therefore, the court considers favorable that the sureties in this case acted through "mere benevolence," "neighbourly feeling," and "ordinary fellow-feeling." They appear, the opinion states, to have gained no benefit from standing as sureties. Based upon these considerations, the Supreme Court reduced the amount of the forfeiture in this case substantially, although, since the sureties clearly took their responsibility too lightly, it upheld the basic forfeiture.[68]

Relying on *Dildar v. State*, the high courts of Karachi and of Lahore have reduced the amount of forfeiture by substantial amounts based largely on the absence of any indication that the applicant for the reduction stood surety for any monetary consideration or benefit. Of course, no countervailing consideration, such as the connivance of the surety in the absconding, can be present. So clearly established seems to be the entitlement to such a reduced penalty that, where no indication appears of monetary gain by the surety, the counsel for the state in the Karachi cases either conceded or joined in supporting the application for the reduction.[69]

Relating to the commercial provision of bail from another perspective is a point in the 1987 case *Muhammad Abdullah v. State*.[70] Here a trial court judge had refused bail to a foreigner in a drug-smuggling case after noting the submission of the prosecution that the proposed surety "was a well-known tout and had given surety bonds in a large number of cases." The clear suggestion is that the would-be surety's reputation as a frequent commercial candidate for suretyship was one of several factors in denying bail. Apparently the proffered surety was further investigated because, as the matter presently stood before the court, he was appealing his own denial of bail on charges of having used forged documents to establish his property status to stand as surety for the accused drug smuggler. The significance of this case for commercial bail bonding is not as much the implicit point of law as the clearly demonstrated view taken by the Pakistani courts of the diminished reliability of financially motivated sureties for securing the presence of the accused. When combined with other indicators, this may result in denial of bail.

Thus, although Pakistan does not follow the main line of the common law tradition in making provision of bail for financial gain a crime, it does attribute some legal effect to compensated bail. Specifically, it is a factor in assessing whether the full bail recognizance of a surety should be forfeited. The absence of indications that bail was provided for a financial motive assists applicants for reduced forfeiture. The presence of such indications removes the basic social reason against harshness, namely the fear that friends and neighbors of defendants will be unduly discouraged from serving as sureties. In addition, as much as a matter of fact as of law, when the grant of bail is under consideration the use of a compensated surety may combine with other factors to cast doubt upon the reliability of the bail arrangements to secure the accused for trial.

Nigeria

The point implied regarding the reliability of compensated sureties in the Pakistani case *Muhammad Abdullah v. State* is independently arrived at and clearly asserted as a matter of law by the High Court of the Imo State of Nigeria in a 1977 case.[71] That court states as the test of whether bail should be granted or refused "whether it is probable that the defendant will appear to take his trial." It then states four usual considerations to which reference should be had. The fourth of these—along with ones relating to the seriousness of the accusation and punishment and the strength of the prosecution case—is "whether the sureties are independent, or indemnified by the accused." The Nigerian case thus states as law what is implicit in the Pakistani case. It also reaches the same conclusion as was reached by the Queens Bench in Ireland 120 years earlier regarding indemnified sureties. All three agree that they are a factor indicative of the unreliability of the bail arrangements for securing the accused's appearance.

CONCLUSION

By the time (principally after 1970) when many jurisdictions created the statutory crime of indemnifying a surety, this offense had a substantial history in common law. This history divides into three stages. In nineteenth-century cases, an agreement to make payment to a surety for bail was treated as an unenforceable illegal contract contrary to the public interest. It then developed in the first decade of the twentieth century into a crime of conspiracy to effect a public mischief. When, in 1974, this category of conspiracy was eliminated by the House of Lords, the crime of indemnifying a surety survived into its final stage with a modified legal foundation as a conspiracy to obstruct the court of justice. In addition to this main line of development, the Victorian Supreme Court views the possibility of indemnification as a factor telling against a surety seeking to mitigate a forfeiture. Pakistan, although not following the common law as to the criminality of indemnification, reaches a conclusion similar to Victoria's as to its telling against mitigating forfeiture. Common to all stages and this supplementary development is the judgment that this is an evil which must be legally prevented.

Thus, in each stage of its development, the common law would have precluded commercial bail bonding as a species of illegal agreement, and in the latter two periods would have made it a crime. Since the essence of the bail bond system is payment of a percentage of the amount of bail, the bondsman has to that extent been indemnified, thus constituting a crime. Not only does the fact that the practice would have been a common law crime tell against it, but the nature of that crime adds to the opprobrium. It would alternately have been viewed as a conspiracy to effect a public mischief and as a conspiracy to pervert the course of justice. Neither description is recommendation for an aspect of a criminal justice system. Since the practice of bail came to the United States from English common law, that it should be modified by institutionalizing in it a procedure that that very law finds either a public mischief or a perversion of justice tells heavily against the alteration. That in some jurisdictions it is a factor considered against mitigating a surety's forfeiture confirms the general view that it is reprehensible.

NOTES

1. Anthony Highmore, *A Digest of the Doctrine of Bail* (London: 1783; rpt. New York: Garland Publishing, 1978), pp. 194–195, 271–272.
2. *Jones v. Orchard,* 139 ER 900 (C.P., 1855).
3. *R. v. Broome,* (1851) LTR 19 (Chamb.).
4. *Jones v. Orchard,* at 904.
5. *Cripps v. Hartnoll,* 2 B&S 697 (C.Ex.C., 1862).
6. Ibid., at 698–699, 702.
7. *Wilson v. Strugnell,* 7 QBD 548 (Q.B., 1881).
8. *Herman v. Jeuchner,* 15 QBD 561 (Q.B., 1885).
9. Ibid.
10. *Consolidated Exploration and Finance Company v. Musgrave,* 64 JP 89 (Ch., 1899).
11. Ibid.
12. *R. v. Stockwell,* 66 JP 376 (C.Cr.C., 1902).
13. *R. v. Porter,* 3 Cr App R 237 (K.B., 1909).
14. Ibid.
15. *R. v. Foy, The Times,* 1 Jun., 1972 (C.A., 1972); [1972] Crim L R, 504.
16. *D.P.P. v. Withers,* (1974) 3 All ER 984 (H.L., 1974).
17. *R. v. Southampton Justices, ex parte Green,* 2 All ER 1073 (C.A., 1975).
18. *R. v. Head and Head,* [1978] Crim LR 504 (C.A., 1977).
19. *Archbold Criminal Pleading Evidence and Practice,* 42nd ed., 1985, s. 24–39; Edgar L. Bradley and J. J. Senior, *Bail in Magistrates' Courts* (Chichester: Barry Rose Publishers, 1977), p. 36.
20. *Archbold,* s. 24–39.
21. See, for example, Gerald Nash, *Magistrate's Courts* (North Ryde N.S.W.: The Law Book Co., current), II, sec. 2831, 2861/1; Edward F. Ryan and Philip P. Magee, *The Irish Criminal Process* (Dublin: The Mercer Press, 1983), pp. 182–183; John A. Griffin, *Criminal Procedure in Papua New Guinea* (Sydney: The Law Book Company, 1977), p. 111; Alfred V. Lansdown, *South African Criminal Law and Procedure* (Cape Town: Juta), V, 341, fn. 5a; *In the Matter of an Application for Bail: Republic v. Kiluwa* (1975) [1977] LRT n. 21, at 79–80; Dhaka Law Reports, *The Law on Bail,* 2nd ed. (Dhaka: Dhaka Law Reports Office, 1985), p. 132; Shaukat Mahmood, *Law of Bail,* 3rd ed. (Lahore: Legal Research Centre, 1987), p. 296; K. C. Mehrotra, *Law of Bails, Forfeiture of Bonds and Habeas Corpus,* 2nd ed. (Lucknow: Eastern Book Co., 1985), p. 282.
22. *R. v. Gallagher* (1856–1858) 7 Ir CLR 19 (Q.B., 1857).
23. Ibid., per Crampton, I., at 22–23.
24. *R. v. Butler,* 14 Cox CC 530 (Q.B., 1881).
25. Ibid., esp. at 531–532.
26. Ryan and Magee, p. 183.
27. Ibid., p. 182.
28. *Fateh Singh v. Sanwal Singh* (1876–1878) 1 ILR (All.) 751 (H.C. All., 1878).
29. Ibid., at 752.
30. Ibid., at 753.
31. *Laxmanlal v. Mulshankar,* 32 Bom 449 (H.C. Bom., 1908).

32. Ibid., at 453–454.

33. *Prosonno Kumar Chakravarti v. Prokash Chandra Datta,* AIR 1915 Cal 695(1) (H.C. Cal., 1914).

34. *Bhupati Charan Nandi v. Golam Ehilar,* AIR 1920 Cal 498 (H.C. Cal., 1919).

35. *Jodhraj v. Bisanlal* 1925 Nag 59 (H.C. Nag., 1924), esp. at 60.

36. *In the Matter of Surja Narain,* AIR 1935 Pat 195 (H.C. Pat. [S.B.], 1935).

37. Ibid., per Noor, J., at 199–200.

38. Ibid., per Wort, J., at 198–199.

39. Ibid., at 197–198.

40. K. C. Mehrotra, p. 282; R. K. Narula, *Jail or Bail* (Bombay: Himalaya Publishing House, 1979), p. 30.

41. *Schuster v. Assistant Collector of Customs,* AIR 1967 Punj 189 (H.C. Punj., 1965), esp. at 190.

42. *Rex v. Booi,* 1932 CPD 398 (S.C., 1932), at 400.

43. Ibid.

44. *Jones v. Kirby,* [1897] NZLR 48 (S.C., 1896).

45. *Ware v. Attorney General,* (1961) NZLR 694 (S.C., 1960), at 695.

46. *In re a Solicitor, ex parte Incorporated Law Institute of New South Wales,* 52 WN (N.S.W.) 182 (S.C. N.S.W., 1935).

47. *R. v. Titterington,* [1954] QWN 6 (S.C. Qld., 1953); 48 QJPR 164.

48. *Re Doueihi,* 20 A Crim R 374 (S.C. Qld., 1986), at 282.

49. *R. v. Titterington,* at 164.

50. Unreported case East Perth Magistrates' Court; "Woman: I was afraid," *The West Australian,* 1 Sept. 1978, p. 19; see also The Law Reform Commission of Western Australia, *Report on Bail* (Perth: 1979), p. 78, f.n. 45. For a discussion of the criminal status of indemnification in Western Australia prior to the *Bail Act 1982* see The Law Reform Commission of Western Australia, *Review of Bail Procedures* (Perth: 1977), pp. 164–166.

51. *R. v. Baba,* [1977] 2 NSWLR 502 (C.A. N.S.W., 1977), at 504.

52. Ibid., at 505.

53. *Re Doneihi.*

54. Ibid., at 382.

55. Ibid., at 383.

56. *R. v. Freeman, Kron and Kron,* (1985) 17 A Crim R 272 (C.A. N.S.W., 1985).

57. Ibid.

58. Ibid., at 278.

59. Ibid., at 278–279.

60. *Re Condon,* (1972) [1973] VR 427 (S.C. Vic., 1972).

61. Ibid., at 432–433.

62. *Re Wilkinson,* (1981) [1983] V.R. 250 (S.C. Vic., 1981).

63. Ibid., at 254.

64. Ibid., at 255.

65. Ibid., at 256.

66. *Dildar v. State,* [1963] PSCR 126 (S.C., 1962).

67. Ibid., at 129.

68. Ibid., at 129–131.

69. *Mazari v. State,* PLD 1987 Kar 267 (H.C. Kar., 1986); *Muhammad Khan v. State,* 1986 P Cr LJ 2028 (H.C. Lah., 1986); *Abdul Karim v. State,* 1983 P Cr LJ 137 (H.C. Kar., 1982).

70. *Muhammad Abdullah v. State,* PLD 1987 Lah 56 (H.C. Lah., 1986).

71. *Okorie Ukachukwa v. Commissioner of Police,* (1977) 2 IMSLR 177 (H.C. Imo, 1977), at 180.

3

Statutory Provisions Against Commercial Bail Bonding

For about a decade beginning in the mid-1970s, a particularly large number of countries undertook extensive reformulations of their bail systems. Many of these, including Canada, England, South Africa, four states and one territory in Australia, and even two American states, used the opportunity to provide statutory basis for prohibiting indemnifying bail sureties. Prior to this period, only the Canadian provision against this was in statutory form. The process of creating the necessary legislation frequently involved in-depth studies of bail problems and of alternative solutions. In many instances the example of commercial bail bonding in the United States was a major consideration in deciding to reemphasize the prohibition of indemnification by making it a statutory crime. Often, although not intended as such, these studies amount to cogent, well-reasoned condemnations of the commercial bail system. The laws themselves demonstrate the determination of legislators in these countries not to let the evils of that system spread to their jurisdictions.

CANADA

Although Canada has a federal system of government, authority to legislate criminal procedure is principally exercised by the central government. Canada, perhaps because of its proximity to the American example, considerably predated other countries in enacting statutory provisions against commercial bail bonding. The 1953–1954 *Canadian Criminal Code*, applicable nationally, lodges this prohibition under Section 119, which creates an indictable offense punishable by up to two years imprisonment for willful attempts in any manner to obstruct, pervert, or defeat the course of justice. The section goes on to specify acts considered to constitute an obstruction or perversion, such as threats or bribes to jurors or witnesses. Among the specified acts are indemnifying, or agreeing to indemnify, in any way and in whole or in part, a bail bondsman. This is criminal whether it occurs before or after release from custody. Also covered by the prohibition is accepting or agreeing to accept such an indemnification on the part of the bondsman. Again this is worded to cover indemnification in whole or in part and indemnification agreed to or accepted before or after release from custody.[1]

Through this provision, Canada had by the mid-1950s statutorily classed bail bonding for compensation with providing bribes or other corrupt considerations to witnesses for their testimony or jurors for their votes. In fact, the broader offense under which these activities are forbidden—willful attempts to obstruct, pervert, or defeat the course of justice—can be found in Canadian statutes in nearly identical terms at least as far back as 1893.[2] However, even the terms of the provision of the 1953–1954 Code have been strengthened by the Canadians. Between 1965 and 1969 a comprehensive review of the Canadian criminal justice system including bail was undertaken by the Canadian Committee on Corrections (the Ouimet Committee).

The Canadian Committee on Corrections Report

The Ouimet Committee report unanimously endorsed the principle reflected in the existing statute of prohibiting professional bail bondsmen. However, it criticized the existing legislation principally in two regards. One of the Committee's objections was that the word *indemnity* in the prohibition as it existed might be construed as limited to a deposit or guarantee against loss if the surety's recognizance was forfeited. If this interpretation prevailed, they feared, payment of a fee to a bail bondsman might elude the prohibitions in the law. The Committee's other main concern on this matter was the apparent omission from coverage of payment to a surety by a party other than the person seeking release. The Ouimet Committee report accordingly recommended retaining the provision against bail bondsmen with amended wording to remove these weaknesses.[3]

The Bail Reform Act of 1971

The various recommendations of the Ouimet Committee formed the basis of a package of reforms of the bail system, known as the Bail

Reform Act, which was passed in 1971 to take effect in early 1972. Those pertaining to surety indemnification entered the *Canadian Criminal Code* as amendments to Section 127. Under these provisions indemnifying a surety and related acts still constitute an attempt "to instruct, pervert, or defeat the course of justice in a judicial proceeding." Indemnification, or agreement to indemnify, is also still prohibited whether in whole or in part, and regardless of the form it takes or the time at which it occurs. This, however, now applies to indemnification or agreement by either the individual in custody or another in respect to him. Additionally, acceptance of or agreement to accept a fee by a surety, whether from the person in custody or from a third party, is also specifically interdicted now. These offenses are triable either on indictment or summarily. They carry a maximum sentence of two years imprisonment applicable in those cases tried on indictment.[4]

Case Law Development

Although peripheral to the matter of surety indemnification, two lower court decisions, *R. v. Cochrane* (1981) and *R. v. Frenette* (1982), throw some light on the Canadian viewpoint.[5] In each case one party provided another money for a cash bail in an instance where the statute makes an exception for that. The provider entered into no bond with the court. Each court ruled that this lender (or donor) was not a surety and consequently had no right to apply for relief from forfeiture of the bond when the accused absconded. The court in *Frenette* noted the statute provided that cash bail is not to be employed where a surety is required. Therefore in each case the provider was at most a creditor of the absconder. Although the point is not discussed in either opinion, if the lender was considered a surety in such instances, repayment of or agreement to repay the money by the accused could run afoul of the provision against indemnifying sureties. This might in part be what the court had in mind in *Cochrane* in saying that as a policy matter "anything which might encourage applications by persons other than formal sureties to be, in effect, reimbursed for moneys they have unwisely parted with to assist friends or associates" should be avoided.[6] In any event, the emphasis on clearly distinguishing a surety from a lender in these cases demonstrates that Canadian law is careful to defend against one who might expect payment from an accused being viewed as a surety.

Commentary

Canada, then, perhaps partly because of its proximity to the United States, moved first to enact statutory provisions which have the effect of outlawing bail bonding. The Ouimet Report makes evident that prohibiting commercial bail bonding as it exists in the United States is the deliberate purpose of the law. This is confirmed by later Canadian commentary on this aspect of the law. Scollin comments that the pertinent paragraphs "strike at professional bondsmen."[7] Powell likewise refers to the prohibition placed on bondsmen, although the term *surety* has been substituted for *bondsman* in the newer Canadian enactment.[8]

ENGLAND

Prior to the mid-1970s in England, the matter of surety indemnification was handled by common law. Other aspects of the bail system were governed by a mixture of common law and statute. In 1971 the Home Secretary established a Working Party to study the bail system and suggest reforms. The Working Party issued its report in 1974. Among the matters it considered in its comprehensive review was that of surety indemnification.

Working Party on Bail Procedures in Magistrates' Courts

In reviewing the existing law on bail the Working Party noted, "It is clear that it is illegal to indemnify bail." They went on to point out that this was true regardless of whether it is done by the defendant or by a third party, and noted that an intention to frustrate the course of justice need not be proven. In support of these contentions they quoted from *R. v. Porter*.[9]

The merits of retaining this prohibition were principally considered in the context of reviewing the retention of the existing noncommercial sureties. Among the alternatives considered was professional bail bondsmen as found in the United States. The Working Party stated their understanding that such a system does not work satisfactorily in the United States, implicitly citing as criticisms the high rates charged by bondsmen and the governing of bail decisions by a commercial assessment of the risks.[10] They therefore resolved that "we would certainly not wish to see its introduction here; nor is there any support for such an innovation."[11] This contributed to their conclusion that no satisfactory alternative to noncommercial sureties had been found.[12]

The Working Party's report was thus amenable to the law against indemnification and hostile to commercial bail bonding which the law acts to prevent. Consistent with this position a provision against indemnification was incorporated into the proposed legislation. Its inclusion proved a completely agreeable aspect of a bill that otherwise aroused professional and public controversy.

The Bail Act of 1976

Section 9 of the Bail Act of 1976 creates a statutory prohibition against agreeing to indemnify sureties in a criminal proceeding. Since indemnification against any liability is forbidden, payment of even part of the amount of the liability to the surety is clearly covered. The offense may be tried either summarily or on indictment. Summary conviction carries up to three months imprisonment or £1000 fine, or both. Conviction on indictment carries up to a year imprisonment or an unlimited fine. The latter punishment can also be imposed in cases tried summarily but committed to Crown Court for sentencing. Both parties to the agreement are subject to conviction.[13] The statute is worded so as to encompass indemnification other than cash, and agreements made either before or after a proposed individual formally enters into the role of surety.[14] Since the agreement constitutes the offense, actual compensation or even the intent to compensate need not be established. Conversely, spontaneous compensation without prior agreement does not constitute an offense, although, arguably, it may have come to do so under the final common law development in the *Withers* case.[15]

The result of the superseding of the common law on indemnification by the statutory provision was to leave English criminal law no more receptive to commercial bail bonding than it had been under the common law prohibition. Although the failure to cover spontaneous payments within its scope renders the English law marginally more vulnerable to some sureties being compensated than the Canadian law, commercial bail bonding could hardly exist based on spontaneous payments.

AUSTRALIA

Australia has a federal system of government in which authority to determine criminal procedure rests principally with the states. Indeed, even federal crimes are tried in state courts and in general under state procedure. Australia's bail systems vary considerably. As in Canada and England, the use of sureties is available in all Australian jurisdictions but it is routine in none. Unlike in those countries, however, a cash deposit may be required of a surety if difficulties with bail justify it, though this is not usual. This possibility renders the pattern of the Australian bail systems somewhat more similar to the American on these occasions. As in Canada and England, most Australian jurisdictions undertook complete revisions of their bail systems between 1977 and 1985. These reviews resulted in comprehensive new bail acts in six jurisdictions during the period: Victoria, 1977; New South Wales, 1978; Queensland, 1980; Western Australia, 1982; Northern Territory, 1982; and South Australia, 1985. Except for the South Australian, each of these laws contains provisions against the indemnification of sureties. A comprehensive revision of the bail law in the Australian Capital Territory is pending in which a similar provision is contemplated. This would leave only South Australia and Tasmania with no legislation specifically against indemnified sureties, although Tasmania has general legislation against perverting the course of justice.

Studies Prior to Legislation

In several of the Australian jurisdictions, studies of various degrees of comprehensiveness were conducted prior to the proposal of the new bail acts. The most thorough of these was issued in Western Australia by the Law Reform Commission in a 1977 working paper, *Review of Bail Procedures*, and in a final *Report on Bail* in 1979.

In its *Review of Bail Procedures*, the Law Reform Commission considers the matter of indemnified sureties in two contexts. One is in discussing the then current law in the state. The other is in considering and evaluating alternative bail arrangements. Both the Western Australia Police Department and the Women Justices' Association of Western Australia had made submissions to the commission recommending creation of a statutory offense covering surety indemnification.[16]

As regards the current law, the commission concludes that in Western Australia—a non-common law code state—an agreement to indemnify a surety was illegal under the then existing law in that it is contrary to public policy. Such an agreement would therefore be void and might involve the commission of a crime. Arguably, it might be prosecuted as conspiracy to obstruct, pervert, or defeat the course of justice. In all events, the commission points out, under circumstances of indemnification an individual would clearly be legally unacceptable as a surety. Individuals who have entered into an agreement to become a surety for an indemnity are disqualified as a class from becoming sureties.[17]

In its consideration of alternatives, the commission directly takes up the issue of commercial bail bonding. In the commission's view, this system has developed in America for two reasons. The first is because indemnification of a surety is permissible. The second is because a cash deposit is normally required for release on bail.[18]

The commercial system has two advantages in the commission's evaluation. It provides an alternative to a private surety for those unable to find one and it adds a further agency to those seeking an absconding defendant. However, weighing against these, the commission notes "it seems to have serious drawbacks."[19] Five of these are identified:

(1) It lends itself to abuses such as collusive ties between bondsmen and organized crime or police, lawyers, and court officials.

(2) It reduces the release decision to a business-oriented consideration of profitability rather than an evenhanded application of justice.[20] As a result, "some defendants who are professional criminals may be able to arrange a surety even for very substantial sums through indemnification agreements, while others, possibly more deserving of release on bail, remain in custody."[21]

(3) In reality, the bondsman is not at risk in most cases. Consequently, the possibility of effective supervision of the defendant is doubtful.

(4) The defendant would feel no moral obligation to appear for the bondsman's sake as he might with a personal surety.

(5) The bondsman is not usually in a position to give a satisfactory reference for the defendant as could a personal surety.[22]

Weighing these factors, the Law Reform Commission concludes that "having considered the United States' experience . . . there are no sound reasons in principal for removing the present prohibition on indemnification of sureties."[23] Even a relaxation of the existing law on surety indemnification can be justified only if an American-style system is desired or if the community is at least prepared to take the risk of its occurring. The commission unequivocally opposes the introduction of professional bondsmen.[24] On the contrary, the commission recommends clarifying the legal liability of an individual who agrees to indemnify a surety by making the act an offense by specific statutory provision.[25] The final report of the commission makes only one recommendation for automatic disqualification of proposed sureties; that is, that a proposed surety should be disqualified where reasonable grounds exist to suspect indemnification.[26]

As to the details of the offense to be created, the commission recommends that indemnification of a surety or agreement to indemnify be made an indictable offense triable summarily. Additionally, it should disqualify the surety. The maximum punishment should not exceed one year's imprisonment or a fine of $1,000. Because of the wide range of possible agreements which might be construed as agreeing to indemnify, requiring the consent of the Attorney General to prosecute is recommended.[27]

Also informative regarding the Australian view on commercial bail bonding is the comparable pre-legislative study undertaken in New South Wales, the *Report of the Bail Review Committee* issued in 1976. This committee considered the alternative of supplementing the existing personal sureties with professional bail bondsmen on the American model. It quickly, however, dismisses the approach as "most undesirable." The only advantage the committee finds worthy of comment is that such a system would avoid the practice of having the police visit the homes of defendants and sureties to assess the value of property potentially available to cover a recognizance. Against this it cites four principal disadvantages. First, it encourages the setting of very high bails in the knowledge that the defendant will pay only a relatively moderate percentage of the amount set. Second, the bondsman rather than a judicial officer effectively decides who is to be kept in custody pending trial and who is to be released. Third, often violent unilateral action is taken by some bondsmen against defendants whom they suspect of absconding. Finally, all defendants end up paying their percentage, which goes to the bondsman. Under the then existing New South Wales system, all defendants are refunded in full any amount they have deposited upon meeting their bail obligation. The committee believes "it would be quite wrong to propose a system which required all defendants to pay for their release."[28]

The Bail Review Committee elsewhere in its report notes that indemnification of a surety by a defendant is an offense under the common law (New South Wales is a common law state). However, it comments—in the context of a personal surety system—that the offense is impossible to detect in practice and undoubtedly often occurs. The committee fails to note the connection between this offense and preventing the rejected alternative of commercially provided bail.[29]

Statutory Provisions

The basic provisions of the statutes in the five Australian jurisdictions specifically legislating against indemnification of a surety are similar, although the wording and format differ. All of them make it an offense for anyone either to indemnify or agree to indemnify a bail surety. Each provides that both the indemnifier and the surety indemnified are guilty of the offense. Since anyone's indemnifying a surety, or agreeing to do so, constitutes the offense, whether the indemnifier is the accused or a third party makes no difference. All of the laws provide that the offense occurs even if the person to be indemnified eventually fails to become a surety.[30] Thus, if the arrangement is discovered and the surety is rejected, prosecution of the offense is not defeated. Western Australia reinforces this point by specifically applying the provision to sureties or proposed sureties.[31] Moreover, whether an agreement occurs before or after the individual becomes a surety is made irrelevant in all jurisdictions. A final point of similarity among the five is that the offense is committed whether compensation is to be in money or some other form.[32]

The penalties attached to the indemnification offense vary considerably. At the lower end of the scale, Victoria punishes the offense with a maximum of $500 fine or three months imprisonment. At the upper end, New South Wales imposes up to $3,000 fine or three years imprisonment if conviction is on indictment, and $2,000 or two years if it is summary. The Northern Territory likewise imposes a $3,000 fine or a three-year maximum imprisonment. In the mid-range, Queensland and Western Australia provide for up to a $1,000 fine or twelve months imprisonment, with the latter specifying the option of both being imposed.[33]

A few other salient differences are noticeable. Western Australia, following the recommendation of its Law Reform Commission, has legislated that a person is not qualified to be approved as a surety where reasonable grounds exist to believe that he has been or will be indemnified. While this is probably the practice elsewhere, raising it to a legislative requirement would clearly help frustrate any attempt at commercial provision of bail.[34] An amendment to the law in that state has provided two alternative defenses for a surety or proposed surety in one situation where an agreement to indemnify exists. If two other people enter in agreement to indemnify a surety and the surety either has no knowledge of it or has knowledge of it but takes all reasonably available steps to prevent the agreement, the surety commits no offense.[35] If, for example, the accused and another agree to indemnify the surety, the surety could argue either lack of knowledge of or the required attempt to prevent the agreement, even though the others would have violated the law. Although the Law Reform Commission recommended that the Attorney General's permission be required to prosecute for indemnifying a surety, the statute has no such provision. This leaves New South Wales as the only jurisdiction requiring ministerial consent to prosecute the offense.[36]

A further point worthy of note pertains to a regulation pursuant to a statute rather than to the statute itself. In Queensland, the *Bail Regulations* provide in the Affidavit of Justification for sureties for the clause, "I have not been indemnified as to bail . . . . " A further clause states, "I am not a party to an undertaking as to bail in any other criminal proceeding."

The latter clause may be altered if necessary. The affidavit containing both clauses is sworn to by the surety.[37] As a result any incipient effort at commercial bonding would promptly come to light or a perjury prosecution against the surety would be possible in addition to the possible indemnification charge.[38] In fact, prosecution in *R. v. Titterington,* discussed in chapter 2, was for perjury on a similar form.[39]

Commentary

Five of the eight major Australian jurisdictions, then, have enacted statutory provisions which have the effect of making commercial bail bonding a crime. In New South Wales, Victoria, Queensland, Western Australia, and the Northern Territory any payment to, or agreement to pay, an individual for becoming a bail surety would run afoul of laws against surety indemnification. Such a provision is contemplated for the Australian Capital Territory as well. Evidence indicates that, at least in some of these jurisdictions, preventing American-style commercial bail was an important consideration in including the particular provision. In Western Australia its adoption was the clear result of a policy decision that the commercial system was undesirable. In New South Wales the same judgment was made as to the merits of that system, although the preventive role of the anti-indemnification clause was not made explicit.

UNION OF SOUTH AFRICA

Although the South African bail system exhibits defects that will be considered later, as it pertains to ordinary common law crimes it is instructive regarding surety indemnification. The Criminal Procedure Act 1977 changed the emphasis of the country's bail law to cash deposit while reducing recognizance to an alternative available upon showing cause of why it should be used.[40] When recognizance is used, one or more sureties can be required as added security.[41] The 1977 act makes clear that deposit of bail money by someone other than the accused is permitted.[42] Thus the South African bail system is closer to the American system than those found in England, Canada, or Australia. Despite such a basic similarity, however, South Africa joins the other jurisdictions in forbidding the indemnification of sureties.

Common and Statutory Law

The basic criminality of surety indemnification is accomplished, as already discussed, by applying the English common law cases. Thus, in the words of one authority, any arrangements or contract under which a third party providing money for bail "purports to become indemnified, whether by means of deposit or contract, is illegal."[43] South Africa supplements this familiar provision with a statutory clause forbidding officials considering bail from accepting bail money from anyone who they believe has been or will be indemnified in any manner against loss, and has or will receive any financial benefit in connection with providing the money.[44]

This provision is usefully compared with the one for similar purpose in Western Australia. Both statutes operate at the level of reasonable belief: "reasonable grounds for believing" in the Western Australia Law, "reason to believe" in the South African. However, South Africa's statute (unlike its common law on the subject) seems to apply only to the provider of a cash deposit and not to a surety by recognizance. In contrast, the Western Australian statute applies to any surety whether by recognizance or with a cash deposit. While the Western Australian provision covers any payment made to a surety by the broad interpretation given the word *indemnification* in the case law, the South African specifically mentions any financial benefit received in connection with providing a bail deposit as well as indemnification as grounds for rejection. Finally, the South African law is cast as an instruction to bail officials not to allow deposit by an indemnified person, while the Western Australian is cast simply as a disqualification to be approved as a surety.[45]

Case Law Development

A 1962 case, *Mapumulu v. Pieterse, N.O.*[46] is instructive as to the general viewpoint reflected in both South Africa's application of the common law regarding surety indemnification and the statutory provision against financial benefits to those providing bail monies. In this case a cash bail deposit was provided by an attorney's clerk for an individual's release. However, whether the money ultimately came from the attorney, the client, or another remained unclear. The court remarked that particularly if the bail money was deposited out of fees paid to the attorney for conducting the case, the proceeding was of questionable propriety. The court's explanation of the reason for the impropriety is particularly enlightening: "Certainly, in so far as an accused person is placed in the position that he loses the amount he has deposited as fees, whether he answers to his bail or escapes, this is undesirable, for the urge upon him to answer his bail is hardly existent."[47] The situation that this court finds so objectionable is, of course, the one that is created on a regular basis in commercial bail bonding with the bondsman in the role that the attorney is hypothecated to have taken here.

Commentary

The South African bail system is of particular interest in regard to surety indemnification because it more closely resembles the American system in its basic workings than those of England, Canada, or Australia. The norm in South Africa, as in the United States when commercial providers are not used, is bail by cash deposit. That country thus shares with the United States one of the two elements which the Law Reform Commission of Western Australia identified as prerequisites for the development of commercial bail bonding.

South Africa, however, applies the common law provision against surety indemnification which makes any agreement to pay a surety an offense. In addition, by statute, bail officials must refuse bail deposits from anyone who there is reason to believe has been or will be indemnified or has received or will receive a financial benefit for providing bail monies. Thus, in spite of an initial similarity to the American system, which might be thought to create a vulnerability to the commercial system's development, that is prevented.

UNITED STATES

The United States provides the prime example of a country dominated by commercial bail bonding. Even most of those jurisdictions which have reformed their bail arrangements to provide alternative means of bail do not forbid the practice, and many indeed actively retain it as an option. At least two states, however, have joined the ranks of those jurisdictions making commercial bail bonding illegal by statute. Case decisions have upheld the constitutionality of these laws. The statutes, in Wisconsin and Kentucky, have notable differences in the way they approach the prohibition.

Statutory Provisions

The Wisconsin statute is quite simple. It provides that all bail sureties shall be natural persons and residents of the state. An exception is created with regard to traffic offenses for automobile associations and the like who offer bail services to members. (This is limited to a total of $200 per year.) The statute then states that no bail surety may be compensated for acting as such.[48]

The Kentucky statute as created by the *Bail-Bonding Act 1976* provides explicitly that, "It shall be unlawful for any person to engage in the business of bail bondsman."[49] It goes on to include within its prohibition anyone who for compensation or other consideration furnishes bail or funds or property to serve as bail, or makes bonds or enters into undertakings as a surety in a criminal case. As in Wisconsin, provision is made for a limited exception for automobile associations and their like in regard to traffic offenses.[50] Violations of the provisions against compensated bail are categorized as Class A misdemeanors for first offenses. These carry a penalty of imprisonment for up to twelve months. Subsequent violations are Class D felonies, the punishment for which is imprisonment for not less than one nor more than five years.[51]

Case Law Development

The Wisconsin and the Kentucky statutes were both subjected to litigation by former bail bondsmen challenging their constitutionality. The litigation regarding the Kentucky law was especially persistent. After an initial trial court victory by the bondsmen, the case was appealed to the Kentucky Supreme Court. That court held that the law abolishing commercial bail bonding is not unconstitutionally unreasonable and arbitrary, but rather is a proper exercise of the police power promoting the public welfare. Whatever is detrimental to the commonwealth is properly considered. This certainly includes the inherent evils and abuses of the compensated sureties in the bail system.[52]

Neither was the abolition in violation of due process. Exercise of the police power almost inevitably curtails property rights, including the abolition of private businesses.[53] In the court's words:

> The bail bonding business by compensated surety is not "an ancient honorable and necessary calling," but one whose evils have been tolerated because of deep-rooted antipathy against the confinement of persons entitled to a presumption of innocence pending trial. Bail bonding by compensated surety has never enjoyed a favorable status but exists because no better system has been provided. It does not have protection as an integral part of the judicial process.[54]

The Kentucky Supreme Court's view of compensated bail sureties thus matches that found in courts and legislatures worldwide.

The bail bondsmen's challenge to the statute next was heard in the Federal District Court for the Eastern District of Kentucky. Here the plaintiffs raised four constitutional points that were addressed explicitly by the court's decision. They claimed that the statute (1) deprived them of liberty and property without due process; (2) impaired contract obligations; (3) violated protection against excessive bail; and (4) violated the separation of powers between the legislative and judicial branches. The court found each contention insubstantial.[55]

To accord with due process, the state's exercise of the police power in outlawing the bail bonding business would have to be based on a reasonable conclusion that this step would further the public welfare. The court looked to the preamble to the statute to find the factors motivating this step. The preamble gives among its reasons for the enactment that "bail bondsmen have . . . reaped huge profits . . . to the detriment of the rights of many citizens and have been a major cause of corruption in the administration of justice." In addition, the commercial bail system has "otherwise fostered widespread abuse of the laws and of the rights of citizens . . . through the corruptive influence of the bail bondsman."[56] Based upon this, the court finds unsound the claim that due process was lacking.

Turning to the impairment of contract, the court reasons that this clause prohibits only statutes that infringe upon existing contracts, not those that act to prevent future ones. Since the anti-bail bonding law provides in great detail for the mechanism to preserve existing bails, the court rules the claim insubstantial. Additionally, even if this were not so, police power is an implied part of every contract in that it enforces the contract. Police power, however, extends to protecting the general welfare and is paramount to any rights created by contracts between individuals, and is not diminished because it may affect a private contract. Contracts are protected from arbitrary restraint, but are not immune from reasonable regulation or even prohibition imposed in the interest of the community.[57]

With regard to protection against excessive bail, the bondsmen are not seeking to be free from this evil. Therefore they lack standing to make this claim. Even if they had it, however, the court points out that the statute contains detailed limits upon bail and criteria to be considered in setting it, but leaves discretion to establish bail amounts to the courts. Therefore, the claim that the law violates this constitutional provision is without merit.[58]

Finally, the separation of powers argument is considered. This claims that by prohibiting courts from dealing with bail bondsmen the legislature impermissibly infringes on the judicial branch, violating the principle of separation of powers. The court begins by saying the requirements of separation of powers under the state constitution are not generally a matter for inquiry under the federal constitution. The only federal requirements would be that the state distribute its powers according to due process and not transgress any other restrictions of the federal constitution which have been applied to the states. Since no such other restriction or due process has been found to be violated here, this claim is also insubstantial. The action was therefore dismissed.[59]

Challenge to the statute was next mounted in the Federal District Court for the Western District of Kentucky. Five constitutional claims were raised of which only two were discussed by the court. One was dismissed as having been precluded by the prior actions.[60] The one issue that was considered at some length was the claim that the statute constituted an unconstitutional bill of attainder. A bill of attainder is defined by the court as "a legislative act which levies punishment against specified individuals or groups of individuals without a judicial trial." The Bail-Bonding Act does not fall within this definition in three important regards. First, it does not pertain to specific individuals or organizations. Rather, it proscribes certain classes of activities in which no individual or organization may engage. Second, it provides no retroactive punishment. Penalties are attached only to engaging in the bailbonding business after the act was in effect. Since by altering their activities people can escape punishment, there is no attainder. Third, the legislature provides no determination of the guilt of the bail bondsmen in place of a judicial determination. Therefore the act is not an unconstitutional bill of attainder.[61]

The only other point on which the district court comments upon the merits is a claim that the bondsmen's equal protection rights are violated by the statute. Since the law applies equally to all citizens, residents of Kentucky or not, this claim is found to be without merit.[62] The court closes by granting a motion for the defendant's attorneys' fees against one of the bonding companies citing the need to deter the relitigating time and again of questions that have already been disposed of.[63]

In the one issue discussed in the final round of litigation, the U.S. Court of Appeals for the Sixth Circuit sustained the decision of the district court and endorsed its reasoning regarding the bill of attainder claim.[64]

Litigation challenging the constitutionality of the Wisconsin law against commercial bail bonding is considerably less prolific. It is confined effectively to one case raising two constitutional claims: violation of due process and violation of equal protection. In deciding these claims, the Wisconsin Court of Appeals applied similar tests for each to a state's exercise of the police power such as abolishing commercial bail bonding. To meet due process requirements once infringement on a basic and substantial individual liberty has been demonstrated, the purpose or objective of the enactment must be a real and proper one and the means to achieve it must have a reasonable and rational relation to the purpose or objective. To meet equal protection requirements infringing such a liberty, a reasonable and practical grounds for the classification made must exist. The classification must be reasonable and practical in relation to the objective. The statute need not employ the classification best serving the general welfare. Doubts must be resolved in favor of the statutory classification. In applying both tests, statutes are presumed constitutional. A challenge must prove unconstitutionality beyond a reasonable doubt. This means, in effect, that the challenger must prove that the exercise of the police power is without any reasonable basis. Conversely, if the statute has any reasonable basis, it will be sustained.[65]

In applying the due process test to the present statute, the court determines that the appropriate question is whether the legislature could reasonably conclude that outlawing commercial bail bonding furthers the public welfare. Such a rational basis is found. After all relevant data have been considered by a court making a bail decision and the amount of bail has been judicially determined, the commercial bail bondsman subverts the process by facilitating the release of good economic risks for one tenth of the judicially determined amount. This is a "denigration of the court's discretion in determining bail."[66] In addition, the "legislature may have reasonably and rationally considered the commercial bail bonding system's potential for abuse."[67] On the one hand, the court concludes, legislation protecting the integrity of judicial bail determinations is clearly in the public interest. Eliminating commercial bail bondsmen is rationally related to this objective. On the other hand, no showing is made that no public interest is served by eliminating bail for profit. Therefore the statute meets due process requirements.[68]

The equal protection issue centers on the difference in the treatment accorded sureties for profit as compared to gratuitous sureties and automobile associations providing traffic offense bails. The court finds that a constitutionally permissible grounds exists for the distinction between commercial sureties and gratuitous individual sureties. Since the latter do not provide release for one tenth of the amount judicially determined to be necessary, they do not subvert the judicial process. Moreover, they lack both the business opportunity and the business motive possessed by commercial bail bondsmen to corrupt police and court officials. The classification is therefore found to be reasonable in relation to the objective of protecting the integrity of the judicial bail determination.[69]

Since a stringent limitation of $200 per year is placed on the bail bonding activities of automobile associations and the like, reasonable grounds are also found to distinguish these from the business of criminal bail bonding. The small amounts involved render this unlikely to seriously subvert the bail process. Similarly, they are not likely to provide an impetus to corrupt or improper activity. The classifications created by the statute are then rationally based. No equal protection claim is established.[70]

Commentary

The fact that two states in the United States, which has no common law against indemnified sureties, have chosen by statute to create such a prohibition tells heavily against commercial bail bonding. The language of the courts in the cases challenging these statutes for unconstitutionality is, moreover, significantly similar to that employed by courts and other official bodies worldwide. Discussion is in terms of subversion and even corruption of the judicial process. This places these American courts' opinions in proximity to the terminology of obstructing and perverting the course of justice found in comparable discussion in Australia, Canada, England, and other common law countries. The Kentucky Supreme Court's view that commercial bail bonding is not an ancient, honorable, or necessary business but one that is tolerated only because no better system of pretrial release has been provided is in line with professional opinion in many countries of common law heritage worldwide.

CONCLUSION

Although the common law provision against indemnified sureties which acts to prevent commercial bail bonding was applied in a number of countries prior to 1970, only one, Canada, had a similar statutory provision. The Canadian Bail Reform Act of 1971 provided a chance to review this provision, and as a result it was strengthened by making clear that any payment to a surety is interdicted. As the preceding Ouimet Committee Report made clear and subsequent commentary confirmed, defense against American-style commercial bail was the objective of these provisions. By classifying compensated sureties under the obstruction or perversion of justice clause, Canada expresses eloquently its view of the neighboring approach to bail.

Five years later, England enacted its statute against indemnified sureties. Here again the Working Party on Bail's report makes clear that it is a deliberate attempt to forestall commercial bail bonding, which is viewed as an evil whose development is to be prevented.

Between 1977 and 1982 four Australian states—New South Wales, Victoria, Queensland, and Western Australia—as well as the Northern Territory included similar legislation in reforms of their bail laws. As the Law Reform Commissions' studies in Western Australia make clear, and as the Bail Review Committee's report suggests, these provisions defend against the development of commercially provided bail. South Africa, with a cash deposit system of bail, basically relies upon the common law prohibition against commercial bail, but included in its 1977 restructuring of the bail law to one normally of cash deposit a provision forbidding indemnified individuals from being accepted as sureties.

Even in the United States, Kentucky and Wisconsin have adopted statutes against compensated sureties in creating legislation to eliminate the commercial bondsman system. The opinions in the cases upholding the constitutionality of these laws speak of such systems in terms strikingly similar to those used by observers in other countries. Commercial bail is seen as a corruption of the judicial process, acting against the public welfare so as to make exercise of the police power of the states against it constitutionally permissible.

Clearly, then, as statutory provisions indicate, and perhaps even more explicity as prelegislation studies urge, a widespread consensus has emerged throughout the common law world that the common law's antipathy to commercialized bail is correct and, if anything, should be made more forceful in statutory form.

NOTES

1. *Canadian Criminal Code, 1953–1954,* s. 119(2)(d),(e).
2. *Taschereau's Criminal Code of Canada* (1893; rpt. Toronto: Carswell, 1980), s. 154(d).
3. Canadian Committee on Corrections, chair. Hon. Mr. Justice Roger Ouimet, *Towards Unity: Criminal Justice and Corrections* (Ottawa: Queen's Printer, 1969), p. 119; Clay M. Powell, *Arrest and Bail in Canada* (Toronto: Butterworths, 1976), pp. 80–81.
4. *Canadian Criminal Code,* s. 127(1); Powell, pp. 1–2, 80–81.
5. *R. v. Cochrane,* 60 CCC 2d 329 (D.C. Sask., 1981); *R. v. Frenette,* 30 CR 3d 123 (Co. Ct. B.C., 1982).
6. *R. v. Cochrane,* at 331.
7. John A. Scollin, Q.C., *Pre-Trial Release* (Toronto: Carswell, 1977), p. 11.
8. Powell, p. 80.
9. Home Office, *Bail Procedures in Magistrate's Courts* (London: HMSO, 1974), p. 11.
10. Ibid., p. 36.
11. Ibid.
12. Ibid.
13. *Bail Act of 1976,* s. 9.

14. Edgar L. Bradley and J. J. Senior, *Bail in Magistrates' Courts* (Chichester: Barry Rose Publishers, 1977), pp. 36–37; "The New Law of Bail," *Justice of the Peace*, 140 (Feb 18, 1978): 97; *Stone's Justices Manual*, I, 168.

15. Bradley and Senior, p. 36; *Archbold Criminal Pleading Evidence and Practice*, 42nd ed., pp. 2092–2093.

16. The Law Reform Commission of Western Australia, *Report on Bail* (Perth: 1979), p. 85, n. 72.

17. The Law Reform Commission of Western Australia, *Review of Bail Procedures* (Perth, 1977), pp. 146, 156, 164–166, 196.

18. Ibid., pp. 147, 166.

19. Ibid., p. 147.

20. Ibid.

21. Ibid., p. 141.

22. Ibid., p. 148.

23. Ibid., p. 166.

24. Ibid.

25. Ibid., pp. 151, 196.

26. Law Reform Commission (W.A.), *Review*, pp. 77–78.

27. Ibid., p. 85.

28. *Report of the Bail Review Committee* (Sydney, 1976), p. 19.

29. Ibid., p. 16.

30. *Bail Act 1978* (N.S.W.), s. 58(2),(3)(b); *Bail Act 1977* (Vic.), s. 31(1),(2); *Bail Act 1980* (Qld.), s. 26(1),(2)(b); *Bail Act 1982* (W.A.), s. 50(1),(2)(a); *Bail Act 1982* (N.T.), s. 45(2),(3)(a).

31. *Bail Act 1982* (W.A.), s. 50(1).

32. *Bail Act 1978* (N.S.W.), s. 58(3)(a)(b); *Bail Act 1977* (Vic.), s. 31(2); *Bail Act 1980* (Qld.), s. 26(2)(a)(c); *Bail Act 1982* (W.A.), s. 50(a)(b); *Bail Act 1982* (N.T.), s. 45(3)(a)(b).

33. *Bail Act 1978* (N.S.W.), s. 58(2)(a)(b); *Bail Act 1977* (Vic.), s. 31(1); *Bail Act 1980* (Qld.), s. 26(1); *Bail Act 1982* (W.A.), s. 50(1); *Bail Act 1982* (N.T.), s. 45(2).

34. *Bail Act 1982* (W.A.), s. 38(c).

35. *Bail Amendment Act 1984* (W.A.), s. 18.

36. *Bail Act 1978* (N.S.W.), s. 58(5).

37. *Bail Regulations 1980* (Qld.), Form 12.

38. See, for example, Law Reform Commission (W.A.), *Review*, p. 165.

39. *R. v. Titterington*, [1954] QWN6 (S.C. Qld., 1953), [1954] 48 Q.J.P.R. 164.

40. *Criminal Procedure Act 1977*, s. 60; *Annual Survey of South African Law* 1977 (Cape Town: Juta, 1978), p. 447; Alfred V. Lansdown, *South African Criminal Law and Procedure* (Cape Town: Juta, 1982), V, 311, 335.

41. *Criminal Procedure Act 1977*, s. 60(2); Lansdown, p. 335.

42. *Criminal Procedure Act 1977*, s. 69(1); Lansdown, p. 341.

43. Lansdown, p. 341.

44. *Criminal Procedure Act 1977*, s. 69(3); Lansdown, p. 341.

45. *Bail Act 1982* (W.A.), s. 38; *Criminal Procedure Act 1977*, s. 69(3).

46. *Mapumulu v. Pieterse N.O.* (1962) [1962(2)] Sa 198 (S.C. L.D.).

47. Ibid., at 200.

48. W.S.A., 969.12(1)(2).

49. K.R.S., 431.510(1).

50. K.R.S., 431.510(4).

51. *Stephens v. Bonding Association of Kentucky*, 538 S.W. 2d 580 (S.C. Ky., 1976), at 581.

52. Ibid.

53. Ibid., at 583.

54. Ibid.

55. *Johnson Bonding Co., Inc. v. Commonwealth of Kentucky*, 420 F. Supp 331 (D.C. E.D. Ky., 1976).

56. Ibid., at 335.

57. Ibid., at 336–337.

58. Ibid., at 337–338.

59. Ibid., at 338.

60. *Benboe v. Carrol*, 494 F. Supp. 462 (D.C. W.D. Ky., 1977).

61. Ibid., at 465.

62. *Benboe v. Carroll* (1977) 494 F. Supp. 462, at 466.

63. Ibid., at 466–467.

64. *Benboe v. Carroll*, 625 F. 2d 737 (C.A. 6, 1980), at 738.

65. *Kahn v. McCormack*, 299 N.W. 2d 279 (C.A. Wis., 1980), at 281–282.

66. Ibid., at 282.

67. Ibid., at 283.

68. Ibid., at 282–283.

69. Ibid., at 283.

70. Ibid., at 283–284.

4

The Recognizance Alternative

The most widely employed alternative to commercial bail bonding is recognizance. This bail form encompasses traditional common law bail and is spread worldwide in former British colonies. In fact, prior to the bail reform movement of the 1970s, alternatives to commercial provision of bail other than this were very rare, being limited to a few noncommercial cash deposit systems such as those in Liberia and South Africa. Consequently, a safe generalization is still that any common law based country that has not revamped its bail system since 1970 probably has a recognizance bail system.

Under the traditional recognizance alternative, the primary sanction motivating the accused's presence for trial is the threat of financial forfeit. An accused seeking pretrial release simply pledges to forfeit a specified amount of money. This debt is incurred conditionally. Upon failure to appear in court the condition of the indebtedness is triggered and the money is declared to be owed. No money or other valuable is surrendered under the traditional recognizance approach unless and until a forfeiture has occurred. Typically bail systems of this type allow one or more persons to be required to stand as third party sureties for the accused's bail. When this is done, they too incur a conditional indebtedness triggered by the accused's failure to appear. Again no payment is required unless a forfeiture occurs. Under the traditional recognizance approach, in addition to these recognizances nonfinancial conditions governing the accused's conduct while on bail can often be imposed, although a number of jurisdictions restrict this possibility, some fairly severely. Some traditional recognizance countries also make strictly limited provisions for cash deposit in certain instances. Even when allowed, these typically must be proposed by the accused. Courts are authorized to accept them, but not to require them. Among the jurisdictions exhibiting traditional recognizance bail systems are: those of the Indian sub-continent; Ireland; the common law countries of Southeast Asia and the Indian Ocean; the common law countries of Africa except for Liberia, South Africa, and Swaziland; the common law countries of the Caribbean and Latin American region; and the common law countries of the South Pacific except for Australia, New Zealand, Papua New Guinea, and the Philippines.

In addition to the traditional recognizance systems, a small number of jurisdictions have modified recognizance systems. These systems keep the predominant reliance upon recognizance, but modify it in a variety of ways. Common modifications include increased authority for courts to require security deposits of various sorts and to impose nonfinancial conditions. Priorities are imposed on the combinations of possible bail terms thus created. Use of third party sureties are placed in the context of these priorities. Criminal penalties for absconding are often created, as may be penalties regarding various ancillary bail matters. Statutory rights regarding bail may be expanded. Procedures may be altered. Among the modified recognizance bail systems are those of the Australian states of Victoria, Queensland, and Western Australia. These jurisdictions revised their bail laws in the 1970s but retained their previous recognizance emphasis.

INDIA

Background

No country, including India, presents a recognizance system that has no elements borrowed from other bail forms. Indian bail law, however, is highly restrictive in controlling such borrowings. Overall, it provides one of the best examples of a traditional recognizance system.

Prior to 1973, bail in India was governed by a *Criminal Procedure Code* dating (with subsequent amendments) back to 1898. Although this law was heavily influenced by English bail practices, it was specifically written for India and differed in substantial respects from the then prevailing English bail system. This earlier version of Indian bail law was, except for that of England, the most widely influential of all bail laws. That law—albeit with post-independence amendments—is still in effect in Pakistan and Bangladesh. Very similar laws modeled upon it govern bail in common law jurisdictions throughout Southeast Asia and the Indian Ocean island states, and its influence extends into

Africa. As recently as 1987 courts in Malaysia and Singapore have referred to Indian decisions interpreting that statute to assist in construing the comparable provisions of their statutes.[1] A Malaysian high court explained the relationship between provisions of that country's bail law and the 1898 statute. Since the two are "almost identical," decisions of Indian courts under the old law are "persuasive authorities" in Malaysia.[2] In more general terms, the High Court of Criminal Revision in Tanzania referred to that country's *Criminal Procedure Code* as being based upon but not slavishly following the earlier Indian Code.[3]

In 1969 the Law Commission of India issued a multivolume study of the country's criminal procedure as its *41st Report*. This dealt in part with existing bail practices and suggestions for their reform. The Law Commission's report served as the basis for criminal procedure legislation, including bail procedure, in the *Criminal Procedure Code of 1973*. The new code made relatively few major changes in the bail law, principally organizing, unifying, and clarifying the law. Some case law was made statutory and some disputed points were settled, but fundamentally the existing bail system was retained. Thus India continues to have a recognizance bail system of a basically traditional sort.

In spite of India's having had for about a hundred years a single bail law embodied in one *Criminal Procedure Code* for the whole country, it is a federal system. States' needs are accommodated to some degree in amendments to the code altering bail provisions within their jurisdictions. Additionally, the high courts immediately below the Supreme Court have jurisdictions based on states or combinations of states. Thus, differences in the interpretation of bail provisions can and do exist among states.

Terms of Bail

Indian bail under the *Criminal Procedure Act 1973* relies on the personal recognizance of that individual as its basic sanction to compel appearance of the accused. An arrested person seeking release on bail pending trial enters into an agreement to forfeit an amount of money upon failing to appear in court as specified. If the defendant then does not appear as required, the recognizance is forfeited and the debt to the state is incurred by the defaulter. The forfeiture may be abated in whole or part, however, if the court finds that this is warranted. To this end an opportunity is provided for the accused to explain his absence. The decision is a matter for judicially exercised discretion. Factors beyond control making the accused's appearance impossible, such as a medical emergency, constitute good reason for remission. Other factors to be considered are the length of the accused's absence, the nature of the offense charged, the degree of inconvenience to the court, and the effort and expense of the state in securing the accused.[4]

Although the accused's recognizance is usually combined with other bail terms (particularly sureties), the Indian Supreme Court has urged much greater use of personal recognizances without such supplements. In a 1979 case the court termed antiquated the concept that pretrial release could only be ordered with sureties. It encouraged release on personal recognizance without surety whenever courts are satisfied that accuseds have roots in the community so as to be unlikely to abscond. The Court proceeded to list indications that would determine this. In addition to those indicative of a heightened incentive to abscond, which would be considered anyway in deciding to grant bail, the Court also emphasizes these five areas:

1. Length of residence in the community
2. Employment status and financial ties
3. Family ties and relationships
4. Responsible community members willing to vouch for the accused's reliability
5. Other factors indicative of community ties[5]

The amount at which a bail recognizance may be set is limited by two considerations established by Section 440 of the code: the amount may not be excessive, and it must be established with regard to the circumstances of the case. Within these limits the court has broad discretion in establishing amount of bail. This discretion, however, may not be exercised in an arbitrary fashion—judicial exercise of the discretion is required. This includes objectivity, detachment, and scrupulous avoidance of extra-judicial considerations. A major consideration in establishing the amount of a bail recognizance under Indian law is the seriousness of the charge. However, the amount at which bail is set should not be determined exclusively based on this. Indian courts have condemned mechanically setting bail amounts based upon schedules keyed to the nature of the offense. Other factors to which the attention of courts is mandated include the defendant's financial means and capacity, the probability of the accused's absconding, and the individual's position in society. Thus the poor, the aged, the young, women, and the infirm should be dealt with liberally by bailing courts. Reduction of excessive bail may be sought by application to the higher courts.[6]

As a second sanction enforcing bail, courts in India can—and normally do—require among the bail terms one or more third parties to be provided as sureties. Sureties also enter a recognizance pledging to forfeit a specified sum if the defendant fails to appear. The purpose of sureties, however, is well established in Indian case law to be securing the appearance of the accused. Their monetary liability is merely a sanction against their own failure to achieve this purpose and not itself the objective of requiring sureties. It is also not a security of the debt the accused incurs by forfeiture.[7]

Sureties regularly constitute an additional guarantee for appearance of defendants except where they are thought unnecessary. Moreover, they are mandatory whenever bail is granted after an accused's recognizance has been forfeited for breach of bail conditions without sufficient justification. Reflecting sureties' adjunct position, an accused may not be released on the surety's recognizance without personally executing a recognizance. So fundamental is this view of sureties that until 1979 a major dispute existed among Indian courts as to whether a recognizance by sureties was even enforceable when the accused's recognizance was omitted. The Supreme Court in that year finally overruled a considerable body of case law by holding that it was.[8] The adjunct perception taken of sureties is one of a number of factors in Indian bail tending to militate against commercial provision of bail. It does so conceptually by emphasizing the personal liability of a defendant in all cases, even those involving sureties.

Various aspects of suretyship under the Indian approach stem from the view taken of its purpose. Before releasing a defendant on bail with sureties, Indian law requires that magistrates or judges be personally satisfied in their judicial capacity of the adequacy of persons proposed as sureties to fulfill that role. This includes but goes beyond their possession of adequate property to be able, if necessary, to pay the amount of their recognizance. It also includes being reliable as regards securing the accused's appearance. Courts consequently will sometimes consider the respectability of candidates for suretyship. Evidence on the various aspects of reliability as well as on solvency, consequently, may be taken by courts and must serve as the basis upon which discretion in accepting sureties is exercised. The view that the purpose of sureties is principally to secure appearance and that their financial obligation is a derivative sanction to enforce it underlies this concept that sufficiency includes reliability, and reliability includes respectability. Otherwise, sufficiency would equate with solvency.[9]

Who meets this standard is for the discretion of the court, so long as that is judicially and not arbitrarily exercised. Other suspects, or persons of bad character, therefore, do not constitute the sufficient sureties required by the law for the accused's release.[10] For similar reasons, proposed sureties who have entered an agreement to be indemnified are ineligible to stand in the role. As already discussed, such individuals are viewed as having a lessened stake in the accused's appearance than the court has deemed necessary. They are correspondingly less than reliable as sureties, and consequently constitute insufficient sureties. Commercial bail is thus further repressed.

Acting toward this same result, moreover, is the restriction that artificial persons such as corporations cannot serve as sureties. Only natural persons are suitable for this role. One dimension of suitability is being of sufficient vigilance. Since the ultimate threat in default of payment of the recognizance is imprisonment, and since artificial persons cannot be imprisoned, the obligation of vigilance cannot be enforced against them. Even more telling, the court deciding the leading case expresses concern that permitting artificial persons to be sureties would create the opportunity for wealthy accuseds to indemnify a corporation to stand as surety and then jump bail. The court's curt dismissal of this is simple: "That could not have been the intention of the Legislature."[11] Although this ban on artificial persons as sureties does not directly prevent commercial provision of bail, it limits funds available for such activities to personal capital. Thus, it restricts the possibility of such activity to *ad hoc* private arrangements or at most a petty enterprise.

A second aspect of suretyship in India that originates in the view taken of its purpose is the issue of the surety's power regarding the person released. Courts have disagreed as to whether a person who is unable to exercise control over the defendant to be bailed is an acceptable surety. Some have rejected sureties who are unable to exercise control. Others have declined to consider the question of whether a proposed surety is in a position to exercise control over the movements of the one released, limiting their inquiries to questions of solvency and respectability only. Once accuseds are released, sureties have a considerable yet limited control over their movements. This extends to the power to hold an accused until he can be transferred to the authorities or brought to court. It does not include authority to hold a defendant in private custody until an appearance date. Although the law expresses no authority for a surety to control an accused, this has been imputed by courts based on the surety's purpose. The object sought is to assure the defendant's appearance, not merely to raise money by forfeiture. It is to create reasonable pressure on accuseds to appear, not to fill jails with them. The same purpose establishes the limits of control by being embodied in an implied contract between accused and surety. Thus, a surety can control the accused's movement to the minimum necessary extent and for the minimum time necessary to obtain relief from the suretyship. This restraint may extend to forcibly bringing the accused before the authorities or confining him while help is sought. It does not extend to prolonged, forcible confinement. Upon these premises, Indian courts in a variety of cases have emphasized the advantageous position for fulfilling the purpose of sureties occupied by relations, friends, or caste-fellows of the accused.[12] The logic of this view again militates against commercialized bail.

The method of discharge provided under the *Criminal Procedure Code* for sureties seeking to be released from their liability also reflects the purpose attributed to suretyship. Under the code a surety can appeal to the magistrate at any time to be discharged from that liability. Upon this application the magistrate must issue an arrest warrant for the accused. No discharge can be granted the surety before the accused appears before the court. Once this is accomplished, though, the discharge must be granted—no hearing on the merits of the application is authorized, and no discretion to deny discharge is created. The surety's presence before the court is not mandatory for the discharge to proceed, although the presence of the accused is. Thus all questions of substance and procedure relating to discharge are resolved by the purpose of suretyship: has or has not the accused been brought before the court?[13]

Finally, a similar recurrence to purpose is reflected in the treatment of surety forfeitures and their mitigation. If the accused does not appear as required, the surety's recognizance is forfeited. Therefore every surety recognizance must include a promise to pay such a monetary penalty if the commitment to produce an accused is breached. Courts have enjoined strictness in enforcing this liability, fearing that any relaxation will encourage individuals to accept suretyships without a proper sense of responsibility. In fact, forfeiture is virtually automatic once the accused's absence is known to the court. Apart from questions of the existence of a valid surety recognizance, no proof of fact is necessary for forfeiture once this knowledge occurs.[14]

However (also related to purpose), sureties must then be given an opportunity to show cause why payment of the penalty they have incurred by the forfeiture should be remitted. If between the forfeiture and the show cause hearing sureties produce the accused, they are entitled to some consideration in the amount of payment, since they have at least belatedly fulfilled their purpose. Even in this situation, nevertheless, some part of the penalty may be enforced for their actual failure to meet their obligation. Payment of the total amount is not in any case automatically required. The decision on amount is a matter of judicially exercised discretion after applying the mind to the circumstances of the case. Factors to be considered in addition to those pertaining to the accused's recognizance are steps taken by the surety to secure the accused's attendance or, alternatively, the surety's lack of capacity to take adequate steps, any indications that the surety connived in the accused's absconding or was negligent in preventing it, and whether the amount of surety was excessive along with the surety's poverty or, alternatively, ability to pay.[15] Except for the last, each of these relate to the attempt to fulfill the purpose of a surety or culpability in the failure to do so.

Another major component of bail sanctions under the Indian *Criminal Procedure Code* is at the same time a principal reason for the relatively unadulterated recognizance nature of the system and an important part of its defenses against commercial bail bonding. This is the strict restraint placed upon cash deposits. The code authorizes courts to permit those defendants of whom they have required a recognizance with or without sureties to substitute a deposit of cash or government notes. The amount of this security deposit need not be the same as that of the initial recognizance. How much it should be will be determined at the time of the substitution. It may even be for a larger amount than the recognizance because the benefits of the sureties' function are forgone by the court in accepting a deposit. This provision has repeatedly been interpreted by the courts to mean two things. First, the courts are not required to accept an offer of cash. Second, and even more important, they have no authority to require a cash deposit as a bail term. The proposal for cash bail must be initiated by the defendant; the court may then accept or reject it. This ban on courts requiring cash is not escaped simply because an accused makes a counteroffer for a lesser amount after a court has demanded a larger cash deposit. Once the magistrate resolves to require cash, the cash security is illegal even though the operative offer came from defense counsel. Since defendants are not required to produce cash, their motivation to raise bail through a commercial bondsman is minimized and the court may reject cash if its origins are suspect.[16]

The prevailing view holds that a cash deposit substitutes for the recognizance by any sureties as well as by the principal, although some contrary judicial opinion exists. In practice, the typical use of cash deposits is to facilitate the release of those defendants who cannot produce sureties but are unlikely to abscond. In accepting the alternative, courts have been cautioned to see that those released do not in effect escape justice by paying a price for their liberty. The preference remains for sureties who have a personal stake in assuring that the accused meets appearance obligations. Securing that justice is not delayed or defeated continues to be the objective, not the forfeiture of money. However, in situations where defendants are strangers in the area in which they seek bail, compelling them to find a suitable surety is perceived to create unhealthy developments and complications which are even more to be discouraged than cash deposits.[17] Sureties thus do not secure their potential indebtedness with cash deposits and generally are unlikely to serve in cases involving cash, further removing the threat of commercialism from this system.

The resistance of Indian bail law to cash deposits extends also to the freezing of security money in a bank account. Magistrates have no power to order money of the accused in bank accounts to be frozen as security. Moreover, ordering an accused to deposit cash with the court or in a fixed bank account within the state constitutes excessively onerous bail terms which, depending upon circumstances, can amount to unlawful denial of bail.[18]

Penultimately, among the major aspects of bail terms to enforce attendance in India is the imposition of nonfinancial conditions of conduct upon an accused. Under limited circumstances, India exploys these conditions as supplementary means of securing bail. They work to incapacitate in varying degrees an accused's absconding and to provide early warning of its occurrence if attempted. India, on one hand, creates fairly extensive powers to impose such conditions on bail in the more serious cases where bail is discretionery. On the other hand, in less serious matters where bail is a right, India restricts such conditions. This restrictiveness tends to reinforce the recognizance emphasis of the country's bail system and to render its version less eclectic than some others that make a freer use of nonfinancial bail terms.

India, as will be further explained with regard to bail eligibility, divides offenses into two categories for bail purposes. Bailable offenses are generally less serious and, unless an exception pertains, convey a right to bail. Nonbailable offenses are the more serious, and bail is placed at the court's discretion. The *Criminal Procedure Code* treats these two classes of offenses differently for purposes of bail conditions. In granting bail for nonbailable offenses, the code gives courts extensive powers to impose whatever nonfinancial conditions of conduct they consider necessary to achieve particular purposes. Conditions are specifically authorized to accomplish three goals: (1) They may be designed to secure the attendance of the accused before the court as required. (2) They may aim at ensuring against the accused's committing an offense similar to the one being charged while awaiting trial. (3) They may also seek to otherwise advance the interests of justice.[19]

These three objectives are not considered to exhaust all possible acceptable reasons for bail conditions. However, conditions must be imposed in an exercise of judicial discretion and may not be arbitrary. Conditions must be fair and reasonable to ensure that a grant of bail is not abused. Vagueness in the conditions can also render them legally ineffective. Conditions relating to court attendance would include not leaving the country, not leaving the court's jurisdiction without permission, surrendering passports, or periodic reporting to the police. Conditions to prevent similar offenses might forbid association with certain persons or entry by the accused into certain locations.

The interest of justice is broadest in scope and the most complex of the objectives of conditions.[20] It relates to securing the ability to fairly and properly investigate the case and conduct the trial. These must be balanced against the personal liberties of the accused. Conditions should be structured so as to avoid unfair advantages to either party: interference with both the investigation and the accused's personal liberty should be minimized. Acceptable conditions include those protecting witnesses or evidence from tampering by the accused, requiring the accused to make himself available to the police for interrogation or for identification by witnesses when required, and requiring the accused's submission to medical examination. Unacceptable conditions include requiring the accused to accompany the police to some particular place, and those in violation of a number of applications of Article 20 of the Indian Constitution protecting against compelled testimony. These latter encompass a number of variations. A defendant may not be required by a bail condition to answer truthfully all questions—including incriminating ones—which the police ask, to show the police where they can recover incriminating articles, to repeat before a magistrate a confession made to the police, or to produce incriminating documents.[21]

In contrast to this very broad authority to impose bail conditions on conduct for nonbailable offenses is the virtually total restriction on placing such conditions on bail for bailable offenses, even by superior courts. Numerically, these constitute the overwhelming proportion of crimes. The section of the code dealing with bailable offenses creates a right to bail whenever a detained individual is prepared to offer it. The court's right to require sureties is implicit in the section's wording. Indian courts have reasoned for bailable cases much as Philippine courts have, that for all cases where bail is a right, no discretion exists to make it conditional. The Indian judicial reasoning is simply that if conditions are imposed and the accused rejects them, bail is in effect denied, which is contrary to the mandatory nature of bail in these cases. Therefore, no discretion to create conditions exists; only the amount of bail and the use or omission of sureties are discretionary. The nature of the potential condition does not affect this result. Conditions struck down cover a wide range of otherwise common bail conditions, including not entering specified areas, reporting to the police, and not participating in activities such as led to the charge.[22] The result of this treatment of bailable offenses is that imposition of nonfinancial bail conditions is limited to more serious types of offenses. Thus, for the broad range of matters, recognizance—whether that of the principal or of the sureties—is not only the principal but the only available bail sanction.

For those matters where bail conditions may be imposed, the question arises of how they can be enforced. India limits its penalty for contravention of bail conditions to cancelation of bail, although in some other countries conditions may be enforced with forfeiture or criminal punishment. Where bail is canceled, the accused is subject to arrest and denial of bail, or granting of it on less favorable terms. Since cancelation is the only mechanism for enforcement in India, an added reason arises for not permitting conditions if a right to bail pertains.[23]

A final general sanction enforcing adherence to bail requirements is arrest and cancelation of bail. This includes the enforcement of nonfinancial bail conditions just discussed, but these constitute a small portion of the applicability of this sanction. In its most fundamental use it can be employed against those who fail to appear in court as required. Even in bailable cases, where the accused initially had a right to bail, upon failure to appear the accused's bail will be forfeited. Once this occurs, the court has discretion to order arrest and commission to custody. This has been held to amount to a cancelation of bail. Thereafter the code provides that the right to bail is lost and courts are free to refuse bail. If bail is granted, courts may order that it be for a higher amount. Sureties must be required by the court even if they were not required for the previous release.[24]

This applicability of cancelation of bail extends under India's law well beyond actual failure to appear. Superior courts (High Courts and Sessions Courts) can in both bailable and nonbailable cases cancel the bail and order arrest when they consider it necessary. Magistrates' courts may cancel their own bails for nonbailable offenses, may cancel bails granted by superior courts for nonbailable offenses where those courts specifically delegated power to do so for violation of a bail condition, or may (according to the predominant view) cancel bails in most cases which they are trying, bailable or not, where the ends of justice will be defeated unless re-arrest occurs. (However, the Orissa High Court in 1986 took the contrary position on this last power in bailable cases.[25])

Decisions to cancel bail are matters of judicially exercised discretion and may not be taken arbitrarily without good reason. Case law has established with some thoroughness what constitutes justifiable reasons, although the facts and circumstances in the particular case, not some fixed rule, determine the decision. Apart from more technical reasons, such as changes in the adequacy of bail sureties or amounts, or in the seriousness of the charge, most justifications come down to a misuse of the liberty of bail or a reasonable apprehension that it will be misused. Well-established manifestations of misuse are the bailed accused committing the same offense or reasonable grounds appearing that he might do so. Preventing the accused from thus being a danger to the community validates this as a reason for cancelation. The accused's hampering or potential hampering of the investigation activities is another justifying manifestation. Activities such as forcibly preventing searches of areas under the defendant's control would fit this category. Likewise, an adequate justifying reason is the accused's tampering with the evidence in the case. This might involve intimidating witnesses, interfering with the crime scene, or destroying or removing evidence. Extending the actual failure to appear in court, any attempt to escape to a foreign country, go into hiding, or avoid the control of sureties justifies cancelation. A final such reason for the courts to intervene is the accused's committing an act of violence for revenge against the police, witnesses, or prosecutors. Whatever reason is relied upon must be supported by evidence and established on a balance of probabilities.[26]

Viewing its various components in combination, India presents a nearly archetypal traditional recognizance bail system. Bail of an accused who has been arrested is nearly always based on that individual's personal recognizance. Under this a debt to the state is incurred contingently. Upon failure to appear as required, the contingency is realized and the amount of the recognizance is forfeited. Prior to that no payment is required, and if the appearance requirement is met no payment is ever required. In addition to the accused's recognizance the courts can, and usually do, require one or more sureties. These are individuals, preferably relatives or friends of the accused, who are willing to enter into a similar recognizance arrangement to secure the accused's appearance. Here again, payment is only required upon failure to produce the accused. Payments to sureties render them unacceptable and contracts to pay them are illegal and therefore unenforceable. Cash deposits may never be required by a court. They may be accepted at the court's discretion but need not be. The predominant opinion is that they substitute for and may not be combined with sureties. Nonfinancial conditions to control conduct can be made an aspect of bail for offenses not involving a right to bail. All conditions, financial or not, may be appealed by an aggrieved defendant. Finally, an accused who does not appear as required or who violates a nonfinancial condition is subject to arrest and cancelation of bail.

Eligibility for Bail

Questions of eligibility for bail in India are governed by an amalgam of constitutional, statutory, and case law. On the constitutional level, limited protection is provided for bail right. Article 21 protects against deprivation of personal liberty except according to procedure established by law. Article 22 requires that any detention of more than twenty-four hours be based on the authority of a magistrate. A major exception is created to this, however, for detention under any law providing for preventive detention. Article 13 provides that any law which removes or abridges a fundamental right conferred is void to the extent that it does so.

In a landmark case in 1978, the Indian Supreme Court reversed its previous position and in effect greatly increased the scope of these protections beyond the modest protection immediately apparent on the face of Articles 21 and 22.[27] This was done by applying to these articles requirements enunciated in Article 19 that restrictions on rights be reasonably related to attaining specified objectives; most pertinently, state security, public order, and prevention of incitement to an offense. As previously read, these Article 19 requirements applied only to specific rights such as speech, assembly, association, mobility, and the like as covered in that article. Moreover, any abridgment of the personal liberty rights in Articles 21 and 22 had also to meet the equal protection requirements under Article 14. Major components of equal protection are, the court reasoned, reasonableness and nonarbitrariness. Procedure for removing the personal liberty rights must therefore be right, just, and fair, and may not be arbitrary, fanciful, or oppressive. Laws restricting bail may therefore be reviewed by the courts for whether they contain reasonable restrictions imposed for the public interest as well as for whether their procedure for removing the liberty right is reasonable, just, and fair.[28]

In a 1986 case, the Supreme Court distinctly stated its view of the role of the court in reviewing decisions made under preventive detention statutes. The detaining authority is not the sole judge of what national security or public order require, but neither are the courts. When power is given to an authority to detain upon certain facts and the authority decides in a manner neither irrational nor unreasonable, then the court cannot substitute its own opinion. The proper question is whether anyone instructed in law could reasonably have taken the authority's view. Preventive detention the court terms "hard law." But it is hard law produced by bad circumstances—a necessary evil in modern society. Nevertheless the hard law must be properly and legally applied. A balance should be struck between social defense and infringing the liberties of the citizen. Preventive detention law may not be interpreted into inoperability.[29]

Another case of the same year refined the focal issues of such a judicial review. In the absence of procedural defects, the court's attention should be directed to the causal connection between the fact alleged as grounds for detention and the purpose of detention under the relevant law. The sufficiency of the grounds and the truth of the grounds are not proper objects of the court's inquiry, since the statutory requirement for detention is the subjective satisfaction of the authority of the need for detention. However, the opinion about this need may not be formed to serve a collateral purpose or to advance a motive ulterior to what is provided by the law. Consequently, the grounds alleged and the purpose of detention of the law must be linked by a creditable chain, which courts should examine. The procedural safeguards provided by the law must be followed by the detaining authority and are subject to court review. These safeguards include presentation to and examination by the authority of the documents relied upon in support of detention, opportunity given the defendant to make representations, and due consideration by the authority to defense representation. If these requirements are met, if the causal connection is established, and if the authority has acted on a bona fide belief in the need to detain, then the detention must be sustained by the court.[30] Conversely, if the relevant material is not placed before the detaining authority or that authority does not apply its mind to the facts, a clear case exists for courts to void the detention.[31]

Most preventive detention statutes fall into a class that might be broadly called political crimes, such as national security, terrorism, and firearms law offenses. Another important area carrying preventive detention is smuggling and foreign exchange violations. Some states allow detention of habitual, serious criminals. The broad scope of ordinary, common law offenses in India is covered by a combination of rights and discretions established by statute. Key to this is the dichotomy between bailable and nonbailable offenses previously mentioned.

Under the Indian *Criminal Procedure Code,* bailable offenses carry a right of the accused to be granted bail that is mandatory on courts before whom they appear. In fact, an extensive obligation exists for police to grant bail for these offenses without a court appearance. For this right to grant of bail to apply, all that must be established is that the accusation is for a bailable offense and that the accused is prepared to give satisfactory bail. Bail, then, is a matter of right with the court normally having no discretion to deny it.[32]

The offenses which are covered by this right to bail are specified in the First Schedule appended to the *Indian Penal Code* for offenses against that code. Generally the less serious offenses are classed as bailable. However, a number of bailable offenses can be found which carry a greater possible punishment than some nonbailable offenses. Some idea of the level of offenses to which the right to bail pertains can be derived from the fact that for offenses not covered by the First

Schedule or by other statutory provisions, offenses carrying less than three years imprisonment are made bailable.[33]

The requirement that bail be granted does not necessarily assure that the accused will be able to meet the terms upon which it is granted. Still, bail may not be excessive, nor may it impose unnecessary impediments to release.[34] Furthermore, the right to bail may be lost even for bailable offenses by failure to appear as required. In one of the most important changes made by the 1973 code, courts were authorized to deny bail after a violation of appearance requirements in these cases.[35]

In matters involving most nonbailable charges, the granting of bail is discretionary. Even when bail is denied, an order may not be made forbidding bail on any terms until the disposal of the case. Such an order is without legal authority, and has been condemned as an arbitrary exercise of power bordering on perversity. However, under certain circumstances limits are placed on discretion toward both requiring and forbidding it. Bail may not be granted by a magistrate in cases where reasonable grounds occur to believe the accused has committed an offense punishable with either death or life imprisonment. Reasonable grounds here means a genuine case and a triable case. This requires that the court be satisfied that evidence amounting to a *prima facie* case will ultimately be produced. The maximum possible punishment is used to establish whether an offense fits this classification. Discretion to grant bail in such cases is thus removed from the magistrate and is in effect reserved to a superior court. A High Court or Court of Sessions has discretionary powers to grant bail in all cases.[36]

Certain categories of persons are exempted from this restriction on magistrates' bailing powers. Magistrates may consider bail for juveniles, women, and the sick or infirm. What constitutes adequate sickness to trigger this exception is not altogether clear. Some courts have insisted that sickness should involve danger to life. Alternative tests employed are that it be untreatable in jail, or be sufficient to result in infirmity. At a minimum, it should be real and not imaginary. The infirmity alternative has been linked to old age as its natural concomitant in at least one bail case.[37]

In the other direction of limiting bail discretion, if a court finds less than reasonable grounds (as described) for believing that the accused has committed a nonbailable offense, but sufficient grounds for further inquiry, bail must be granted. It may be with or without sureties, and although mandatory, the statute preserves the right to impose nonfinancial conditions.[38]

Bail discretion is also limited by a requirement that it be granted in another instance. One suspected of a nonbailable offense who has not been formally charged before a court can be detained during investigation. A magistrate must authorize this and should be satisfied that reasonable grounds justify it before doing so. However, after ninety days detention in matters punishable by over ten years imprisonment (or sixty days in all other cases), magistrates must release such accuseds on bail if they are prepared to furnish it. Various High Courts have described bail in those circumstances as a matter of right which is absolute and indefeasible, and the majority hold that defendants need not even apply for it. The magistrate should monitor the proceedings and bail should be offered them. A late filing of the charge sheet will not defeat the right to release. This provision is not a license for the investigating agency to detain a person for the specified period. Even during that time courts should consider bail applications and scrutinize the reason for detention and the progress of the investigation.[39]

Finally, a *prima facie* right, or presumption, to be granted bail attaches if, in a nonbailable offense triable by a magistrate, the trial is not concluded within sixty days. For this right to pertain the accused must have been in custody throughout the period. This right may be defeated, however, simply by the magistrate directing the accused to be held for reasons that are recorded. A record of habitual absconding would be good reason for directing custody. Even with matters triable by the higher courts, and so not falling under this provision, case law has granted bail to incarcerated defendants as a remedy for undue delay without good cause in violation of an implied constitutional speedy trial right.[40]

Even when by statute bail is discretionary, a strong strain of case law in India enforces a presumption in favor of bail being granted unless good reason exists to the contrary. This general policy of the law that bail should be granted rather than refused has been repeatedly stated by the Supreme Court. Only in matters punishable by death or life imprisonment have concerted arguments been advanced against the application of this presumption. Nevertheless, in other serious matters—e.g., drug trafficking or serious economic offenses—bail may regularly be denied because considerations to defeat the presumption will be present. A variety of principles lie behind this presumption, including the presumption of innocence, the stricture against bail's being used as a punishment, and the requirement that discretion be exercised judicially on relevant criteria. Based on these, the grant of bail becomes the rule; its denial, the exception. Moreover, considerations that are adequate to defeat the presumption in favor of bail have received extensive judicial consideration. Courts must apply their minds to the facts establishing these, and exercise discretion judicially for a lawful denial of bail.[41]

Anticipatory Bail

One aspect of eligibility for bail in India—anticipatory bail—requires particular attention because of its innovative nature and uniqueness to the Indian subcontinent. Under this approach, individuals not under arrest who qualify can anticipate possible arrest and seek bail in contemplation of the possibility. When anticipatory bail has been granted, release on bail under the terms fixed beforehand follows immediately upon arrest.[42] In this sense only, bail is anticipatory. As Indian sources (including the Supreme Court) have taken care to point out, such bail is not anticipatory in the sense of being actually in effect prior to arrest. Courts have no power to prevent the arrest from occurring.[43]

Prior to the 1973 code, although anticipatory bail was known to Indian practice, the majority of High Courts which considered it had held it to be unauthorized. The Law Commission's report had, however, recommended that it be authorized by legislation, resulting in its inclusion in the new code. The commission gave two reasons for recommending it. Principally, it could be used to counteract attempts by influential people to implicate rivals in fabricated cases to either disgrace or immobilize them by confining them in jail while awaiting ordinary bail. In addition, even in uncontrived cases it could be used to avoid the unnecessary confinement while awaiting ordinary bail of those who were not likely to abscond or abuse their release.[44]

In granting anticipatory bail, the court orders that, in the event of a future arrest on the charge, the suspect shall be released on bail on the terms and conditions it has established. If, following the grant, a magistrate issues a warrant against that person on the same charge, the code requires that it make provision for bail accordingly. Alternatively, if that individual is later arrested without a warrant for the same offense and offers the bail established, the law directs the officer in charge of the police station to effect release.[45]

The code itself specifies a variety of conditions which a court granting anticipatory bail can attach to protect the interests of justice. These are in addition to the three categories of conditions that can be imposed in an ordinary bail for a bailable offense. In anticipatory bail, the accused may be ordered to be available for interrogation by the police as required. An order not to tamper directly or indirectly with witnesses by inducement, threat, or promise may be included. A prohibition against leaving the country without the court's permission is also authorized. As with regular bail, violation of any condition of anticipatory bail can result in its cancelation.[46]

Anticipatory bail creates an entirely new dimension for the question of eligibility for bail. The *Code of Criminal Procedure* provides that anyone having reason to believe that he may be arrested for a nonbailable offense may apply to a superior court (High Court or Court of Sessions) for anticipatory bail. Anticipatory bail is not available for bailable offenses where bail will eventually be mandatory anyway, nor is it available from a magistrate's court. Once an individual has applied, the court applied to has discretion to grant the bail, setting the terms as it sees fit or refusing it. Although the general rule in favor of granting bail applies to anticipatory as well as regular bail, courts must be satisfied that it is necessary in the interest of justice before allowing it.[47]

Despite the granting of anticipatory bail being discretionary, it should not be made merely because someone expects arrest for a nonbailable offense. The anticipation must be reasonably based upon existing facts. An accusation must exist; a merely imaginary or possible future accusation is not adequate grounds to fear arrest. Moreover, some exceptional factor should characterize the case to justify bail being granted. It should not be used merely to avoid the normal process of arrest and investigation or to hinder the investigation. As with regular bail, the judicial exercise of discretion required for anticipatory bail decisions involves an assessment of all of the considerations of the case. For anticipatory bail, since it is likely to interfere to some degree with the investigation, this includes in an enhanced way the difficulties faced by investigative agencies and the probable effect they may have on the public interest. The considerations to be contemplated in anticipatory bail decisions are consequently not altogether identical with those in regular bail decisions. Anticipatory bail adds a further dimension to the matter of considerations in denying bail.[48]

Considerations in Denying Bail

Due to the substantial range of offenses for which bail is discretionary, either to a magistrate or to a superior court judge, and given the presumption in favor of bail when it is discretionary, a substantial body of Indian case law has refined the considerations to be evaluated in reaching bail decisions. The reasons for bail decisions must be recorded. Although each case must be judged on its own facts, and the balance and predominance among facts will vary with the circumstances in the particular matter, the following considerations are regularly thought pertinent:

1. The nature and seriousness of the charge. The more serious the charge, the less appropriate is bail. Closely related to this, but sometimes considered separately, is the likely severity of the punishment.

2. The nature of the prosecution evidence. A strong case militates against bail more than a marginal one does.
3. Particular circumstances relating to the accused. These could be such as to either increase or decrease the likelihood of bail. They include age, health, sex, character, means, community standing and ties, employment, family relationships, and prior record, both generally and as regards bail.
4. The likelihood that the accused will abscond if released.
5. A reasonable apprehension of danger of the accused's tampering with witnesses.
6. A danger to the interest of the state or public.
7. The probability of the accused committing repeat offenses if released.
8. Protracted detention, especially if the prosecution has been dilatory.
9. Opportunity to prepare a defense.

While no one of these considerations is likely to determine a bail outcome, a balance of several of them pointing in a particular direction might well do so. All are not of equal importance, moreover. If an accused is unlikely to abscond, normally bail will be granted unless serious reasons exist under another consideration. Although a few cases (e.g., *Ram Chandra v. State*) distinguish between considerations justifying denial and factors used to establish these, this distinction is not commonly drawn in Indian cases as it is in English. As here, the two are typically mixed.[49]

Cases in which anticipatory bail is sought add further considerations to the exercise of bail discretion, although various courts including the Supreme Court have also stressed that the considerations governing regular bail apply to anticipatory bail as well. Two additional considerations have emerged prominently in the case law. Since anticipatory bail inevitably interferes to some extent with the police investigation, the extent to which it will interfere in the case should be considered. Likewise, since the purpose of anticipatory bail is clearly established, an objective compatible with that purpose should be advanced. If an accusation is motivated by something ulterior to furthering justice, anticipatory bail is supported. The Supreme Court has indicated that if an accusation has been made to injure or humiliate an individual by contriving his arrest, anticipatory bail should generally be granted. The converse does not hold; India, unlike Pakistan, does not make a bad faith accusation a necessary condition of bail. At this point, the more usual considerations such as likelihood of absconding or tampering with evidence take over. Again, however, no rigid rule that it must be granted in the absence of a fear of flight can be made.[50]

Procedural Considerations

A series of procedural arrangements are in place to implement India's recognizance bail system, some of which relate directly to the nature of their kind of approach to bail. Of these, perhaps the most directly related to the essence of the system are those dealing with forfeiture of bail. Because the accused's recognizance and that of any sureties are society's chief security for the accused's appearance, procedures for forfeiture are at the heart of systems of this type.

Under the *Criminal Procedure Code*, forfeiture of an accused's recognizance or that of any sureties takes place, courts have explained, in two stages. The finding of forfeiture occurs for both as soon as the accused's failure to appear is established to the satisfaction of the court. Although technically this must be proven by evidence and the proof recorded, given the lack of the accused's presence, the only possible defects are those relating to the existence of a recognizance valid under the code. Forfeiture is therefore virtually automatic in the face of an absent accused.[51]

The matter then proceeds to the second stage, which is the realization of the debt specified in the recognizance as penalty for default. Here, in spite of being controlled by the same provision, some difference necessarily occurs between the procedure applicable to the accused and that applicable to sureties. The accused's bail is canceled and arrest warrants are issued. When the accused appears or is brought before the court, he must be allowed to show cause why payment of the penalty should not be required. The opportunity to do this must be offered by the magistrate even if the accused is prepared to pay immediately. The magistrate can then require payment or remit the penalty in whole or part.[52]

When the recognizance of sureties is at issue a somewhat different procedure pertains. Once the recognizance has been forfeited, the court is required to serve notice on the surety to pay the penalty or show cause why payment should not be required. So essential is this notice that its absence vitiates the forfeiture proceedings. The prevailing view in Indian law, unlike that in some countries, is that the showing of cause cannot precede the initial order that forfeiture has occurred.[53]

India provides by statute for a lacuna in the common law regarding appeal of a forfeiture. The *Criminal Procedure Code* creates an appeal from bail forfeiture in a magistrate's court or a Court of Sessions. Further review is possible at the discretion of the higher courts. Since forfeiture proceedings are essentially civil in nature, a refusal to forfeit a recognizance can also be appealed.[54]

Like forfeiture, cancelation of bail has its procedural requirements. As previously discussed, an accused who fails to appear in court, who attempts to abscond, who violates nonfinancial bail conditions, or who abuses the liberty of bail is subject to arrest and cancelation of bail. Apart from failure to appear, which is evident, cancelation must be based on sufficient grounds amounting to a balance of probabilities. Material must be placed before the court to establish a strong *prima facie* case for the grounds for cancelation, and the accused must be given an opportunity to show cause why cancelation should not take place. Discretion to cancel must then be judicially exercised. Cancelation of bail does not prevent the accused's reapplying for bail and its being regranted. If this is done, it may be granted upon more stringent terms and, indeed, where no sureties were previously required they become mandatory.[55]

Other provisions of the Indian code deal with the procedural implementation of the various aspects of bail rights, rather than of the particular bail form. Salient among these is the requirement that a person arrested without a warrant who is not released on bail by the police be brought before a magistrate to consider release without unnecessary delay, and in any event within twenty-four hours exclusive of travel time to the court. If an arrest is with a warrant, the terms upon which the accused should be released are commonly endorsed upon the warrant by the issuing magistrate. The twenty-four-hour detention limit is a constitutional as well as a statutory right, and the police must notify those arrested for a bailable offense of their right to bail. In addition, the officer in charge of a police station must notify the pertinent magistrate of all persons arrested. Thus, unless suspects are released under the duty of the police to grant bail for bailable offenses, a procedural structure calculated to implement their right to bail within twenty-four hours is entered. The same structure provides judicial review of detention within the same period for all others as well.[56]

Other major procedural implementations of bail rights take over if bail is not granted but the accused is not charged before a court. Notable here is the limit of sixty days in most cases, and ninety days in those punishable by over ten years imprisonment before the granting of bail becomes mandatory. Even these limits are reached incrementally by remands of no more than fifteen days. The ninety-day maximum for such detentions is a constitutional as well as a statutory provision. As mentioned previously, the more widely accepted view among High Courts places the burden to monitor and implement this limit upon the magistrate granting the remand. The Supreme Court has indicated that magistrates should at least point out to accuseds their entitlement to have bail granted, and see to the implementation of their right to be provided counsel to apply for it.[57]

In a more general way, the rights and presumptions regarding bail are protected by provisions for appealing the various aspects of the denial of bail, or the granting of it upon unacceptable terms, and for reapplying after an unsuccessful application.

Results of the System

As regards the recognizance nature of the Indian bail system, practice seems to agree well with the statement of the law. Indian authorities portray the usual result of the system to be the release of accuseds on recognizance with sureties. Release without sureties is implied to be in the nature of an exception to normal bail.[58]

In the absence of any public statistics on bail results, some support for this view of bail practice is derived from the terms of bail in the post-1973 cases employed here as legal references in which details of bail terms can be discerned. Bail terms can be determined in twenty-three cases (including five anticipatory bails) involving over thirty-three defendants (three cases indicate only several) and over thirty-five separate bails. Since only one of these cases seems likely to involve a bailable offense, and even that may not, the picture presented is of bail for nonbailable offenses rather than for all bails. Thus, use of nonfinancial conditions will be overrepresented for the overall system, and to a lesser extent use of sureties may be.

Only one instance of cash deposit occurs among these post-1973 cases, and this was overturned because the court had illegally demanded it. Recognizance without sureties appears in three cases. In one of these (the possible bailable offense), this was only an interim arrangement to facilitate finding a surety. In the other two, nonfinancial conditions were imposed even though sureties were not required. In a further case not included in the total, omitting sureties was urged by the court, but no actual bail order was made. A single surety was required in fourteen cases, whereas two were required in seven. Nonfinancial conditions were imposed in eight of the regular bails and four of the five anticipatory bails.

The impression which emerges from this, then, at least for more serious cases, is as the law suggests it should be. Indian bails typically involve release on the accused's recognizance with a surety, and not uncommonly in nonbailable cases, two sureties. Occasionally, however, sureties are not required for these graver matters even where nonfinancial conditions are imposed. Nonfinancial conditions are employed in something under half of the regular bails, but most of the anticipatory bails.

Summary

The Indian bail system functions almost completely by recognizance. The accused's recognizance is fundamental to release, but third-party sureties who also function by recognizance are typically required. Nonfinancial conditions of conduct can be required in cases where no right to bail applies. Bail by cash deposit can never be required by the courts. If an accused offers a deposit—usually because he cannot obtain the necessary sureties—the court may, but need not, accept the offer. A defendant who absconds, is about to abscond, violates a nonfinancial condition of conduct, or abuses the liberty of bail is subject to arrest and cancelation of bail or alteration of bail terms.

OTHER TRADITIONAL RECOGNIZANCE SYSTEMS

Pakistan and Bangladesh

The Pakistani and Bangladeshi bail systems are in most important regards similar to the Indian system. This is partly due, as previously mentioned, to the root of all three bail laws in the 1890 Indian *Criminal Procedure Code*. Similarity is also fostered by the generally parallel nature of post-independence amendments to the law. Finally, it is advanced by the mutual attention paid by courts in each of the countries to the decisions of courts in the others. An Indian High Court judge explained the relationship concisely in commentary upon a Pakistani bail decision shortly after the two countries separated: "That decision, being one of a foreign court, is not strictly speaking binding upon me as an authority but the reasoning on which it is based may well be adopted by learned counsel—as parts of his arguments."[59] In spite of these impetuses to uniformity in bail matters, some differences and dissimilarities of emphasis are noteworthy.

The emphasis on recognizance and sureties found in India is also present in Pakistan and Bangladesh, as is the insistence that courts have no authority to demand cash bail.[60] However, a generally more restrictive view of nonfinancial conditions of conduct is taken in these latter two countries. The statutory provisions explicitly allowing nonfinancial conditions in nonbailable cases in India are not present in the statutes of those countries. Thus, authority to impose conditions depends upon a complex interaction of case holdings. The result in Pakistan is that nonfinancial conditions are at least arguably lawful in nonbailable cases, but they must be made as conditions for the granting of bail rather than imposed by the bail recognizance itself. Consequently, although conditions of conduct while on bail may not be absolutely precluded, conditions able to be fulfilled prior to release—such as surrender of a passport or providing a surety of a particular sort—seem more usual. In fact all nonfinancial conditions are relatively rare. The only exception to this is in anticipatory bail cases where nonfinancial conditions are fairly commonly imposed.[61] In Bangladesh the case law stops just short of precluding all conditions on conduct.[62]

Another salient difference in the sanctions by which bail is enforced between India and Pakistan regards cancelation of bail. Unlike India, courts in Pakistan have no authority to cancel bail for bailable offenses on grounds of abuse of bail liberty. Authority is not created by statute and no inherent power to rearrest the accused and to cancel bail is recognized at any court level. Earlier case law had applied the same protection against cancelation of bail to nonbailable cases where a right to bail applies due to lack of reasonable grounds or length of delay. In a 1987 case the Lahore High Court distinguished these from bailable cases, disagreed with the leading case to the contrary, and held that these carried no immunity from cancelation.[63] Bangladesh comes closer to the Pakistani position against cancelation of bail in bailable offenses than to the Indian.[64]

Eligibility for bail in Pakistan and Bangladesh is also structured much as in India with a few notable variations. The most serious nonbailable offenses constitute the principal area of difference. The Pakistani code adds to the capital and life imprisonment exclusion from the courts' discretion to grant bail cases of offenses punishable by more than ten years. It also extends the exclusion to all courts, including courts of superior jurisdiction. Thus, where in India such cases are in effect reserved for superior courts, in Pakistan they are made completely ineligible for bail. Pakistan provides, however, an exception to this exclusion in addition to the one for juveniles, women, the sick, and the infirm found in India. In a noncapital case, if the accused has been continuously detained awaiting trial for a period exceeding a year, a right to be granted bail is activated. For capital offenses the period of continuous imprisonment is two years. This bail right, however, does not apply to previously convicted offenders or where the court opines either that the accused or a person acting on his behalf has occasioned the delay, or that the accused is a hardened, desperate, or dangerous criminal.[65] The Bangladeshi provision is similiar to the Pakistani, except that it does not exclude cases punishable by less than life imprisonment from the courts' discretion. It also omits the provision for mandatory release after continuous imprisonment of one or two years.[66]

Pakistani courts have held that, under the provision limiting continuous incarceration, once the specified time has expired bail is the accused's of right. No discretion remains, except as provided by statutory exception, to refuse bail whatever the nature or seriousness of the crime. Until that point, however, no discretion exists to grant bail under this provision. Probable future delay cannot be anticipated.[67] A final major difference between Pakistan and India regarding eligibility for bail is that no eventual right to bail limits the possible remands to custody prior to an accused's being charged in court in Pakistan to the sixty or ninety days set in India. This is covered only by principles and provisions more generally applicable to prolonged pretrial detention. Delay in itself is not a grounds requiring bail, although inordinate, unjustified, scandalous, or unconscionable delay amounting to an abuse of process, can be. The statutory provisions limiting time in continuous custody to one or two years already discussed also applies.[68] The statutory provision on this point in Bangladesh resembles that in Pakistan in lacking the limit found in India.[69]

Anticipatory bail is generally more restricted in Pakistan than in India. A major statutory difference between the laws in Pakistan and India was created by a 1976 amendment to the Pakistani *Criminal Procedure Code*. Whereas in India anticipatory bail may be granted to anyone reasonably anticipating arrest who otherwise qualifies for it, the amendment in Pakistan has deliberately sought to restrict the general power of the higher courts to grant pre-arrest bail. Under the amendment, such bail can only be granted for offenses where a case has been registered.[70] Thus, beginning with the statute itself, Pakistan takes a more restrictive approach to the grant of anticipatory bail than does India.

Within the context of this more constraining statute, one of the most notable contrasts between Pakistani and Indian case law regarding anticipatory bail is that the Supreme Court in the former country has taken a narrower view of when pre-arrest bail is appropriately granted. In Pakistan an accusation in bad faith has been made a virtually indispensable prerequisite for pre-arrest bail. Indeed, in several Supreme Court opinions anticipation of an arrest due to an ulterior motive has been called most essential, or a necessary condition, for anticipatory bail.[71] In India, as previously seen, a bad faith accusation is consideration in, but not a necessary condition for, the bail grant.

This narrower view of the applicability of anticipatory bail in Pakistan appears to reflect a concept of its purpose which is more narrowly focused than that prevailing in India. Common to the concept of purpose in both countries is the desire to provide relief from the inconvenience and disgrace of detention for the victim of a falsely motivated charge. To this India adds a secondary consideration of providing relief under any unusual circumstances to an accused individual who is not likely to abscond or otherwise abuse bail set prior to arrest. This secondary purpose of pre-arrest bail seems absent from the concept behind the approach to such release in Pakistan.

In contemplating the considerations used to guide discretion in granting or denying bail in Pakistan, one stands out in contrast to India. This is the prominent emphasis given the shared principle of consistency, or equality of treatment. Various wordings of the principle have been given, but in essence it is that "equality of treatment [is] to be meted out to all accused persons who are charged with the commission of similar offenses in a case," and discrimination must be justified on some grounds.[72] Alternatively put, "no discrimination can be made between different cases of a similar nature and . . . the Court should adopt a uniform standard in their disposal."[73] As a result, unless grounds exist to distinguish between co-accuseds, if one is granted bail the others should be; if one is denied bail, the others should be.[74]

Malaysia, Zambia, and Tanzania

Malaysia, Zambia, and Tanzania, as well as a number of other jurisdictions including Sri Lanka, Singapore, Brunei, and Fiji, have bail statutes basically similar to the pre-1973 Indian code. In some of these, where the Indian statute was deliberately followed, the attendant case law is also viewed as persuasive interpretation. The most notable differences in common amongst all of these countries and the current Indian bail system is their lack of anticipatory bail and their treatment of other aspects of bail eligibility, especially with regard to nonbailable offenses.

Malaysian bail law is among those closest in most respects to that of India before 1973. One striking aspect of bail law in that country, however, deals with eligibility for bail in drug trafficking cases. The usual provisions against bail in capital cases are found in Malaysia, and as has received some attention worldwide, Malaysia applies the death penalty to drug trafficking. This in itself would result in notably restricting bail in drug cases.[75] However, the drug law in that country imposes even greater restrictions on bail in these matters.

Under the *Dangerous Drugs Act*, drug charges punishable with death or imprisonment for more than five years may not be granted bail. Under five years an offense may be bailed unless the Public Prosecutor certifies that a grant of bail to the accused is not in the public interest. The provision is structured to override any conflicting law. Thus, the provision of the *Criminal Procedure Code* exempting women, juveniles, and the sick or infirm from the ban on bail applicable to capital or life imprisonment cases—similar to those found in India and Pakistan—does not apply to drug cases in Malaysia. Even a pregnant woman could not be granted bail under the *Criminal Procedure Code* exemption.[76]

Furthermore, this restriction on the granting of bail is not limited to courts of inferior jurisdiction. High Courts as well are deprived of any discretion to grant bail in these drug cases.[77] This contrasts with their extensive discretion in other matters where lower courts lack bailing powers.[78]

Among these related bail systems, the greatest contrasts with India and Pakistan in regard to terms of bail that may be imposed are found in Zambia and Tanzania. Consequently, these two countries are of interest on this point, in spite of the dated nature of the legal materials available in establishing the details of their systems. Although both of these countries adhere to the basic recognizance with sureties as the normal bail arrangement, they expand the role given to other bail terms in the direction of the modified recognizance systems.

The Zambian *Criminal Procedure Code* contains the usual wording authorizing courts to accept deposits. It then, however, proceeds to refer to "bail or deposit required by a subordinate court." A 1979 High Court case provides a clear instance of a cash deposit being required from four defendants, although no point of law is stated supporting this practice. A similar instance is found in Sri Lanka.[79] Other provisions of the Zambian code authorize imposing nonfinancial conditions on bail. Whatever conditions seem reasonable and necessary in the particular case may be required under the accused's recognizance by any court level, regardless of the level of offense. Similar provision is made to append nonfinancial conditions to cash deposits. Authority to forfeit the deposit for breach of the conditions is included.[80] Thus, terms of bail in Zambia are expanded over those of India by a somewhat ambiguous possibility of cash deposits being required, and by clear provision for nonfinancial bail conditions enforceable for forfeiture in all cases.

In Tanzania the standard statutory wording to permit cash deposit is used without the reference to cash being required as found in Zambia. Nevertheless, in several cases coming from the High Court of Tanzania during the early 1970s (a period of considerable available case material) cash bail was demanded. This indicates that, in contrast to the view of the Indian courts, this statutory wording is not seen as an obstacle to requiring cash security for bail. Interesting in this context is that a Tanzanian case contains one of the best African discussions of *R. v. Porter* on the illegality of agreements to indemnify sureties.[81] The Tanzanian statute does not make the specific provision for nonfinancial conditions as found in Zambia. The High Court has, however, held that a court may refuse to grant bail unless the accused agrees to conditions of conduct such as reporting to the police. At the same time, that court cautioned that such conditions could not be made binding on third-party sureties—they cannot be penalized if the accused violates the conditions.[82] Thus Tanzania, like Zambia, provides for greater use of cash deposits and nonfinancial conditions than usual under the Indian model.

Nigeria

Nigerian jurisdictions are structured in a federal arrangement with separate Criminal Procedure Codes for the federal and nineteen-state court systems. In addition to their discrete statutes, decisions of courts in one state are not binding upon courts in another although they can be, and regularly are, used as persuasive arguments.[83] Simplifying this pattern for bail matters, however, is the fact that the laws of the federation and the nine southern states regarding bail are very similar, as are those of the ten northern states. Both groups are traditional recognizance systems similar in substance to India's before 1973, although the northern states follow roughly the statutory pattern and wording of the pre-1973 Indian law, while the southern states do not. A further force for interstate similarity is created by the federal constitution, although that was suspended by a 1984 decree.

Terms of bail in Nigeria are marked by a few distinguishing variations. Release on self-recognizance without sureties is provided for in the statutes but is rarely encountered in the reported cases.[84] Somewhat more commonly found is the specification in bail terms of the nature and location of the property that the surety must own and how ownership must be established. The High Court of Lagos State has held that to establish qualifications of this sort that are impossible for a surety to meet amounts to denial of bail.[85] No statutory provisions are made to impose nonfinancial conditions on the conduct of the accused. These are, however, occasionally imposed by High Courts.

With regard to cash deposit, the northern and southern states' laws differ. The statutes of the northern states contain the frequently created authority to allow courts to accept them. Those of the southern states do not include such clauses. In reviewing the provisions applicable in the Northern states, a state High Court explained very forcefully the basic principle:

> The Court does not have the power to order . . . deposit of a sum of money. . . . The provision . . . is an advantage which the accused

> person may take himself in case he finds difficulty in getting sufficient surety or for some other personal reasons he appeals to court, that instead of entering a bond with or without sureties he should be allowed to deposit the amount.... The Court may allow him to do this. It is illegal of the Court to demand cash deposit without request of the accused. In the case before me the ... Magistrate was not empowered to order security ... on his own motion other than at the request of the accused.

Differing from the view expressed in India, the court here indicates that the amount of the deposit should be that already fixed for the recognizance.[86]

Only one other instance of cash deposit is reported. In this 1986 case the Court of Appeal of Nigeria upheld bail on a recognizance with sureties with specifics of what the sureties must establish regarding ownership. It also indicated, however, that if a cash deposit was offered in a given amount it would vary the terms of bail to accept it.[87] This reflects a less-guarded attitude to cash bail than seen in India, and yet clearly stops short of court demands for cash bail encountered in, for example, Tanzania.

Eligibility for bail in Nigeria provides an interesting contrast to the Indian approach in certain respects. It is, however, complicated because certain constitutional provisions regarding it were suspended, albeit with a commitment for their reinstatement. Under the suspension, statutes made to implement the constitutional provision remain in effect unless repealed. Two principal rights pertaining to bail are created by these constitutional provisions for persons accused of any but a capital crime. The accused must be brought before a court within a reasonable time unless otherwise released. (A reasonable time is defined by the provision as one day unless the arrest occurs more than forty kilometers from a court with jurisdiction.) Thereafter those detained must be tried within two months or released either on bail or unconditionally. Anyone unlawfully detained is entitled to compensation and a public apology from the appropriate person or authority.[88]

Prior to the constitutional suspension, courts had numerous opportunities to interpret the application of these provisions to bail cases. The Federal Court of Appeal has held that a person who is not released must be brought before a court within the constitutionally specified period whether or not that person has been granted bail by the police. Once granted bail, however, that person's custody is lawful until the terms of bail are met.[89] State high courts have divided over whether bail must be granted after an accused has been held in custody for over two months without trial on a capital charge. The high courts of Benue

State, Oyo State, and Plateau State have held that it need not be[90]; the High Court of Lagos State has held that it should be allowed.[91]

The unusual point about all violations of bail rights under the Nigerian constitution is the provision for compensation and apology. The High Court of Oyo State has held that in case of violations payment of some compensation for the unlawful detention is mandatory.[92] The court further held the Commissioner of Police responsible for compensation and damages even though a magistrate provided the remand in custody. The magistrate would only be liable if acting in bad faith. The amount of damages depends upon the following:

1. What is adequate to repair the injury to the accused's reputation
2. What will atone for the assault on the accused's character
3. The circumstances leading to the unlawful detention

In addition to this amount, exemplary compensation might be warranted if the detention is the result of a stubborn decision to act contrary to law.[93]

Considerations in granting or denying bail in Nigeria are very similar to those used in other countries, allowing for the levels of categories of eligibility established by the various state statutes.[94] One aspect in Nigeria is important in the context of defending against commercial bail. According to the High Court of Imo State, a major factor to be considered in determining whether an accused is likely or not to appear as required is whether the sureties are independent or indemnified by the accused. This factor, along with the seriousness of the charge of its punishment and the strength of the prosecution case are the bases for evaluating this consideration.[95] Where sureties have been paid, bail should be denied. Thus, Nigeria reflects the worldwide distrust of compensated provision of bail as running contrary to the logic underlying the securing of the accused's appearance.

A point regarding the forfeiture procedure in Nigeria requires comment. Although the rights to a notice to show cause, to be told of the nature of the breach alleged, to be heard, and to have any forfeiture order based on evidence were well established, a 1983 Federal Court of Appeal case considerably strengthened them. Under the decision in this case, since the consequence of forfeiture could be imprisonment (in the default of payment) the provisions of the Constitution guarding fair trial should be enforced by the court for forfeiture proceedings. This includes—enhancing the already recognized rights—strict proof of the surety's guilt as in a criminal proceeding, notice in the language he understands, and adequate time and facility to prepare and conduct a defense.[96] The rights afforded in forfeiture proceedings under Nigerian case law are thus among the strongest found in recognizance systems.

Zimbabwe

Terms upon which bail is granted in Zimbabwe represent a degree of modification from a purely traditional system. Certain such alterations are noteworthy. The frequently encountered provision permitting courts to accept cash deposits as substitutes is modified in two ways. Deposits by a third party on behalf of an accused are specifically permitted, as are deposits of securities as well as cash. A wide authority is created to impose nonfinancial conditions of conduct upon bail whether by recognizance or deposit. Indeed any matter relating to the accused's conduct may be regulated where necessary or desirable in the interests of justice. The more usual conditions—surrender of passport, reporting, avoiding specified places, and not communicating with the accused or prosecution witnesses—are specifically authorized. Zimbabwe is among the countries where default on any bail condition is enforceable by forfeiture of recognizance.[97] Criminal penalties for bail defaults have been explicitly held unlawful. Not only are they without statutory authority, but imposing both a fine and forfeiture for a bail violation has been ruled unjust and unreasonable and tantamount to punishing twice for the same default.[98]

An atypical aspect of bail eligibility in Zimbabwe lies in executive involvement. The Home Secretary and Attorney General are authorized to preempt the courts' discretion to grant bail in a range of national security, political, and politico-economic offenses. Similar provisions for the preemption of the judicial function of bail by an executive official are found in other jurisdictions, including Sri Lanka, South Africa, and Zambia. The courts in Zimbabwe, while accepting the validity of this provision, have repeatedly insisted that the executive demonstrate to them reasonable grounds for suspicion that the accused committed a crime that would fall within the ambit of the power to preempt judicial bail.[99]

In a manner that is unusual for a traditional recognizance system, Zimbabwe provides a clear statutory indication of the main considerations guiding the exercise of the discretion to deny bail. It may be refused if the accused is likely to fail to appear, to interfere with evidence, or to commit an offense. These considerations are not meant to be exclusive, however, and denial may be based on any good and sufficient reason.[100] The Zimbabwe High Court has held that an accused's extensive record of committing similar crimes while on bail creates a presumption against his being bailed under the third consideration. Consequently, he should bear the onus of satisfying the court that repeat offenses will not result from his release.[101]

An unusual procedural approach applies to the mitigation of forfeitures in Zimbabwe. If an accused fails to appear or violates another bail condition, courts are confined to considering whether it is willful or deliberate. If they are satisfied of that, they have no discretion in the matter of forfeiture. If they are not satisfied, they may refuse forfeiture. The rather strict test of willful or deliberate is whether default was due to circumstances beyond the accused's control or so compelling as to materially interfere with his freedom of choice. The courts lack authority to inquire beyond this issue, and lack the usual authority to consider whether sureties are blameless or culpable in the default. The authority to mitigate forfeiture even in part is placed entirely in the Attorney General. As a result, the most the courts can do is to recommend that the Attorney General give serious consideration to remission where that result seems appropriate.[102]

Ireland

The provision regarding acceptance of cash deposits in Ireland, even more clearly than in most other traditional recognizance systems, precludes demands by a magistrate for such deposits. The *Criminal Procedure Act* specifies that a sum equal to the amount fixed for the recognizance may be accepted in lieu of sureties. This wording makes clear that the amount of bail has already to be set in the form of a recognizance. Cash deposits are limited to substitutes for sureties where these have been required. The court's discretion is limited to accepting the substitution or not.[103] Imposition of nonfinancial conditions of conduct is a well-established practice supported by case law. Evidence of their necessity is required to justify their use.[104]

In addition to these bail sanctions, which are more or less typical of traditional recognizance systems, another one was added in 1984 that moves Ireland away from the purely traditional systems. The *Criminal Justice Act* of that year created an offense of failing to appear in accordance with the terms of a bail recognizance. The offense is punishable as a summary offense by up to a year's imprisonment or a £1000 fine or both. Any sentence imposed under this provision must be made consecutive to the sentence for the original (or any other) offense. A reasonable excuse for not appearing constitutes a defense.[105]

Ireland does not create any constitutional or statutory right to bail, so the granting of bail by a court is discretionary. Nevertheless, it is a judicial act which requires that various matters be considered and discretion exercised according to law.[106] Bail for a few serious offenses is reserved for a superior court (the High Court).[107]

The law governing the exercise of discretion regarding bail creates what amounts to a presumption of or qualified right to bail. Some suggestion of this is implicit in the statute,[108] but it is much more clearly enunciated in the case law. The unconvicted person has a fundamental right to personal liberty. This can only be lost when necessary for the state to effectuate its duty to guard the common good. Consequently, an accused should not be unnecessarily kept in custody; release on bail should therefore be allowed whenever it can safely be done.[109] Thus, in the absence of a recognized consideration warranting denial of bail, it should be granted.

Ireland has only two considerations justifying denial of bail. One is the probability that the accused will fail to appear for trial. The other is the likelihood that the accused *would*—as opposed to *could*—interfere with the course of justice if released. Such interference might take the form of tampering with witnesses, jurors, or physical evidence.[110] The Irish Supreme Court has rejected a third consideration recognized in varying degrees by many other countries: the possibility of the accused's committing a further crime if released. That court has stated that the use of this consideration is a form of preventive justice which has no place in the country's legal system and is alien to the true purpose of bail.[111] For denial of bail, one of the two accepted considerations must be established by the prosecution based on definite evidence. A vague possibility is not enough.[112]

Summary

The traditional recognizance systems other than India's exhibit a range of variations from the specific bail arrangements prevailing in that particular system. Bail in each of these is characterized by release upon the accused's executing a recognizance: a commitment to forfeit a specified amount upon failure to appear in court as required. Typically one or more third parties are required as sureties executing a similar recognizance. In most of these countries, not requiring sureties is somewhat of an exception to normal practice and is reserved for especially low-risk cases. However, regular use of sureties is not necessarily inherent in bail of this type. Studies done of the English system prior to the 1976 *Bail Act* show that sureties were not required in a clear majority of cases, and in some courts in an overwhelming majority of them.[113]

In addition to the basic recognizance core, almost all of the jurisdictions involved allow nonfinancial conditions of conduct to be attached in some instances. However, use of these may be very restricted as in Pakistan, or widely authorized by statute or case law as in Zambia and Tanzania. A frequent middle ground is linking use of conditions to the lack of a right to bail on the Indian model. The status of conditions also varies depending on whether they can be enforced only by the arrest of the accused and reconsideration of bail (e.g., Malaysia), by forfeiture of the accused's recognizance only (e.g., Tanzania), or by forfeiture of the recognizances of sureties as well as principal (e.g., Zimbabwe).

Limited use of cash deposits as an alternate form of bail is found in most recognizance systems. Typically this is permitted only on the initiative of the accused. The court's role is passive in that it cannot require cash. In practice, courts in a few jurisdictions such as Tanzania seem to take a more active role. Judicial opinion in several countries makes clear that cash is to be used as a substitute for sureties to allow release of strangers who are unable to obtain them. Ireland expresses this usage in its statute itself. A few bail laws, like Zimbabwe's, make provision for other forms of security deposit.

A final supplementary sanction is provided in Ireland. Although most traditional recognizance systems, like Malaysia, forbid imposing a punishment on bail violators, Ireland provides by statute for a criminal punishment upon conviction for absconding. Thus, the Irish system moves to this extent away from the traditional and toward the modified recognizance approach.

Bail rights vary widely. In some instances a statutory right to bail applies to all lesser offenses, or after prolonged pretrial detention to a wider range of crimes. Bail in serious matters, conversely, is often reserved to superior courts. Though the exact limits of these provisions vary, capital offenses and often those punishable with life imprisonment are included in such provisions. Even where bail is discretionary, moreover, a presumption, or *prima facie* right, to be granted bail is almost universal. The considerations for defeating this are basically similar virtually everywhere. They include the threat of absconding and of interfering with justice. A more debatable third consideration is the danger of commission of a further crime. This is sometimes limited to serious crimes or similar crimes.

MODIFIED RECOGNIZANCE SYSTEMS

Background

As is evident, deviation from the traditional common law model of recognizance bail is found in all countries basically adhering to that form. Modification occurs by statute amending the approach as found in Ireland, or in the expanded availability of conditions in Zambia and Zimbabwe, or the limited use of conditions based on case law elsewhere. There are a few jurisdictions that, while retaining basically recognizance systems, have restructured their bail arrangements by statute to such a degree as to produce a recognizable subtype within the recognizance approach. Most notable of these are the Australian states of Victoria, Queensland, and Western Australia. The Victoria *Bail Act 1977* was the first of these modifications and served to a considerable extent as the model, particularly for the Queensland law.

Australia: Victoria

The statutory provision governing the core financial sanction motivating adherence to bail in Victoria is an elaboration on traditional recognizance bail. It provides a set of four alternative terms upon which defendants may be released. These are arranged by ascending degree of onerousness. Courts are directed to consider terms of release in the sequence given, and not to impose terms more burdensome than are required in the public interest by the nature of the offense and the circumstances of the accused. Possible bail terms in the order given are the following:

1. Release on the accused's own recognizance without sureties or deposit of money or other security.
2. Release on the accused's recognizance with a deposit of money or other security.
3. Release on the accused's recognizance with one or more sureties.
4. Release on the accused's recognizance with both a deposit of money or other security and one or more sureties.

Thus, the statutory preference is for release by recognizance alone, and even the more burdensome terms are based upon recognizance.[114]

The *Bail Act,* in addition to the core financial terms of release, authorizes the imposition of nonfinancial conditions of conduct in conjunction with any level of financial terms required. Nonfinancial conditions must, however, be necessary to achieve one or more of four authorized objectives. These are (1) securing the accused's appearance, (2) assuring against offenses by the accused while on bail, (3) preventing danger from the accused to the safety or welfare of members of the public, and (4) securing against the accused interfering with witnesses or otherwise obstructing the course of justice in relation to himself or others. Violation of conditions of conduct subjects an accused to arrest without a warrant and possible forfeiture and revocation of bail.[115] Courts are required by the *Bail Act* to provide the person to be released with written notice of the bail conditions and of the consequences of failure to comply with them, and to satisfy themselves that the accused understands both the conditions and consequences of violations. Nonfinancial conditions as well as financial ones may be altered or supplemented by the court in the interest of justice.

Where sureties are required, the courts are authorized to consider the suitability of individuals proposed for the role. The statute specifies three aspects of suitability, although other dimensions are not precluded from consideration: (1) the adequacy of the sureties' financial resources, (2) their character and previous record, and (3) their proximity to the accused. The last may be proximity in terms of kinship, place of residence, or other relationship. This emphasis on a proximate relationship between surety and accused as a dimension of suitability reflects the widespread preference in noncommercial systems for sureties who, it is hoped, can exercise some moral suasion over the accused.

A 1978 amendment to the *Bail Act* ostensibly deals with demonstrating the surety's financial adequacy but in effect creates an additional level of bail terms. By this provision courts may require sureties to demonstrate their financial adequacy by a deposit of cash or bank account passbook. Thus, to the ascending list of bail alternatives, providing surety with cash deposit can be implicitly added. Victoria, as previously explained, makes indemnification of sureties, or agreement to indemnify them, an offense by statute.[116]

Sureties in Victoria are entitled by law to notice of bail conditions and consequences of violations much like the accused. They retain the right to arrest the accused and bring him before the court seeking their discharge. Members of the police are directed by the act to assist sureties if requested. Alternatively, sureties may seek discharge from the court which can then issue a warrant for the accused and allow discharge upon the accused's being brought before it.[117]

In the case of all forfeitures, whether on the part of the accused or of sureties, and whether of a recognizance or of cash or other deposit, Victoria is among those jurisdictions taking the view that forfeiture occurs immediately upon the accused's failure to appear. Courts have no discretion to refuse forfeiture. As the Victorian Supreme Court explains, "the recognizance is self-executing and . . . it is forfeited on failure to comply with the condition" of appearance.[118] Once forfeiture has occurred, however an opportunity to show cause for mitigation is provided. The accused or surety is given three months in which to apply for the forfeiture to be moderated or rescinded. This may be done where the court concludes that requiring the individual to pay the amount would be unjust under all the circumstances.[119]

As in the traditional recognizance systems, a further sanction enforcing appearance is liability to arrest and possible cancelation of bail or release only on more unfavorable terms. The police may arrest without a warrant upon reasonable grounds for believing that the accused is likely not to appear as required. Upon actual failure to appear the court may issue a warrant for arrest.[120]

Finally, like Ireland among the more traditional recognizance systems, Victoria supplements its other means of enforcing bail by constituting failure to appear as a criminal offense. Anyone bailed who fails to appear without reasonable cause is subject to up to twelve months' imprisonment. A copy of the declaration of forfeiture of the accused's recognizance is *prima facie* evidence of the failure to appear. The burden of showing reasonable cause then rests with the defendant. Several ancillary offenses are also created. To protect against prejudicial pretrial publicity resulting from a bail hearing, the court may order that the evidence taken, information given, representations made, and reasons stated not be published under penalty of a fine or imprisonment of up to three months. Failure by either accused or sureties to provide notice of a change in address or business is punishable by the same penalties. Entering into recognizance under a false name may be punished by up to fifteen years' imprisonment.[121]

Most aspects of eligibility for bail in Victoria are controlled by statute. However, one aspect has been determined based upon a federal constitutional provision. The Victoria Supreme Court, following that of Queensland, held unconstitutional a provision of the *Bail Act* creating a presumption against bail for anyone not ordinarily a resident of the state accused of an indictable offense. The Victorian court agreed with that of Queensland that the provision violated Section 117 of the Constitution by discriminating solely on the basis of residence in another state.[122] The provision was consequently repealed.

A strong presumption is created against the granting of bail in treason and murder cases. Only the Supreme Court or a judge of that court can consider bail in treason cases. To these is added the magistrate (or coroner) who commits the accused for trial in murder cases. However, even these specified judicial officials can only grant bail if satisfied that exceptional circumstances exist which justify doing so. This has been held by the Supreme Court to require a showing of special or unusual circumstances if refusal of bail is to be avoided. The burden of proof to establish these rests on the accused seeking bail under these charges.[123]

A presumption against granting bail is also created for certain other offenses, although these are not reserved to any specific classes of judge to consider:

1. Aggravated burglary and any other indictable offense involving the use of threatened use of a firearm, offensive weapon, or explosive.
2. A range of offenses involving production of or dealing in opium, cocaine, and cannabis, or their derivatives.
3. Any crime against the *Bail Act* itself.
4. Any indictable offense committed while at large awaiting trial for another indictable offense.

Bail may be granted for these only if the accused can show cause why detention in custody is not justified. A court granting bail in these instances must record its reason in the recognizance. In addition to these constraints a 1986 amendment to the *Bail Act* created an even stronger presumption against bail for a variety of the most serious offenses involving the importation, production of, or trafficking in large quantities of dangerous drugs. Bail may only be granted for these if a court is satisfied of the existence of exceptional circumstances which justify it. The amendment did not explicitly require a recording of reasons, but this has been subsequently recommended.[124]

For all other offenses a *prima facie* right to bail is created by the *Bail Act*. Bail is to be granted unless specified considerations require its denial. Courts should refuse bail principally in two instances:

1. The accused is in custody for failing to answer bail, unless that accused can satisfy the court that the failure was from causes beyond control.
2. The court is satisfied of the presence of an unacceptable risk of the accused's failing to answer bail, committing an offense while on bail, endangering the safety or welfare of members of the public, or interfering with witnesses or otherwise obstructing justice in his own case or another's.

Provisions are also included to deny bail to incarcerated convicts, to those requiring protective custody, and to those about whom obtaining sufficient information to decide a bail issue has not been practicable.[125]

In assessing the risk with regard to a consideration justifying denial of bail, all matters appearing relevant to the court may be considered. The Victorian Supreme Court has held this to include any evidence that the court considers credible or trustworthy under the circumstances, including hearsay, whether or not it would be admissible under ordinary rules of evidence.[126] Nevertheless, without limiting the breadth of factors available to be used, the *Bail Act* highlights certain ones for consideration where relevant. Two of these are commonly found in traditional systems: the nature and seriousness of the offense and the strength of the prosecution's evidence. The other two specified in Victoria are the accused's character, antecedents, associations, home environment and background; and the accused's history regarding previous grants of bail.[127]

Procedurally, not only must accuseds be brought before a magistrate within twenty-four hours if not released, but if not granted police bail on terms that they are actually able to meet they must be advised of their right to apply to a magistrate. Defendants are protected against prejudicial revelations in proceedings before the court, not only by the possible ban on publicity already mentioned but also by a statutory prohibition against their being questioned by the court or anyone about the offense charged. An accused who is granted bail by a court and who is unable to meet bail terms within twenty-four hours may, subject to some limitations, apply to have them varied. Various routes for both prosecution and defense to seek review of bail decisions are provided.[128]

Australia: Queensland and Western Australia

Both the Queensland *Bail Act of 1980* and the Western Australian *Bail Act of 1982* create modified recognizance systems of the general sort found in Victoria. Both of these differ in some particulars from the Victorian. The Western Australian differs to a greater extent than does that of Queensland, which was directly modeled on the Victorian statute. Although the Western Australian legislation was put in place in 1982, its effective date was still being delayed at the end of 1988.

An important basic difference from the other two jurisdictions occurs in Western Australia as to what is secured by bail. Not only are defendants required to appear in court as specified, but upon failure to do so they are also required (1) to notify a court administrator of the cause for that failure and (2) to appear at the court when it is sitting. Both additional requirements must be met as soon as practicable after the initial failure.[129]

The alternative terms of bail by which appearance is secured are presented in this same list format in Queensland and Western Australia that was seen in Victoria. Similar instructions about minimizing onerousness are also given, although Western Australia lacks the explicit instruction that bail terms should be considered by courts in the order presented. Some differences occur in the sequence of alternative terms between that state and the other two (which are identical). Western Australia lists the following:

1. Release on the accused's own recognizance.
2. Release on the accused's recognizance with one or more sureties, also by recognizance.
3. Release on the accused's recognizance with sureties and a cash deposit by either accused or surety.
4. Release as in 3, but with a passbook (or equivalent) deposited instead of cash.
5. Release as in 3, but substituting some other security by means of a mortgage, charge, assignment, or other transaction.[130]

When this sequence is compared with the others, two important differences appear. Western Australia, by placing a recognizance with sureties before any use of deposit, reverses the order of the other two states. Implicitly this accords with the judgment of the traditional system that a third-party surety by recognizance is normally preferable to any demand for a deposit. However, by apparently linking use of a deposit to a required surety, Western Australia does not manifestly provide, like the other two, for an accused's making a deposit without seeking a surety. Thus, the principal use contemplated for deposit by the traditional systems—the stranger unable to locate a surety—is not evidently accommodated.

Differences of detail also are present in provisions for nonfinancial conditions. Queensland and Western Australia, unlike Victoria, make explicit that these are not to be made more burdensome for the accused than is necessary. Western Australia allows conditions to be imposed to prevent danger to the property of members of the public as well as to their safety and welfare as in the other two states. It adds a separate provision for conditions to ensure during its occurrence the proper conduct of the trial. The others would have to justify such conditions under the general prevention of obstructing the course of justice. Western Australia also makes explicit provision for bail conditions to ensure compliance with orders for drug or alcohol abuse treatment when these have been ordered.[131]

In bails involving the use of sureties, a few differences emerge as salient from the general similarity of the three bail acts. Although in Queensland as in Victoria a surety may establish sufficiency of means by a deposit, unlike Victoria, nothing in the Queensland wording suggests that the court may order that this be done. A more minor difference is that Queensland mentions only a deposit of money while Victoria provides for either a deposit of cash or a bank passbook.[132]

Regarding the arrest powers of sureties, Western Australia is generally more restrictive than the other two states. Although sureties retain a power of arrest in that state, they may only exercise it subject to two conditions: (1) the accused is either unlikely to appear as required or has breached some other bail condition, and (2) seeking the aid of a police officer would cause a delay that would defeat preventing the breach of bail. They are further obliged to deliver the accused to a police officer as soon as practicable after the arrest. In one dimension only, however, this power is wider than in the other two jurisdictions—it applies to breach of conditions other than appearance itself.[133]

Accuseds who fail to appear as required and their sureties are subject to forfeiture of their recognizances. The sequence of immediate forfeiture and subsequent opportunity to show cause is identical in Queensland to that described in Victoria. Western Australia provides a different and in some respects unique sequence. For the defendant's recognizance, forfeiture is linked to conviction for the offense of failing to appear. Upon conviction the court, even without a prosecutor's application, is instructed by the *Bail Act* to order the forfeiture. This provides the forum for the accused to show cause why it should not be ordered. The grounds specified for mitigation again contrast with those employed in Victoria and Queensland. Only one is given: that forfeiture would cause excessive hardship to the accused or his dependants by reason of circumstances which have changed since the recognizance was entered. Upon satisfaction that this is the case, the court may either decline forfeiture or forfeit only in part. After one year from a nonappearance, if the defendant has still not appeared, forfeiture in full is automatic without any order being necessary.[134]

Forfeiture of sureties' recognizances are also handled differently in Western Australia than in the other two states. Upon the accused's failure to appear, application is made for forfeiture. The accused is then summonsed to show cause against the forfeiture. Only thereafter is forfeiture in whole or in part in order. Thus, unlike the other jurisdictions, no forfeiture is ordered before the showing of cause against it. The reasons acceptable in sureties' showing of cause are also different in Western Australia from Victoria and Queensland. A 1984 amendment to the *Bail Act* apparently deletes the traditional justification that the surety took all reasonably available steps to secure the defendant's compliance. As a result, two grounds are available for sureties to argue. They can show that the defendant had reasonable grounds for failure to appear or that they or their dependents would suffer excessive hardship due to changed circumstances since they entered the recognizance.[135]

Like Victoria, Queensland and Western Australia supplement their bail sanctions with a criminal offense of failing to appear without reasonable cause. Queensland punishes the offenses more heavily than does Victoria, with possible imprisonment of two years, while Western Australia expands the possible sentence to three years. The alternative possible fine is $1000 in Queensland and $3000 in Western Australia. In addition, Western Australian courts are given discretion to fix an amount to be paid by defendants toward defraying the expenses created by their apprehension. The most significant difference among the three systems, however, is the creation of a second offense carrying the same punishment under the Queensland and Western Australian statutes. The additional offense is committed when the accused, having failed to appear as required, also fails to appear as soon as is practicable when the court is sitting. Queensland restricts this offense to instances where reasonable cause is shown for the initial default. Thus, conviction for both failures is precluded. Wording of the Western Australian statute does not contain this limitation. Therefore, a persistently absent defendant might violate both provisions.[136]

Eligibility for bail in Queensland differs in only relatively minor details from that seen in Victoria. Queensland adds two uncommon offenses to the list exempted from the *prima facie* right to bail reserved for a Supreme Court judge. In addition, it includes specified serious drug offenses on that list whereas Victoria, although exempting them from the right, does not reserve them. In contrast to these two states, Western Australia creates no *prima facie* right to bail. All bails are at the discretion of the court. The accused has only the right to be brought before a court as soon as is practicable and to have bail considered whether or not an application for it is made.[137]

The considerations to be used in the exercise of bail discretion differ in how they are to be used depending upon whether a *prima facie* right to bail is created or not. Thus, in Queensland, as in Victoria, bail should be granted unless the court is satisfied that a specified consideration is present. In contrast, in Western Australia the law requires that discretion be exercised having regard to whether, if the defendant is not kept in custody, a specified condition may apply. Clearly, this perspective is less conducive to bail's being granted.[138]

As to the considerations themselves, large similarities exist in all three states and virtual identity exists between Queensland and Victoria. To the consideration of danger to the public safety or welfare of members of the public seen in Victoria, Western Australia adds property. Western Australia enters as a separate consideration whether the prosecutor has put forward grounds for opposing bail. A final and clearly desirable consideration in the state is whether any condition of bail which might be imposed could eliminate a possible grounds for denying bail.[139]

Queensland statistics provide some confirmation that the recognizance emphasis of that state's bail law is reflected in practice. The number of bail recognizances forfeited in magistrates' courts in Queensland for the six one-year periods from 1 July 1981 to 30 June 1987 ranged from 26,792 to 29,661 and averaged 28,523. These represented between 15.5 percent and 18.9 percent of all appearances before these courts. This overstates greatly, however, the number of true forfeitures due to a scheme for processing drunkenness cases known as "10 cent bail," which was introduced in the 1973–1974 reporting period. Under this approach, habitual drunks are released on nominal bail of 10 cents secured with a cash deposit which is in due course forfeited without recording a drunkenness conviction. Comparing the 1972–1973 period (before this scheme was introduced) with the 1974–1975 period afterward, drunkenness convictions were reduced by 11,885 and bail forfeiture increased by 16,737, indicating a transfer from one category to the other of somewhere in between the two figures. A realistic estimate of normal bail forfeitures might then be about half the annual number stated, with their percentage of the total appearances also about halved. Even this result would demonstrate prevalence of a recognizance system.[140] Use of sureties in the state, as well as in Western Australia, is rare.[141]

Summary

Although modified recognizance systems keep their emphasis on recognizance, this is altered in several ways. The primacy of recognizance is demonstrated by the fact that whatever other impetuses to respond to bail may be added, the accused's recognizance remains at the core of release on bail. It is further demonstrated by the fact that, unless need is found to supplement it, it is the form of release preferred by these statutes. In at least one respect the accused's recognizance receives even clearer emphasis in these systems than in traditional common law recognizance bail systems. In most traditional systems sureties are normally required unless reason to dispense with them is found. In these systems the accused's recognizance stands without them, unless reason to require them is found.

The modified recognizance systems make other supplementary terms of bail more available than do the traditional. Nonfinancial conditions of conduct may be added as needed without the restrictions in many traditional systems where bail is either of right or is granted by a lower court. Use of cash deposits to secure the bail recognizance is not restricted to the accused's initiative in the modified systems as it generally is in the traditional. Courts may require deposit if a recognizance alone is thought inadequate incentive to appear. Finally, forfeiture of a recognizance or its threat can be supplemented by the threat of punishment on a criminal charge of absconding. How these alternatives are combined into a package of bail terms for an individual case is generally controlled by a statutory requirement that onerousness of bail terms be minimized as much as possible. The use of a hierarchical listing of terms by burdensomeness—as in Victoria and Queensland—structures the requirement of minimizing the burden.

The modified systems, like the traditional ones, are capable of being linked to various degrees of right to bail. Victoria grants a *prima facie* right to bail for most offenses. Western Australia makes all bails discretionary.

CONCLUSION

All three modified recognizance systems and many of the traditional ones have laws or practices that either make illegal or otherwise directly inhibit commercial provision of bail. In addition, however, the recognizance system which they adopt in place of the commercial alternative militates against its development. Since under a recognizance system defendants and sureties are not actually required to raise cash unless they default, the incentive to turn to a commercial source of bail is greatly lessened. In that the modified systems do not routinely require sureties, the temptation to attain them by hire is further reduced. Curtailment of the commercial route to sureties allows the courts in both varieties of recognizance countries to place a very reasonable emphasis on the relationship existing between the accused and potential sureties. Characteristics such as sureties' personal knowledge of defendants and influence over them can then be considerations in their acceptability.

To the extent that cash can be demanded (as opposed to passively accepted) by courts, the immunity of the recognizance system from commercial bail is compromised. This is perhaps the reason why in general those recognizance jurisdictions most open to the courts' requiring cash have the most explicit provisions against surety indemnification. However, even in the recognizance jurisdictions with laws most conducive to deposit demands, they are legally inhibited and relatively rare. The possibility of commercial bail bonding surviving as an ongoing business under any of these systems is extremely small. Even the Queensland "10 cent bail scheme," which greatly inflates the number of bails involving cash, is most unlikely to attract commercial exploitation.

NOTES

1. *Lim Kiap Khee v. Public Prosecutor,* 1988 (1) MLJ 198 (H.C. K.L., 1987), at 199 E-G; *Public Prosecutor v. Chou Tai Chuan,* 1988 (1) MLJ 511 (H.C. K.L., 1987), at 512 H-E; *Mohamed Razip v. Public Prosecutor,* 1988 (1) MLJ 84 (C. A. Sing, 1987), 85 F-86 G.

2. *Lim Kiap Khee v. Public Prosecutor,* at 199 E-G.

3. *Republic v. Mahmood Mohamed,* 1973 LRT n. 79 (H.C. C.R., 1972), at 347.

4. *Criminal Procedure Code 1973,* s. 88, s. 441; K. C. Mehrotra, *Law of Bails, Forfeiture of Bonds and Habeas Corpus,* 2nd ed. (Lucknow: Eastern Book Company, 1985), pp. 24, 269, 271, 272; Vindeshwari Prasad, *The Law of Bails,* 3rd ed. (Allahabad: Hind Publishing House, 1985), pp. 88, 89, 258, 263, 265–267; K. K. Singh, *Law of Bails* (Allahabad: National Law Agency, 1986), pp. 326–328, 351–352, 370–371, 374–377.

5. *Hussainara Khatoon v. State of Bihar (1),* AIR 1979 SC 1360 (S.C., 1979), esp. at 1363–1364.

6. *Criminal Procedure Code,* s. 440; *Hussainara Khatoon v. State of Bihar (1),* at 1364; Mehrotra, pp. 215–216; Prasad, pp. 273–274; Singh, p. 321.

7. *Criminal Procedure Code,* s. 88, s. 441; *Chimanlal v. State,* 1987 Cri LJ 2002 (H.C. Bom., 1987), at 2004–2005; Prasad, pp. 263, 265, 266–267; Singh, pp. 323, 330–332, 333.

8. *Criminal Procedure Code,* s. 446A; R. K. Narula, *Jail or Bail* (Bombay: Himalaya Publishing House, 1979), pp. 82, 83; Mehrotra, pp. 293–294; Prasad, pp. 277, 304–305; Singh, pp. 326–328.

9. *Abdul Karim v. Emperor,* AIR 1933 Sind 320 (H.C. Sind, 1933); Mehrotra, pp. 280, 282; Singh, pp. 326, 338.

10. *State of Rajasthan v. Lalsingh,* 1987 Cr LJ 269 (H.C. Raj, 1986), at 270–271; *Emperor v. Din Mohammed,* 11 Cr LJ 198; Mehrotra, p. 282.

11. *Schuster v. Assistant Collector of Customs,* AIR 1967 Punj 189 (H.C. Punj., 1965), at 190; Prasad, p. 266; Singh, p. 337.

12. *Chotey Lal v. Emperor,* AIR 1948 All 72 (H.C. All., 1947), at 73–74; Mehrotra, p. 283; Narula, pp. 84–85; Singh, pp. 333–335.

13. *Criminal Procedure Code,* s. 444; Mehrotra, p. 286; Prasad, p. 288; Singh, pp. 341–343.

14. *Criminal Procedure Code,* s. 446; Mehrotra, p. 297; Prasad, pp. 299, 305; Singh, pp. 330–331, 355–356, 361, 369, 371.

15. *Criminal Procedure Code,* s. 446; Mehrotra, pp. 298, 299–300; Prasad, pp. 309–311; Singh, pp. 351–352, 354–355, 360, 374–377.

16. *Criminal Procedure Code,* s. 445; *R. R. Chari v. Emperor,* AIR 1948 All 238 (H.C. All., 1948), esp. at 239; *In the Matter of Surja Narain,* AIR 1935 Pat 195 (H.C. Pat., 1934), esp. at 200; 1935 Cri LJ 730; Mehrotra, pp. 217–218, 277–278; Prasad, pp. 274–275; Singh, pp. 169, 325, 343–345.

17. *Criminal Procedure Code*, s. 441, s. 445; *Abdus Sattar v. K. E.*, AIR 1938 Oudh 195; *In the Matter of Surja Narain*, esp. at 199–200; *R. R. Chari v. Emperor*, at 239; Mehrotra, pp. 277–278; Singh, pp. 325, 344–345.

18. *Keshab Narayan v. State of Bihar*, 91 Cri LJ 1857 (S.C., 1985); *Niamut Khan v. Crown*, AIR 1951 Nag 206 (H.C. Nag, 1949); Mehrotra, p. 284; Singh, p. 341.

19. *Criminal Procedure Code*, s. 437(3).

20. *Nilu v. State*, 89 Cri LJ 1590 (O.H.C., 1983); *In re Saradamma*, AIR 1965 AP 144 (H.C.A.P., 1965); Mehrotra, pp. 313–315; Prasad, pp. 174, 176–179, 245–246; Singh, p. 202.

21. *In re Saradamma*, at 447; Mehrotra, pp. 214–215; Singh, p. 202.

22. *Criminal Procedure Code*, s. 436(1), s. 439(1)(a); *In re Saradamma*, at 446; *R. v. Genda Singh*, AIR 1950 All 525 (H.C. All, 1949); *In re District Magistrate of Vizigapatam*, AIR 1949 Mad. 77 (H.C. Mad., 1947), at 78; *In re Kola Appolokonda*, AIR 1942 Mad. 740 (H.C. Mad., 1942); Mehrotra, pp. 213, 238–240; Prasad, pp. 172–173, 175–177, 219–220; Singh, p. 158.

23. *Criminal Procedure Code*, s. 437(5); *Nilu v. State*; Singh, p. 158.

24. *Criminal Procedure Code*, s. 89, s. 436(2), s. 446(A); *Johny Wilson v. State of Rajasthan*, 1986 Cri LJ 1235 (H.C. Raj., 1985), esp. at 1240–1243; Prasad, pp. 196, 199, 221–222, 269–270.

25. *Criminal Procedure Code*, s. 437(5), s. 439(2), s. 482; *T. H. Hussain v. M. P. Mondakar*, AIR 1958 SC 376 (S.C., 1958), esp. at 379–380; *Madhab Chandra Jenna v. State of Orissa*, 1988 Cri LJ 608 (H.C. Oris., 1986); Mehrotra, pp. 78, 231–232; Prasad, pp. 175–176, 202–203; Singh, pp. 174–175, 184–185, 211.

26. *Criminal Procedure Code*, s. 443; *State (Delhi Administration) v. Sanjay Gandhi*, AIR 1978 SC 961 (S.C., 1978); *Gurcharan Singh v. State (Delhi Administration)*, AIR 1978 SC 179 (S.C., 1977), at 186–187; *Public Prosecutor v. George Williams*, AIR 1958 SC 376 (S.C., 1958), upholding below AIR 1951 Mad. 1042 (H.C. Mad., 1951), at 1044; *State v. P. Sugathan*, 1988 Cr LJ 1036 (H.C. Ker, 1987); *Kashmeri Devi v. Delhi Administration*, 1988 Cri LJ 1649 (H.C. Delhi, 1987), at 1651; *Vishwanath Tiwary v. State of Bihar*, 1988 Cri LJ 333 (H.C. Pat., 1986), at 335–336; *Raghubir Singh v. State of Bihar*, 1987 Cri LJ 157 (S.C., 1986), at 169–170; *Jaram Tiwary v. State of Bihar*, 1987 Cri LJ 254 (H.C. Pat, 1985), at 256, 257; *T. H. Husain v. M. P. Mondkar*, at 379–380; *Tahir v. Shaukat*, 1986 Cri LJ 1815 (H.C. All., 1986), esp. at 1816–1817; *Johny Wilson v. State of Rajasthan*, at 1241; *Nilu v. State*, at 1593–1595; *Paras Ram v. State*, AIR 1951 HP 13 (H.C. H.P., 1950), at 15; Mehrotra, pp. 220–227, 232–236, 237–238; Prasad, pp. 192–194, 203–208; Singh, pp. 117–118, 211–215.

27. *Maneka Gandhi v. Union of India*, AIR 1978 SC 597 (S.C., 1978).

28. Ibid.; Mehrotra, pp. 2–3; A. M. Bhattacharjee, J., "*Maneka Gandhi* and Law of Bail," *Criminal Law Journal* (1983), pp. 14–19.

29. *Raj Kumar Singh v. State of Bihar*, 1986 Cri LJ 2042 (S.C., 1986), esp. at 2045–2047; Also *Asmanbhai Dawoodbhai v. State of Gujarat*, 1988 Cri LJ 938 (S.C., 1988), at 949–950.

30. *Saraj Pal v. State of Maharastra*, 1986 Cri LJ 2047 (S.C., 1986), esp. at 2054, 2056, 2057, 2059–2061.

31. *Sita Ram v. State of Rajasthan*, 1986 Cri LJ 860 (S.C., 1986), esp. at 862; *Debabrate Das v. Joint Secretary, Government of India*, 1986 Cri LJ 2085 (H.C.D., 1986), esp. at 2087.

32. *Criminal Procedure Code,* s. 436; *T. H. Hussain v. M. P. Mondkar,* at 378; Mehrotra, pp. 77–78, 134; Prasad, pp. 215–217, 218, 220; Singh, pp. 162–163.

33. *Indian Penal Code,* First Schedule, Pt. I, Col. 5, Pt. II; Mehrotra, p. 37.

34. Mehrotra, p. 28; Prasad, pp. 216–217.

35. *Criminal Procedure Code,* s. 436(2); Mehrotra, pp. 79–80; Singh, p. 170.

36. *Criminal Procedure Code,* s. 437(1), s. 439; *Santosh Bhaurao Raut v. State of Maharashtra,* 1989 Cri LJ 205 (H.C. Bom., 1988), at 206; *Ram Sahodar v. State of Madhya Pradesh,* 1986 Cri LJ 279 (H.C. M.P., 1985); *Uthaman v. State of Kerala,* 1983 Cri LJ 74 (H.C. K., f.b. 1982), esp. at 76; Mehrotra, pp. 156–159; Prasad, pp. 227–229, 242–243.

37. *Criminal Procedure Code,* s. 437(1); *State v. Gadadkar Barai,* 1989 Cri LJ 627 (H.C. Orissa, 1988), at 628–629; Mehrotra, p. 159; Prasad, pp. 228–229; Singh, p. 203.

38. *Criminal Procedure Code,* s. 437(2)(3); Mehrotra, p. 157; Prasad, pp. 228–229.

39. *Criminal Procedure Code,* s. 167; *Gursewak Singh v. State of Punjab,* 1988 Cri LJ 1605 (H.C. P. & H., 1987); *P. N. Ogechi v. The State (Delhi Administration),* 1986 Cri LJ 2081 (H.C.D., 1986), esp. at 2083–2085; *Vijay Kamar v. The State,* 1983 Cri LJ NOC 11 (H.C. J. & K., 1982); *Harpindar Singh v. The State (Delhi Administration),* 1983 Cri LJ 53 (H.C.D., 1982), at 56–57; *N. Sureya Reddy v. State of Orissa,* 1985 Cri LJ 939 (H.C.O., 1984); Mehrotra, pp. 82–87.

40. *Criminal Procedure Code,* s. 161; *Robert Lendi v. Collector of Customs,* 1987 Cri LJ 55 (H.C. Delhi, 1986), esp. at 59–60; *N. Ibo Ton Singh v. U. T. of Manipur,* AIR 1969 Man. 6 (H.C. Man., 1967), at 8; *Mang Karai v. State,* AIR 1967 Tri 32 (H.C. Tri, 1967), at 33; *Sant Ram v. State,* AIR 1952 J & K 28 (H.C. J. & K., 1951), at 29; *Emperor v. Hutchinson,* AIR 1931 All 356 (H.C. All., 1931), at 358–359; *Ramroopsingh v. State of Madhya Pradesh,* 1987 Cri LJ 1256 (H.C. M.P., 1986), esp. at 1257; *Sita Ram v. State of Uttar Pradesh,* 1987 Cri LJ 645 (H.C. U.P., 1986); Mehrotra, pp. 92–93.

41. *Renjander Singh v. State,* 1988 Cri LJ 749 (H.C. Delhi, 1987), esp. at 755; G. Narsimhula v. Public Prosecutor, AIR 1978 SC 429 (S.C., 1977), esp. at 430–432; *Baba Singh v. State,* AIR 1978 SC 527 (S.C., 1978), esp. at 529, 531; *State of Rajasthan v. Balchand,* AIR 1977 SC 2447 (S.C., 1977), at 2448; *N. Iboton Singh v. U.T.,* at 8; *Mang Karai v. State,* at 33; *Sant Ram v. State,* at 29; *Abdul Hamidkhan v. State of Gujarat,* 1989 Cri LJ 468 (H.C. Guj, 1987), at 476; *Income-tax Officer v. Gopal Dhamani,* 1988 Cri LJ 1079 (H.C. Raj, 1987), esp. at 1082, 1084; *Ratansingh v. State,* AIR 1959 MP 216 (H.C. M.P., 1959), at 218; *Sagri Bhagat v. State of Bihar,* AIR 1951 Pat 497 (H.C. Pat., 1950), at 449; *Paras Ram v. The State,* AIR 1951 HP 13 (H.C. H.P., 1950), at 15; *Nagendra v. King-Emperor,* AIR 1924 Cal 476 (H.C. Cal., 1923), at 479; *Ram Chandra v. State,* 1952 AIR MB 203 (H.C. M.B., 1952), at 204; *Emperor v. Hutchinson,* at 360–361; *Amat Singh v. State,* 1985 Cri LJ 550 (H.C.D., 1985), esp. at 552.

42. F. E. Devine, "Anticipatory Bail: An Indian Civil Liberties Innovation," *International Journal of Comparative and Applied Criminal Justice* 14, (1), 1990.

43. *Gurbaksh Singh v. State of Punjab,* AIR 1980 SC 1632 (S.C., 1980), esp. at 1637, 1638; *State of Karnataka v. Aswathappa,* 1989 Cri LJ NOC 122 (Kant) (H.C. Kant., 1987); *Durga Prasad v. State of Bihar,* 1987 Cri LJ 1200 (H.C. Pat., 1987), esp. at 1203, 1205; *C. T. Mathews v. Government of India, Home Department,* 1985 Cri LJ 1317 (H.C.K., 1984); *Hidayat Ullah v. The Crown,* AIR 1949 Lah 77 (H.C. Lah. f.b., 1948), at 81–82; Pannalal Dhar, "Anticipatory Bail," *Criminal Law Journal* 89 (1983): 35–36; L. K. Hatolkar, "Concept of 'Bail' and Some Conflicting Views," *Criminal Law Journal* 89 (1983): 37–40.

44. Law Commission of India, *41st Report*, vol. I (New Delhi: Ministry of Law, 1969), pp. 320–321; *Hidayat Ullah v. The Crown*, at 82–83; *Amir Chand v. The Crown*, AIR 1950 E Pun 53 (H.C. E. Pun., 1949), at 59–60; Narula, pp. 93–94; Hatolkar, p. 38.

45. *Criminal Procedure Code*, s. 438(1),(3); *Pokar Ram v. State of Rajasthan*, 1985 Cri LJ 1175 (S.C., 1985), at 1176.

46. *Criminal Procedure Code*, s. 438(2).

47. *Criminal Procedure Code*, s. 438(1); *R. L. Jalappa v. Delhi Police*, 1989 Cri LJ NOC 35 (Kant., 1988); *Madan Monan Benera v. State*, 1988 Cri LJ 1574 (H.C. Orissa, 1987); *Padma Charan v. S. Ram Mohan Rao*, 1987 Cri LJ 923 (H.C. Orissa, 1986); *V. Nandanan v. DIG of Police, Hyderabad*, 1986 Cri LJ 1050 (H.C.K., 1985); *Pokar Ram v. State of Rajasthan*; *Rama Swaroop v. State (Delhi Administration)*, 1986 Cri LJ 526 (H.C.D., 1985); *Thayyanbadi v. S. I. of Police, Panoor*, 1985 Cri LJ 1111 (H.C. K., 1985).

48. *Pokar Ram v. State of Rajasthan*, at 1176–1177, 1178; *Gurbaksh Singh v. State of Punjab*, at 1648–1649; *Rama Swaroop v. State (Delhi Administration)*, esp. at 532, 534–535; *V. Nandanan v. DIG of Police*; *Thayyanbadi v. S. I. of Police, Panoor*; Mehrotra, pp. 167–172; Singh, pp. 220–232.

49. *Hussainara Khatoon v. State of Bihar (1)*, AIR 1979 SC 1360 (S.C., 1979), at 1364; *Gurcharan Singh v. State (Delhi Administration)*, at 186–187; *Kalyan Singh v. State of Madhya Pradesh*, 1989 Cri LJ 512 (H.C. M.P., 1988), at 514; *Rama Swaroop v. State (Delhi Administration)*, esp. at 535; *H. Husain v. M.P. Mondkar*, at 379; *Uthaman v. State of Kerala*, at 76–77; *Askok Kumar Binny v. State*, 1983 Cri LJ NOC 27 (J & K) (H.C. J. & K., 1982); *Ran Chandra v. State*, AIR 1952 MB 203 (H.C. M.B., 1952), at 204–205; *Sagri Bhagat v. State of Bihar*, AIR 1951 Pat 497 (H.C. Pat., 1950), at 499; *Pabas Ram v. the State*, at 15; *Emperor v. Hutchinson*, at 361–362; *Nagendra v. King-Emperor*, at 480; *Prashant Kumar v. Mancharlal*, 1988 Cri LJ 1463 (H.C. Bom., 1987), at 1465; Mehrotra, pp. 196–213; Prasad, pp. 186–189, 229, 233–241; Singh, pp. 167–169, 184–185. Regarding consideration 4 see *Juria v. State of Orissa*, 1985 Cri LJ 1487 (H.C.O., 1984).

50. *Pokar Ram v. State of Rajasthan*, esp. at 1176–1178; *Gurbaksh Singh v. State of Punjab*, at 1648–1649; *K. K. Jajodia v. State*, 1988 Cri LJ 968 (H.C. Delhi, 1987), at 972–974; *Rama Swaroop v. State (Delhi Administration)*, esp. at 532; *V. Nandanan v. DIG of Police Hyderabad*, esp. at 1052, 1054; Mehrotra, pp. 168–173; Singh, pp. 238–239; 242–243.

51. *Criminal Procedure Code*, s. 446; *Sadananda v. State of Karnataka*, 1986 Cri LJ 756 (H.C. K., 1985), esp. at 757–758; *Tarni Yadav v. State*, AIR 1962 Pat 431 (H.C. Pat., 1961), at 432–434; *Ajudhya Prashad v. State*, AIR 1953 MB 4 (H.C. M.B., 1952), at 5; *Barkat Ram v. Bhagwan Singh*, AIR 1949 E Pun 221 (H.C.E. Pun., 1949) at 222; Mehrotra, pp. 290–293, 296–297; Prasad, pp. 281–282, 293–299, 309–310; Singh, pp. 353–354, 355–356, 357–358, 361–362.

52. *Criminal Procedure Code*, s. 446; *Sadananda v. State of Karnataka*, esp. at 757–758; *Tarni Yadav v. State*, at 432–433; *Ghulam Mehdi v. State of Rajasthan*, AIR 1960 SC 1185 (S.C., 1959), at 1186; *Adjudhya Prashad v. State*, at 5; Mehrotra, pp. 290–293, 296–299; Prasad, pp. 295–296, 297–299, 309–311; Singh, pp. 354, 364, 370–371, 374–377.

53. *Criminal Procedure Code*, s. 446; *Sudananda v. State of Karnataka*, esp. at 757–758; *Tarni Yadav v. State*, at 432–433, 434; Mehrotra, pp. 290–293, 296–299; Prasad pp. 295–296, 297–299, 309–311; Singh, pp. 354, 363–364, 364–371, 374, 377.

54. *Criminal Procedure Code*, s. 449; Mehrotra, p. 303; Prasad, pp. 310–311; Singh, pp. 379–381.

55. *Criminal Procedure Code*, s. 89, s. 436(2), s. 437(5), s. 439(2), s. 446A; *Delhi Administration v. Sanjay Gandhi*, esp. at 965–966; *Johny Wilson v. State of Rajasthan*, esp. at 1240–1242; *Nilu v. State*, esp. at 1593–1594; *Tahir v. Shaukat*, esp. at 1817; Mehrotra, pp. 226–237; Prasad, pp. 200–214, 283; Singh, pp. 174–175, 284–298.

56. *Constitution of India*, Art. 22; *Criminal Procedure Code*, s. 50(2), s. 56, s. 57, s. 58; Mehrotra, pp. 2–5; Prasad, pp. 80–82, 85–86; Singh, pp. 52–55, 126–128, 148–149.

57. *Criminal Procedure Code*, s. 167; *Hussainara Khatoon v. State of Bihar (3)*, AIR 1979 SC 1377 (S.C., 1979), at 1379; *P. N. Ogechi v. State (Delhi Administration)*, esp. at 2085; Mehrotra, pp. 82–83; Singh, pp. 99, 103, 107, 113–115, 127–129, 141, 204.

58. Narula, pp. 82–83; Prasad, p. 89; Singh, pp. 170, 203.

59. *Amir Chand v. The Crown*, at 54.

60. *Criminal Procedure Code*, (Pak) s. 513; *Code of Criminal Procedure*, (Bangl.), s. 513; *R. K. M. Reza v. State*, 33 DLR (1981) 146 (H.C., 1980), esp. at 148; *Lakhi Narayan v. Crown*, PLD 1953 Dacca 84 (H.C., 1952), at 95; Shaukat Mahmood, *Law of Bails* (Lahore: Legal Research Center, 1987), pp. 280–281; Dacca Law Reports Office, *The Law on Bail* (Dacca: Dacca Law Reports Office, 1985), p. 98.

61. *Mahmud Ali Qasuri v. State*, PLD 1963 SC 478 (S.C., 1963), esp. at 483, 485, 486; *Lakhi Narayan v. Crown*, PLD 1955 Dacca 84 (H.C. Dac., 1952), esp. at 94–95; Shaukat Mahmood, pp. 4–5, 103.

62. *Code of Criminal Procedure*, s. 497A (2); *Abdus Sukur v. State*, 25 DLR (1973) 119 (H.C., 1971), at 121–122; Dacca Law Reports Office, pp. 36–37.

63. Dacca Law Reports Office, pp. 65–72.

64. *Abdul Shakoor v. Ghulam Rasool*, PLD 1987 Lah 225 (H.C. Lah., 1987), esp. at 227–228; *Mahmud Ali Qasuri v. State*, at 485–486; Shaukat Mahmood, p. 247.

65. *Criminal Procedure Code*, s. 497.

66. Dacca Law Reports Office, pp. 24–25, 31–32, 33, 65–72.

67. *Shakir Ali v. State*, 1988 SCMR 1073 (S.C., 1988); *Mashooque v. State*, PLD 1987 Kar 667 (H.C. Kar., 1987), esp. at 670; *Nazir Hussain v. Ziaul Haq*, 1983 SCMR 72 (S.C., 1982), esp. at 75; *Saleh Muhammad v. State*, 1983 SCMR 341 (S.C., 1982), esp. at 341.

68. *Muhammed Hanif v. Khushi Muhammed*, 1979 SCMR 235 (S.C., 1979), esp. at 238; *Faiz Razool v. State*, 1979 SCMR 67 (S.C., 1978), at 68; *Ghulam Haider v. State*, 1983 SCMR 790 (S.C., 1976); *Talib Hussain v. State*, 1980 SCMR 613 (S.C., 1979), esp. at 615–616; *Mir Akbar v. Kala*, 1978 SCMR 303 (S.C., 1979), esp. at 304; *Barkhurdar v. Liaquat Ali*, PLD 1977 SC 434 (S.C., 1977); Shaukat Mahmood, pp. 48–49.

69. *Code of Criminal Procedure*, s. 167.

70. *Criminal Procedure Code* (Pakistan), s. 498; William Clifford and S. D. Gokhale, *Innovations in Criminal Justice in Asia and the Pacific* (Canberra: Australian Institute of Criminology, 1979), p. 177; compare with *Code of Criminal Procedure 1973* (India), s. 438; *Gurbax Singh v. State of Punjab*, 1978 Cri LJ 20 (S.C., 1977); Mehrotra, p. 172.

71. *Meeran Bux v. State*, 1988 SCMR 1217 (S.C., 1987), at 1218; *Zia-Ul-Hassan v. State*, 1984 PLD 192 SC (S.C., 1982); *Murad Khan v. Fazal-E-Subhan*, 1983 PLD 82

SC (S.C., 1982); *Ali Muhammad v. Yamin*, 1981 SCMR 1139 (S.C., 1976), at 1140; *Khalid Mian v. State*, 1981 SCMR 1098 (S.C., 1981).

72. *Muhammad Aziz v. State*, PLD 1987 Sh C (AJ & K) 45 (Sh. C. A.J. & K., 1987), at 39; compare with India: *Kaylan Singh v. State of Madhya Pradesh*, at 515.

73. *Faiz Razool v. State*, at 68.

74. *Abdul Salam v. State*, 1980 SCMR 142 (S.C., 1979); *Muhammad Fazal v. State*, 1979 SCMR 9 (S.C., 1978), at 10; *Faiz Razool v. State*, at 68; *Muhammad Aziz v. State*, at 39; Shaukat Mahmood, pp. 166–167.

75. *Code of Criminal Procedure*, s. 126(2), s. 126(3); *In re Siuluta*, 1979 ZR 14 (H.C., 1979); *Code of Criminal Procedure Act, 1979*, s. 404, s. 421; *Pathirana v. State*, 1985(2), Sri LR 75 (C.A., 1985).

76. *Code of Criminal Procedure*, s. 124, s. 126(2).

77. *Criminal Procedure Code*, s. 126; *Saidi Gurhl Shabel v. Republic*, 1976 LRT n. 4 (H.C., 1974), at 15; *Jaffer v. Republic*, 1973 EA 39 (H.C., 1972), at 41; *Panju v. Republic*, 1973 EA 282 (H.C., 1972) at 285, 1972 HCD n. 161, at 168–169, sub nom *R. v. Ahmedi Panju*; *In the Matter of an Application for Bail: Republic v. Paulo Kiluwa*, 1977 LRT n. 21 (H.C., 1975), at 79–80.

78. *I. A. Furguson v. Republic*, 1967 HCD n. 245 (H.C., 1967).

79. As illustrative of this see *Che Su binti Duad v. Public Prosecutor*, 1978(2) MLJ 162 (H.C.P., 1978).

80. *Public Prosecutor v. Chew Siew Luan*, 1982(2) MLJ 119 (F.C., 1982); Overruling 1982(1) MLJ 280 (H.C.K.L., 1980).

81. *Loy Chin Hei v. Public Prosecutor*, 1981(1) MLJ 31 (H.C.M., 1981).

82. *Sulaiman bin Kadir v. Public Prosecutor*, 1976(2) MLJ 37 (H.C.K.L., 1975).

83. *Ula-Uku v. Commissioner of Police*, 1986(1) QLRW 146 (H.C. Sok., 1983), at 147–148.

84. The one example is *Oyenuga v. Commissioner of Police*, 1977(3) CCHCJ 277 (H.C. Lag., 1977).

85. *Ogbole v. Commissioner of Police*, 1977(1) CCHCJ 1 (H.C. Lag., 1977).

86. *Onuigbo v. Commissioner of Police*, 1975 NNLR 34 (H.C. Ben-Plat, 1975).

87. *State v. Amaefule*, 1986 CA 7 (II) 1 (C.A., 1986).

88. *Constitution of the Federal Republic of Nigeria*, Art. 321(1), (4), (5), (6), (7).

89. *Eda v. Commissioner of Police*, 1982 3 WCLR 219 (F.C.A., 1981), esp. at 226–228; 1981(2) NCR 414.

90. *Aliji v. State*, 1983 (4) NCLR 447 (H.C. Plat., 1981); *Shom Nyam v. Commissioner of Police*, 1984(5) NCLR 397 (H.C. Benu., 1982); *Commissioner of Police v. Iyanda*, 1983(1) OYSHC 296 (H.C. Oyo, 1983).

91. *Amuda v. Commissioner of Police*, 1981(1) NCR 299 (H.C. Lag., 1981).

92. *Ogor v. Kolawole*, 1983(1) NCR 342 (H.C. Oyo, 1983), at 358; 1985(6) NCLR 534.

93. Ibid., esp. at 361–365.

94. *Ogor v. Kolawole*, at 350; *Attorney General v. Odegua*, 1982(1) NCR 150 (H.C. Bend., 1982), at 157; *State v. Felix*, 1979(1–3) CCHCJ 239 (H.C. Lag., 1979), at 241–242; *Dantata v. Inspector General of Police*, 1958 NNLR 3 (H.C. Kan., 1957), at 3–4; *R. V. Abdullah Jammal*, [1941/2] 16 NLR 54 (S.C., 1941), at 55.

95. *Okorie Ukachukwa v. Commissioner of Police*, at 180.

96. *Kotun v. Federal Director of Public Prosecutions*, 1983(2) FNLR 411 (F.C.A., 1983), esp. as per Mnaemeka-Agu, J.C.A., at 414; *Commissioner of Police v. John*,

1981(1) NCR 139 (H.C. Bauchi, 1981); *Oyenuga v. Commissioner of Police*, 1977(3) CCHCJ 277 (H.C. Lag., 1977); *Tea v. Commissioner of Police*, 1963(2) All NLR 60 (C.A. No., 1963).

97. *Criminal Procedure and Evidence Act*, s. 108, s. 110, s. 116, s. 120, s. 121; *Knight, N.O. v. van Tonden*, 1962(3) SA 719, at 720; 1962 R & N 405.

98. *State v. Sibanda*, 1980 ZLR 413, esp. at 414.

99. *Bull v. Attorney-General (2)*, 1986(3) SA 886 (S.C.Z. 1986), esp. at 891, 892; *Bull v. Attorney-General (1)*, 1986(3) SA 870 (S.C.Z., 1986); *Ndhlovu v. Attorney-General*, 1987(4) SA 302 (H.C.Z., 1987), esp. at 405, 407; *Corona v. Minister of Home Affairs*, 1982(2) SA 533 (H.C.Z., 1982), esp. at 537.

100. *Criminal Procedure and Evidence Act*, s. 106(3).

101. *Attorney General v. Phiri*, 1988(2) SA 696 (H.C.Z., 1987), at 699–701.

102. *Criminal Procedure and Evidence Act*, s. 221, s. 222; *State v. Sibanda*, at 415; *Knight, N.O. v. van Tonder*, esp. at 720–721.

103. *Criminal Procedure Act 1967*, s. 26.

104. *Attorney-General v. Duffy*, 1942 I.R. 529 (H.C., 1942), at 534; *People (A.G.) v. Gilliland*, 1986 ILRM 357 (S.C., 1985), at 360.

105. *Criminal Justice Act 1984*, s. 13.

106. *Criminal Procedure Act*, s. 22, s. 28(1), s. 30; *State (Lynch) v. Ballagh*, 1987 ILRM 65 (S.C., 1986), esp. at 70.

107. *Criminal Procedure Act*, s. 29.

108. Ibid., s. 28(1).

109. *People (A.G.) v. O'Callaghan*, 1966 IR 501 (S.C., 1966), at. 513; *People (A.G.) v. Gilliland*, esp. at 359–360; *People (A.G.) v. Crosbie*, 1966 IR 426 (S.C., 1965), at 427.

110. *People (A.G.) v. O'Callaghan*, at 513–516; *People (A.G.) v. Crosbie*, at 429; *Attorney General v. Ball*, 1958 IR 280 (S.C. 1956), esp. at 284, 287; *Attorney General v. Duffy*, at 533, 534.

111. *People (A.G.) v. O'Callaghan*, at 516–517.

112. *People (A.G.) v. Gilliland*, at 360; *People (A.G.) v. O'Callaghan*, at 517–518; *Attorney General v. Ball*, esp. at 283–284; *Attorney General v. Duffy*, esp. at 534; *People (A.G.) v. McCabe*, 1944 IJR 41 (H.C., 1944), at 42.

113. Michael King, *Bail or Custody* (London: The Cobden Trust, 1973), p. 54; A. Keith Bottomley, *Prison Before Trial* (London: G. Bell & Sons, 1970), pp. 56–57.

114. *Bail Act 1977*, s. 5(1).

115. Ibid., s. 5(2), s 17(1), s. 24(1), s. 24(3).

116. Ibid., s. 9(2),(3),(7), s. 31.

117. Ibid., s. 17(2), s. 21, s. 23.

118. *R. v. Baker*, 1971 VR 717 (S.C. Vic., 1971), at 717.

119. *Crown Proceedings Act 1958 (Amend.)*, s. 5(3), s. 6; *Bail Act*, s. 32; *R. v. Baker*.

120. *Bail Act*, s. 24(1)(a), s. 26(2).

121. Ibid., s. 7, s. 29(2)(3)(4); *Crimes Act 1958*, s. 281; *R. v. Sanghera*, 1983(2) VR 130 (S.C. Vic., 1982), esp. at 131; *R. v. Devitt*, A.S.D. 112.01.VI (C.C.A. Vic., 1974).

122. *Bail Act*, s. 4(4)(b); *D.P.P. v. Spiridon*, unreported (S.C. Vic., 7 Sept. 1988), at 12–13; *R. v. Loubie*, 19 A Crim R 112 (S.C. Qld., 1985).

123. *Bail Act (Amend.)*, s. 13; *Re Anderson*, 1978 VR 322 (S.C. Vic., 1977).

124. *Bail Act (Amend.)*, s. 4(2)(aa), s. 4(4)(a),(c),(ca),(d); D.P.P.'s Working Party on Drugs Legislation, "Victoria: Bail in Drug Cases" (Melbourne, 1988), p. 11.

125. *Bail Act*, s. 4(2)(c),(d).

126. *Bail Act*, s. 4(3), s. 8(d),(e); *R. v. Sanghera.*

127. *Bail Act*, s. 4(3), 8(c).

128. Ibid., s. 4(1), s. 8(b), s. 10(2), s. 18, s. 18A.

129. *Bail Act 1982* (W.A.), s. 28(2)(b).

130. *Bail Act* (W.A.), s. 17, Sch. D(1); *Bail Act 1980*, (Qld.), s. 11(1); *Bail Act* (Vic), s. 5(1).

131. *Bail Act* (W.A.), s. 17, Sch. D(2); *Bail Act* (Qld), s. 11(2); *Bail Act* (Vic), s. 5(2).

132. *Bail Act* (Qld), s. 21(6); *Bail Act* (Vic), s. 9(3).

133. *Bail Act* (W.A.), s. 46(1)(2); *Bail Act* (Qld), s. 24(1); *Bail Act* (Vic), s. 21(1).

134. *Bail Act*, (W.A.), s. 56, s. 57, s. 58.

135. Ibid., s. 49.

136. *Bail Act* (W.A.), s. 28(2)(a)(b), s. 51; *Bail Act* (Qld), s. 33.

137. *Bail Act* (Qld), s. 13(1), 16(3); *Bail Act* (W.A.), s. 5, 6, 7, Sched. Pt. C(1).

138. *Bail Act* (Qld), s. 9, s. 16; *Bail Act* (W.A.), Sched. Pt. C(1).

139. *Bail Act* (Qld), s. 9, s. 16; *Bail Act* (W.A.), Sched. Pt. C(1).

140. Australian Bureau of Statistics (Qld), *Law and Order Queensland 1986–1987* (Brisbane, 1988), Tab. 3; Ibid., 1978, Tab. 2.

141. J. M. Herlihy and R. G. Kenny, *An Introduction to Criminal Law in Queensland and Western Australia*, 2nd ed. (Sydney: Butterworths, 1984), p. 49.

5

The Criminal Penalties Alternative

A second alternative to commercial bail bonding substitutes criminal punishment for the liability to financial forfeitures as the principle motivating sanction to assure presence at trial. Under this approach failure to appear as required—absconding—is made a criminal offense. As with any criminal violation, a defendant who breaches bail is subject to conviction and imposition of the prescribed punishment. Two countries, England and Canada, rely upon such punishment as their basic compulsion in bail matters, although both retain the possibility of adding other constraints. In addition, most Australian jurisdictions have added criminal punishment as a secondary alternative to their principal bail form. In New South Wales such punishment is relied upon as the major sanction, producing a system much like that of England or Canada. Scotland exhibits a unique mixture of criminal penalties with, on one hand, nonfinancial conditions and, on the other, a secondary alternative of cash deposit.

ENGLAND

Background

Prior to restructuring its bail system in the late 1970s, England employed a recognizance type of bail, a development of that established by common law. In fact, this former English approach to bail provided directly or indirectly the pattern for recognizance systems worldwide. Although this system produced a relatively low rate of absconding and a per capita percentage of pretrial detainees as low as Sweden and lower than other European countries at the time,[1] it was subject to considerable criticism throughout the 1960s and early 1970s.[2]

As a result of this criticism, a Home Office working party was established in 1971 to study bail. The working party's report, *Bail Procedures in Magistrates' Court,* recommended substantial changes. One of the most important of these was abolishing the taking of a recognizance from the defendant seeking release. Cash deposit was rejected as a substitute. Instead, creation of a crime of absconding punishable by a fine or imprisonment was the alternative recommended.[3] Another important change suggested was establishing a legal presumption in favor of bail unless substantial reason to deny it could be shown. If bail was to be denied, reasons should be required to be given.[4] The working party recommended retaining as a supplementary term of bail the possibility of requiring third parties to stand as sureties by recognizance for the accused's appearance. Likewise, it favored retaining the imposition of nonfinancial conditions as supplementary terms.[5] Thus, though far from totally unmixed, England presents the purest available example of a bail system based upon criminal penalties.

Terms of Bail

The *Bail Act 1976* which came into effect April 17, 1978, follows the working party's recommendation and abolishes the defendant's personal recognizance as a term of bail. In place of this form of financial liability, absconding is made an offense. It is punishable in Magistrate's Court by up to three months' imprisonment or a £2000 fine, or both. If the Magistrates' Court concludes that a heavier sentence is warranted, the absconder may be committed to Crown Court for sentencing, where up to twelve months or an unlimited fine may be imposed. Defendants who fail to appear when and where required are guilty of this offense unless they surrender to custody as soon thereafter as possible and can show, on a balance of probability, reasonable grounds why they could not appear as ordered.[6] Absconding may not be punished as escape or as contempt of court.[7] The court may issue an arrest warrant for an absconder, but arrest without a warrant is also authorized. In fact, the police may arrest without a warrant anyone on bail who they have reasonable grounds to believe is not likely to surrender as required. Bail may then be altered or withdrawn.[8]

English courts have refined various aspects of the concept of absconding. A defendant's being a few (seven) minutes late does not constitute absconding.[9] However, a defendant's failing to appear due to a severe hangover does constitute absconding even though he made no attempt to flee and was brought before the court within three and a half hours.[10] A person who arrives at court as required intending to surrender, reports according to posted instruction but is not taken into custody, and eventually leaves without informing anyone, does not commit an offense, although he is subject to arrest.[11] However, a defendant who merely arrives at the proper time but leaves without reporting and absconds abroad is guilty of the offense.[12] A defendant does not show reasonable cause for failure to surrender because the failure was not deliberate but the result of confusion about the appearance date. The fact that extraneous factors contributed to this confusion and might amount to mitigation still does not constitute something which arose to prevent attendance. He had been provided the correct information and the error was his responsibility.[13]

Sentencing considerations have also been dealt with by the courts in absconding cases. A custodial sentence for absconding was sustained on appeal for a defendant who had been acquitted on the main charge where he had absconded abroad and only returned after the acquittal of his co-defendant. The Court of Appeal approved the trial judge's view that such a sentence was a necessary deterrent to other defendants' absconding to countries without an extradition treaty with England.[14] Conviction for absconding has been held to be a conviction adequate to require activation of a pending suspended sentence. It and the absconding sentence, moreover, may be imposed consecutively.[15]

In addition to the accused's liability to the penalties for absconding, one or more individuals who will stand as sureties for his bail may be required under the current English system. These sureties enter a recognizance for the defendant's appearance and, although the defendant's personal recognizance has been abolished, they function as in a recognizance bail system. English sureties both before and after the system's restructuring could not be required to deposit cash or other securities as a condition of a bail. The *Bail Act* directs that sureties are not to be required as a matter of course but rather only when a particular need for them is indicated. Three considerations are specified for deciding the acceptability of a proposed surety: in addition to financial resources and character (including any previous convictions) is closeness to the defendant in terms of residence, kinship, and other relationships.[16] The last emphasizes the personal nature of suretyship.

Although a court has discretion to forfeit all or part of a surety's recognizance if the defendant absconds, English case law on the liability of sureties remains quite strict. The heavy burden on a surety seeking remission of a forfeiture has been stressed.[17]

A surety who wishes to be relieved of that liability may accomplish this by securing the accused's return to custody and being discharged by the court. Police help may be sought to achieve this. However, merely requesting police help does not discharge the surety. The request should, though, be considered in deciding whether part or even all of the forfeiture should be remitted.[18]

In addition to the penalties for absconding and sureties, the English bail system provides for the imposition of fairly extensive nonfinancial conditions of bail on a defendant released from custody. A court may impose any conditions which seem necessary to secure the accused's surrender to answer bail, to prevent him from committing offenses while on bail, to assure that he does not interfere with witnesses or obstruct the course of justice in relation to himself or others, and to assure that he makes himself available to enable inquiries or reports to be made to assist the court in dealing with the case.[19] The imposition of conditions is justified by a real rather than fanciful risk of one of these considerations requiring it. Substantial grounds for the perception need not be established.[20] The conditions of bail may be altered as the case develops,[21] and the reasons for imposing or varying conditions must be recorded by the court.[22] Enforcement of the conditions is by arrest and possible revocation, or alteration of terms, of bail. No surety may be required for adherence to bail conditions. Arrest may be made in anticipation of a breach of bail condition if this is based on reasonable grounds.[23] Typical conditions include living at a specified address, observing a specified curfew, reporting periodically at a police station, not contacting particular people, not going near particular places, not entering a place licensed to sell alcohol, not driving, and surrendering one's passport and not leaving the country. However, any workable condition reasonably related to a justifiable objective under the circumstances of the case may be imposed.[24]

An innovation in the conditions of bail under the 1976 *Bail Act* breaks in a limited way with the principle of no cash bail. This is the possibility of requiring security of a defendant who appears likely to leave Great Britain. The security may be cash or property deposited with the court by the defendant or by another on his behalf. It is forfeited in whole or in part if the defendant fails to appear. If he later appears and is able to show reasonable grounds for his earlier failure, all or part of the forfeiture may be remitted.[25] All interest earned on a deposit is payable to the person making it, even if the security is later forfeited.[26] Some examples of situations where the deposit provision has been used are a deposit of £10,000 required of a French citizen accused of check fraud,[27] and deposits of £3,000 and £5,000 required of two Italians accused of multiple drug charges.[28] A U.K. citizen charged with unlicensed export of military vehicle engines who wished to visit the United States was required to deposit £25,000 plus obtain a surety.[29] Deposits of as much as £60,000–£100,000 have been reported to have been required under this provision.[30]

In sum, then, England has a bail system which relies upon the imposition of criminal penalties for its fundamental sanction motivating the appearance of the accused. A defendant who fails to appear as required is guilty of absconding and subject to fine or imprisonment as for any other offense. In addition to this basic provision, personal sureties can be required where warranted by the particular case. These secure the defendant's appearance by a recognizance, although the defendant's own recognizance has been replaced with the threat of the punishments. Where needed to secure appearance, prevent commission of crime, or prevent interference with the course of justice, nonfinancial conditions can be added. Finally, if a given accused is particularly likely to leave the country, a cash deposit can be required.

Eligibility for Bail

The matter of eligibility for bail in English Magistrates' Courts must be seen in the context of the overall system in which about 70–73 percent of defendants are dealt with by summons. Even for indictable (more serious) offenses, this procedure is used in 21–22 percent of cases. In addition, bail is granted by the police in 23–25 percent of all cases and 63–65 percent of indictable offenses. Thus, about 4–6 percent of defendants overall, and 13–15 percent of defendants in more serious cases, come before the magistrates in custody.[31]

The *Bail Act 1976*, reversing the presumption of the previous system, creates a broad but qualified statutory right to bail for most unconvicted defendants. The right applies only to bail granted by a magistrates' court or by Crown Court. The only offense for which bail may not be granted is treason.[32] Where the statutory right applies, bail must be granted unless an exception provided by the *Bail Act* applies.

Offenses punishable by imprisonment are distinguished from those which are not, and for the former the right to bail is subject to greater qualifications. Whether or not an offense is subject to imprisonment an exception to the right to bail occurs with any of the following situations:

1. Based on the accused's appearing to have absconded in a previous case the court believes that he would again fail to appear.
2. The accused has absconded or breached other conditions of bail in the present case.
3. The accused is in custody for his own protection.
4. The accused has been sentenced to imprisonment on another matter.[33]

In addition to these exceptions, if an offense is subject to imprisonment, exceptions also apply for the following:

1. The court has substantial grounds to believe that the accused would fail to answer bail, commit offenses while on bail, or interfere with the witnesses or obstruct the course of justice either in his own case or another's.
2. Insufficient time exists to gather information to make the bail decision.
3. The case has been adjourned for reports or inquiries impracticable to carry out without the accused's being in custody.[34]

Substantial grounds for believing that the accused will abscond, commit a crime, or interfere with justice is to be assessed objectively. The test is whether grounds of substance are present which would satisfy a reasonable person on the balance of probabilities that one of these events would occur. Strict rules of evidence do not apply.[35]

The reasons for a refusal of bail must be recorded and a copy given to the defendant.[36] A 1988 amendment to the *Bail Act* requires that reasons also be recorded when bail is granted in cases of murder, manslaughter, rape, or attempted murder or rape, where the prosecution has opposed bail.[37]

When bail is granted, excessive bail may not be required. However, the mere fact that the accused cannot meet the terms of bail does not prove them excessive. A number of other considerations are pertinent to setting bail terms. Therefore, notwithstanding the accused's inability, the bail terms may be no more than what is necessary.[38]

Considerations for Denying Bail

In deciding whether an exception to the right to bail applies such that bail may be denied, all relevant factors are to be considered. Under the *Bail Act*, courts are instructed to have regard to whichever of four sets of generally applicable considerations are pertinent to the given case. First is the seriousness of the offense and the probable manner of its punishment. Alternatively, if the issue is a prior default on bail or its conditions, then its seriousness is considered. Second is the character and background—including previous convictions, associations, and community ties—of the defendant. Third is the defendant's record regarding the fulfillment of obligations under previous grants of bail. Finally, the strength of the evidence that the accused committed the offense or bail default is to be considered.[39] The considerations relied upon to establish an exception to the right to bail is included in the reasons for refusal recorded and presented to the defendant.[40]

Procedural Considerations

The procedural matters peculiar to the form of bail system found in England are, of course, those connected with imposing the penalties on absconders. Procedure for dealing with an absconder under this system is adapted to the criminal status of the act. Since absconding is an offense, the procedure for handling it involves conviction and sentencing.[41]

If the absconding is from a Magistrates' Court, a bench warrant is issued when the defendant fails to appear. The matter is handled in most respects like any summary offense. Upon arrest for absconding, the accused is brought before the court at which proceedings on the principal charge for which the bail was granted are to be heard. However, the court in cases of absconding initiates proceedings on its own motion following an expressed invitation by the prosecutor. An information is used only in cases of police rather than court bail. The prosecutor conducts the proceedings, and if the absconding is contested presents the evidence. Trial normally follows immediately the proceedings on the principal charge. After conviction, if the magistrates believe a sentence in excess of their powers is necessary, they may commit the defendant to Crown Court to be sentenced.[42]

If the absconding is from Crown Court, a choice of two procedures is open. The matter may be treated as a summary offense before a Magistrates' Court, or it may be treated as if it were a contempt of court before the Crown Court. If the second alternative is adopted, the defendant should be afforded the opportunity to give an explanation, and submission from counsel should be invited.[43] Appeal is available and follows the normal route for any other offense.

The other area of procedure of particular significance in the English bail system is comprised of those aspects relating to the implementation of the statutory right to bail created by the *Bail Act*. An individual who has been arrested and charged and is not released on bail by the police or pursuant to bail terms endorsed on an arrest warrant must be brought before a Magistrates' Court as soon as is practicable. Typically, this would be at the court's next sitting. Where evidence does not warrant charging, a delay of twenty-four hours is permitted. This may be extended to thirty-six hours for serious offenses if authorized by a ranking police officer for statutorily provided reasons.[44] Since the right to bail is presumed, bail must then be considered, at least in a formal sense, in all cases even if the defendant does not apply for it.[45]

A defendant who is denied bail is remanded in custody for a normal maximum period of eight days. After each remand his bail status must be reviewed. However, in a decision that has caused considerable controversy, *R. v. Nottingham Justices, ex parte Davis* (1980), a Queen's Bench divisional court held that a full review of the issue of bail need be conducted at the third and subsequent appearances only where a change of circumstances has occurred.[46] *R. v. Reading Crown Court, ex parte Malik* (1980) applied the same principle to the Crown Court.[47] The principle has been applied as well to prosecution seeking withdrawal of bail.[48] These holdings do not imply, however, that, given the new circumstances justifying review, the bail decision should not rest on the totality of circumstances both new and old.[49] A change in the circumstances refers to circumstances disclosed to the court; a newly existing fact is not required.[50] The altered circumstances must be related to the reason bail was denied in the particular case. Where bail was denied because of the danger of the defendant committing further crimes, a change in the circumstances affecting his likelihood of appearance will not be grounds for a full review.[51]

The *Criminal Justice Act 1988* draws together the implications of these various holdings by stating that if bail has been denied, courts have a duty at each subsequent hearing to consider whether it should be granted. At the first hearing after the one at which the denial occurred, the defendant may present any argument in support of bail. However, thereafter courts need not rehear arguments advanced previously.[52] In an attempt to clarify when a full argument has been conducted, the *Criminal Justice Act 1982* amends the *Bail Act* to require magistrates to certify whether this was done whenever a remand in custody is made.[53] However, the provision has been faulted for not requiring details of the arguments heard so that new circumstances can be identified.[54]

A degree of legal assistance is provided to those asserting their right to bail. An unrepresented defendant who is denied bail upon his first appearance in Magistrates' Court is entitled, subject to a means test, to legal aid at his second appearance if he may again be refused bail.

Additionally, legal aid may be granted, also subject to a means test, for other bail applications, but it is not mandatory. If a defendant has already been granted legal aid for his defense, this will cover bail application.[55] Duty solicitor schemes may also provide legal advice on bail but will typically stop short of mustering the case for its being granted.[56]

An extensive opportunity for a defendant dissatisfied with a bail decision to have it reconsidered or reviewed by a higher court has been established. Both the Crown Court and the High Court can entertain such bail applications, which are normally handled by a single judge sitting in chambers. The High Court can also vary conditions of bail.[57] Legal aid may be provided for applications to Crown Court.[58] After exhaustion of remedies in these courts, judicial review may be sought from a divisional court of the Queen's Bench. However, this is available to oversee the decision-making process rather than to merely reevaluate the factual considerations in a properly exercised discretionary judgment.[59]

Procedural matters pertaining to sureties in England are handled generally as in the recognizance jurisdictions. In the split between those jurisdictions allowing a surety to argue for mitigation of the amount of forfeiture at the time of forfeiture and those allowing argument only after forfeiture, the position of English law bridges the two. Argument at either time or both is possible.[60] Although, strictly, no appeal exists against an order to forfeit a surety's recognizance, a limited review under a motion for *certiorari* to a Queen's Bench divisional court is sometimes available. This may rest only on a claim that the Magistrates' Court or the Crown Court has abused its jurisdiction by either failing to consider something that should have been considered or considering something which should not in ordering the forfeiture, by an error of law, or by reaching a conclusion that no reasonable court could reach.[61]

Results of the System

England provides a uniquely high level of information about the results of its bail system. Of those remanded by Magistrates' Courts between 1980 and 1985 inclusive, an average of 13.5 percent for all offenses and of 14.8 percent for indictable offenses were held in custody. This produces a bail rate of 86.5 percent and 85.2 percent respectively.[62] Of those committed for trial for indictable offenses, the average for those years is 79.8 percent committed on bail and 20.5 percent in custody.[63] Absconding rates for persons remanded on bail for indictable offenses at Magistrates' Courts have remained fairly constant at around 4 percent. They are slightly higher for summary offenses and particularly for summary motoring offenses. Whether these are enough to raise the overall rate for absconding in a particular year from 4 percent to 5 percent varies.[64] Of those committed for trial and bailed by magistrates, only 0.9 percent failed to appear in 1985. For those committed for sentencing, 0.8 percent absconded in that year.[65]

Private studies supplement the official statistics on some points. Two studies conducted during the period 1981–1982 indicate a level of legal representation in the vicinity of 83–88 percent of defendants when bail matters are considered. One of the studies attributes this to a duty solicitor scheme functioning in the court studied. Bail was found to be granted subject to conditions, both nonfinancial and financial, in 38 percent of bails in one study and 26 percent in the other (just over a third of these being financial).[66] A study shortly after the system came into effect in 1978 found 34 percent of the bails conditional, with less than one sixth of the conditions being financial.[67]

Summary

The English bail system, then, functions principally by criminal punishment for absconding. Financial conditions of bail, chiefly in the form of sureties, are used in only a small percentage of cases. Nonfinancial conditions are much more common; still, they are added in only a distinct minority of cases. A high percentage even of those defendants who reach Magistrates' Court in custody are released. Nevertheless, rates of absconding are low. Some degree of legal assistance is provided to most defendants while bail is under consideration, though this may well be restricted to the limited help provided by a duty solicitor.

CANADA

Background

The Canadian bail system is like the English in that it relies upon criminal punishments for its basic sanction in motivating the appearance of an accused. In fact, the Canadian legislation altering its bail system is some six years older than the English. Thus Canada can be credited with the original such system. However, the Canadian break with its predecessor system was less complete than that of England.

As a result Canada presents more mixture with elements of other types of bail in its approach.

As determined by the distribution of authority within Canadian federalism, bail for most offenses serious enough for bail to be employed is controlled by federal statute. Thus, the basic bail law for the whole country is the same. However, a court system structured on provincial lines has the authority to interpret this law. Since the courts of each province have coordinate jurisdictions to render the interpretations, differences among them sometimes develop. In addition, the provinces have their own bail systems for the offenses covered by provincial laws. However, since these mostly deal with minor matters not requiring bail, the provincial bail arrangements are relatively less important than those of the federal Criminal Code.

Prior to the 1970s Canada employed a recognizance-based bail system. Three alternatives were presented for the discretionary use of a magistrate or judge. The accused could be released upon entering into a recognizance with sureties, upon entering into a recognizance with a deposit, or upon simply entering into a recognizance.[68] In 1965 the Canadian Commitee on Corrections, known as the Ouimet Committee, was charged with studying this system. Its report issued in 1969 formed the basis for a package of amendments to the law regarding bail known as the *Bail Reform Act 1970–1971–1972*. Subsequently, amendments have been made to the bail legislation, the most important being those of the *Criminal Law Amendment Act 1974–1975–1976*.

The *Bail Reform Act* in effect created a change of direction for the Canadian bail system within the framework of the older approach. The alterations of the most significance for comparative purposes were those dealing with bail terms and those limiting the discretion to deny bail. Regarding the former, the possibility, on one hand, of release of an accused without a recognizance was not only created but was given statutory preference. On the other hand, criminal penalties for breaches of bail were included. Thus, the possibility of an accused's being released without financial terms but subject to punishment for breach of bail resulted. Along with this the use of cash deposits was restricted. On the latter point, automatic consideration of bail was introduced. The grounds upon which release could be denied were specified and reasons for denial were required to be stated. Additionally, the burden to demonstrate these was placed on the prosecution in most instances.

Finally, in a development independent of the *Bail Reform Act*, a change in the status of the right to bail occurred in 1982. Prior to that year the right to reasonable bail, unless there was just cause to deny it, and the freedom from arbitrary detention were protected by the *Canadian Bill of Rights 1960*. This was a classic example of a flexible constitutional document. It provided that unless Parliament declared otherwise laws should be interpreted and applied in such a way as not to abridge the rights they created. This was superseded by the *Canadian Charter of Rights and Freedoms 1982*.[69] The *Charter* is a rigid constitutional document and involves protection for the same two rights. As rigid constitutional provisions, however, they override conflicting legislation. Any statutory provisions to the contrary will be declared void by the courts.

The Canadian bail system, then, functions basically as a criminal penalties system. However, by retaining the accused's recognizance as an alternative form of release, it remains a somewhat more mixed approach to bail. Taken in conjunction with the English system it demonstrates some of the range of alternatives available within this type of system.

Terms of Bail

The Canadian *Bail Reform Act*, which became effective January 3, 1972, contrasts significantly with the English bail legislation in that it does not abolish the alternative of an accused's being required to enter into a bail recognizance for release. It does, however, provide for the possibility of release on a simple undertaking to appear without a recognizance or other conditions being imposed. Not only is this possibility provided, but it is given statutory preference for most offenses. The accused is to be released on such an unconditional undertaking unless the prosecutor shows cause why detention or release subject to the imposition of conditions is justified.[70]

The *Bail Reform Act*, having established the priority of an unconditional undertaking, proceeds to list in order of onerousness alternative terms of bail and to direct that a magistrate shall not proceed in most matters to a more burdensome level unless the prosecution shows cause why the next less onerous will not suffice. This list of alternatives begins with the undertaking plus nonfinancial conditions. It then proceeds through the accused's recognizance and his recognizance with sureties to his recognizance with a deposit.[71] Moreover, bail terms that a defendant cannot meet have been equated in case law with the issuance of a detention order. They in effect deny the accused release from custody, which may constitute a violation of constitutional rights.[72]

Complementing the emphasis on release without financial liability thus created, the Canadian *Criminal Code* establishes an absconding offense. Anyone released on an undertaking or recognizance by a magistrate or judge who fails to attend as required without a lawful excuse is guilty of an offense. This offense may be tried summarily or on indictment. If tried on indictment it is punishable by a maximum of two years imprisonment. If tried summarily, the maximum is a $2,000 fine or six months' imprisonment. The burden of proof to establish lawful excuse lies on the accused.[73]

The preference given in most cases to bail by nonfinancial undertakings and the offense created for absconding are brought together under the Canadian system by the form for the undertaking. Contained in that form is a quotation from the pertinent subsection warning the accused of the offense and the punishment created for either absconding or for violating conditions if the undertaking is with them.[74] No such written warning is contained in record of the bail decision given to defendants in England.

Provisions for arrest of a defendant who fails to appear are similar to those in England. The Canadian law provides for arrest either on a warrant issued by the magistrate upon reasonable and probable grounds to believe that the accused has violated or is about to violate his bail or without a warrant by a police officer having the same grounds.[75]

Canadian courts have elucidated various dimensions of the absconding offense created by the *Bail Reform Act*. Within the first year of operation of the act, an Ontario County Court had determined that before the question of a defendant's lawful excuse is reached the prosecution must establish that the time and place for his appearance was within that defendant's knowledge.[76]

This suggests a further issue, one of the most important addressed by the Canadian courts for developing the concept of the offense, that is, whether *mens rea* must be proven to establish the offense. Alternatively viewed, does forgetfulness either negate the offense or provide an excuse for it? A judge of the British Columbia Supreme Court in chambers has held that it does. *Mens rea* was found to be an essential element of the offense. Therefore, if an accused honestly forgot the obligation to appear, *mens rea* was negated and a lawful excuse for failure to appear was provided.[77] This interpretation was further developed by an Ontario County court. A defendant had failed to appear as the result of honest, unintentional but negligent forgetfulness. The court held that the prosecution had failed to prove *mens rea* beyond a reasonable doubt, as it must do. Mere negligence in failing to take sufficient measures to remember the correct day and place of appearance does not establish an offense. Although the court found that genuine forgetfulness would not constitute a lawful excuse, that question should not have been reached because the prosecution had not established all elements of the offense. Therefore, even though legislative action to remove *mens rea* from the offense might be desirable, and stricter conditions of bail might be imposed on such a defendant, no offense was proven.[78]

Not considered in these two cases was a solution to this dilemma previously adopted by an Ontario Provincial Court of on one hand not attributing *mens rea* when the accused is completely without wrongful intention and on the other hand not routinely accepting forgetfulness or carelessness as a complete defense. This solution adopts from Australian and New Zealand law a threefold division of *mens rea* in place of the usual twofold division. Under this analysis, between offenses where a positive state of mind must be proven and offenses of strict liability is a third category in which the prosecution need not prove *mens rea*. Rather, it is implied *prima facie* by commission of the prohibited act. However, unlike strict liability offenses, the defendant may escape liability by proving a reasonable mistake of fact that frees him of fault and makes the act innocent. Under this alternative, negligence is sufficient to establish liability, but a reasonable mistake of fact is a substantive defense.[79]

In applying this concept to the offense of failing to answer bail, the test proposed by the Provincial Court is, "Did the accused use honest and reasonable efforts to recall his trial date and to attend Court in accordances therewith?" For those accused appearing on the wrong date, this can be restated as, "Notwithstanding honest and reasonable efforts to recall his trial date had he formed the honest and reasonable belief of the incorrect trial date?"[80] A defendant failing to appear as required would be required to prove on the balance of probabilities that one of these alternatives was met to establish a complete defense. Lack of deliberate intent would remain to mitigate sentence for the offense.[81]

Viewed in their entirety, undoubtedly the most striking difference between bail terms in the Canadian and English systems is the retention of the possible use of the accused's own recognizance in Canada in contrast to its abolition in England. Under the Canadian law in most matters if the prosecution shows cause why release on an undertaking even with nonfinancial conditions should not be allowed, the magistrate is justified in requiring the accused's recognizance in the amount and subject to the nonfinancial condition deemed necessary.[82] The Canadian view of recognizance remains close to its common law roots.[83] Therefore, when used, it functions much as in the recognizance-based systems.

In Canada, as in England, third parties can be required to stand as sureties for the accused's release. Sureties can be required in Canada only upon the prosecution showing cause as to why the accused's recognizance without sureties is inadequate.84 Requiring a surety in an amount greater than the accused can arrange can constitute a violation of that individual's constitutional right to release on bail.85 Unlike England, the Canadian statute provides for the court to require a particular person to stand as surety. Thus, the accused's wife or any one member of his family might be required to be included among his sureties.[86] A further important difference between Canada and England is that whereas sureties in England stand independently of a recognizance by the accused (since that has been abolished), sureties in Canada—as in recognizance systems—are always in addition to the accused's recognizance.[87] An attempt to circumvent this by granting the accused a recognizance for nil amount with sureties for $1,000 failed. Since the accused acknowledged no indebtedness if he failed to meet his bail, he was not bound by the recognizance he was supposed to have entered. The sureties, however, were bound.[88]

Federalism introduces a consideration into Canadian suretyship not found in unitary England. Where a surety's only available property is real or immovable property in another province, a judge of the Ontario Court of Appeals has indicated, the surety is not really put at risk of having his property taken in event of a forfeiture. Consequently, that individual cannot be a sufficient surety for an accused's release.[89]

Generally, the liabilities, duties, responsibilities, and rights of Canadian sureties are like those in England and the recognizance bail countries.[90]

Use of a cash or security deposit is available in a broader range of cases in Canada than in England, although it is only to be progressed to when cause is shown why a recognizance even with sureties is inadequate. As originally structured, use of a deposit was only available when the accused was not ordinarily resident in the province, or alternatively within 200 kilometers, of his place of custody.[91] To this was added in 1975 any other case with the consent of the prosecutor.[92] Commentary indicates that the purpose of this addition is to allow a defendant who is unable to provide the required sureties to substitute an offer of cash deposit.[93] However, unlike the Indian approach, nothing in the wording of the provision seems to limit the initiative in resorting to cash to the defendant, and in several of the reported cases there is nothing to indicate that it was.[94] Nevertheless, requiring as a condition of release a deposit that is impossible for the defendant to provide violates the right to reasonable bail under the Charter of Rights by in effect denying the right to release from custody.[95]

Nothing in the statute or its amendments gives authority to require cash or security deposits of sureties.[96] In fact, persons loaning money to a defendant to make a cash deposit have been carefully distinguished by the courts from a surety.[97]

Canada, like England and the modified recognizance countries, permits nonfinancial conditions to be imposed. If justified, they can be included in a bail order at any level of financial imposition from the simple undertaking through recognizance with sureties or deposit. The Canadian statute specifies certain common conditions that may be imposed, but also provides that any other reasonable condition considered desirable is permissible.

Conditions in Canada are subject to the constitutional retraints of the *Charter*. As already seen, they must be possible for the defendant to meet. In addition, if a condition would curtail a basic right of an individual protected by the *Charter*, the prosecution must show a compelling reason why it should be imposed. A speculative concern of danger is not justification enough. The restriction must be shown to further an important or substantial state interest unrelated to the suppression of the right. Moreover, the limitation on the basic freedom must be no greater than what is necessary or essential to protect the public. The infringing condition must be precisely drawn, without any unnecessary erosion of rights.[98]

Beyond these constitutional constraints, the Quebec Court of Appeals has held that conditions can be imposed only when justified by the same purposes that the act specifies for justifying detention. These are to ensure the accused's appearance, to protect the public interest (including preventing illegal interference with the proceedings), and to protect the public from further criminal acts by the accused. In the case of protecting the public, what is controlled by the condition must be causally connected with the potential crime to justify the condition. However beneficial the control measure may be, if there is no such causal connection it is beyond the power of a magistrate to impose.[99] In deciding on conditions to prevent further crime, relevant considerations are the nature of the offense, the accused's criminal record, other indications of violent or antisocial behavior by the accused, and the surrounding circumstances.[100]

A major difference between Canada and England with regard to the enforcement of conditions is that failure to comply with a condition of bail without lawful excuse is, in Canada, punishable in the same way as absconding. Violating a bail condition, whether it is imposed by an undertaking or a recognizance, constitutes an offense punishable either summarily or upon indictment. The maximum penalty which may be imposed is two years' imprisonment if it is proceeded against on indictment and $2,000 fine or six months if tried summarily.[101] A restriction in the original law limiting proceedings on indictment for violations of conditions to those previously convicted of a bail violation was removed in a 1985 amendment to the law.[102] As with the penalty for absconding, a warning about the offense of, and punishment for, violation of bail conditions is contained in the form for the accused's undertaking.[103] In addition to punishment for this offense, a violation of bail conditions in Canada (unlike England) serves as the basis for forfeiting the accused's recognizance—including any cash or security deposit—and that of any sureties.[104] The accused may be arrested for a conditions violation with or without a warrant on the same terms as for absconding, and the undertaking or recognizance will be canceled unless he can show cause why it should not be.[105]

Although the terms of bail in Canada fall into the same general category as those employed by England, important variations exist between the two systems. The fundamental similarity that serves as the basis for classifying the two systems together is their basic reliance on the imposition of criminal penalties to motivate the accused's presence at trial. Even on this point several differences exist. Canada retains the possibility of the accused's being required to enter into a recognizance, whereas England has abolished this. Canada also extends the possiblity of criminal punishment to violations of other conditions of bail, which England does not. In both countries nonfinancial conditions and sureties can be required. Both of these additions in the Canadian system are subject to constitutional rights found in the *Canadian Charter of Rights and Freedoms*, whereas England does not have the rigid constitutional form of rights protection. In both countries cash or security deposits may be required in some cases. England is considerably more restrictive on this point, limiting them to cases where reasonable grounds suggest that the accused will leave the country.

Eligibility for Bail

Like England, bail in lower courts of Canada must be seen in the context of an overall system that places emphasis on the use of summons, appearance notices (a form of quasi-summons issued by the police), and release on bail by the police of a large proportion of defendants.[106] For those defendants who do appear before the magistrate for consideration of bail, Canada adds a dimension of consideration to the matter of eligibility not present in England in that the *Canadian Charter of Rights and Freedoms* creates pertinent constitutional rights capable of overriding statutory provisions. Two such rights have regularly been applied by Canadian courts, in addition to others occasionally considered. One of these is the right of everyone under

Section 9 of the *Charter* not to be arbitrarily detained. The other is the right under Section 11 of any person charged with an offense not to be denied reasonable bail without just cause.

The Supreme Court of Canada has held that the protection of reasonable bail under Section 11 of the *Charter* applies to anyone prosecuted by the state for a public offense involving punitive sanctions. This includes criminal, quasi-criminal, and regulatory offenses under both federal and provincial law. Matters which are criminal in nature are covered even if the consequences of conviction are relatively minor. Excluded from this coverage are private, domestic, or disciplinary matters intended primarily to maintain integrity or discipline, or regulate conduct, within a limited private sphere of activity. The one exception to this is where a true penal consequence has been attached to the matter. Consequently, if imprisonment or a fine of sufficient magnitude to indicate the purpose of redressing a wrong to society is involved, the matter would be covered. The right to reasonable bail thus applies to any criminal proceeding and to any other matter where a true penal consequence follows upon conviction.[107]

Within this constitutional context, Canadian statute creates a qualified right of the accused to be released pertaining to most offenses under most circumstances. Nevertheless, where detention can be demonstrated to be justified by criteria specified in the statute, release can be denied even where the right pertains. The prosecution bears the burden of showing cause to detain the defendant for this broad range of offenses,[108] and it must be given a reasonable opportunity to present evidence to accomplish this.[109] The most common offenses excluded from the qualified right to bail are drug trafficking, drug importing and exporting, and murder (each including the attempt, the conspiracy to commit, and accessory after the fact). Other less common offenses excluded from the right include treason, sedition, piracy (plus a few offenses related to each), and accepting a bribe by the holder of a judicial office.[110] For all of these offenses the presumption is that bail will not be granted unless the defendant can show cause why detention in custody is not justified. In addition, for all of these crimes except the drug offenses, only a judge of a superior court of criminal jurisdiction can grant release from custody to an accused.[111]

In addition to the crimes specifically excepted from the right to bail, any indictable offense is excluded if it was committed while the accused was on release for another indictable offense, or if the accused is not ordinarily a Canadian resident. Finally, the right to bail does not apply to offenses of absconding or violating the conditions of bail. These situations are treated like drug trafficking offenses, with the presumption being against release and with the burden being on the accused to show why detention is not justified (but with no reservation of release to a superior court judge).[112] The accused may not be deprived of reasonable opportunity to show cause why his detention is not justified.[113]

The reverse onus provision, where the burden of proving that detention is unjustified is placed upon the accused for certain matters, has been one of the most heavily litigated aspects of Canadian bail law. In 1982, the Appeal Division of the Nova Scotia Supreme Court found the provisions contrary to the *Charter* protection of the rights under Section 11.[114] The weight of judicial opinion and the courts in most provinces have, however, found the provision constitutional. In *R. v. Bray* (1983) the Ontario Court of Appeal (a court of comparable jurisdiction to that in Nova Scotia) sustained the provision in another murder case. This court reasoned that the *Charter* did not address the matter of burden of proof. If adequate statutory reasons for denial of release exist, just cause is present. Furthermore, the right to bail under Section 11 is not absolute. It may be subjected to reasonable limits prescribed by law if these are demonstrably justified in a free and democratic society. The reverse onus is such a reasonable limitation.[115] The Quebec Superior Court has upheld reverse onus in murder and drug cases,[116] and similar conclusions were reached by courts in British Columbia and Manitoba.[117] Other constitutional objections to reverse onus, such as arbitrary detention and violation of the presumption of innocence, are also considered in some of these cases. The most extensive reasoning on these other points is provided in *R. v. Frankforth*. Here placing the burden on the accused is held not to represent arbitrary detention because the detention is not arbitrary, understood as unreasonable or capricious. The detention is not at the whim of the court, but rather rests on authorization specified by Parliament.[118] The presumption of innocence is not violated because no finding of guilt or innocence is involved in the bail decision.[119]

Considerations for Denying Bail

Where the prosecution seeks to defeat the qualified right to bail, the Canadian law specifies two criteria as being the only grounds justifying detention in custody. The primary grounds is that detention is necessary to assure the accused's attendance at court. The secondary grounds is that detention is necessary in the public interest or for the protection or safety of the public. All circumstances are to be regarded in assessing the latter, but specifically pertinent is any substantial likelihood that the accused, if released, will commit a crime or interfere with the administration of justice.[120]

The presence of either the primary or secondary grounds has been held to constitute just cause under the *Charter* to deny bail. Even in a free and democratic society, there are reasonable limits on an individual's right to release that therefore render them just cause for denial.[121] Moreover, as the only grounds, if one or the other is not present there is no discretion to deny bail.[122] Several cases have established that these same grounds serve as criteria for detention regardless of who has the burden of proof. Thus, even in murder, drug trafficking, or commission of an indictable offense on bail cases where reverse onus applies, they determine the relevant considerations.[123] The degree of proof required regardless of the onus is the balance of probability.[124]

Probably the most extensive judicial consideration regarding the criteria for detention has been devoted to the concept of the public interest. At the threshold, the public interest is not the same as the protection and safety of the public. These are separate concepts and each requires individual consideration.[125] A widespread judicial consensus on the meaning of "the public interest" has emerged.[126] This is based on the reasoning in *Re Powers and the Queen* (1972).[127] Under the definition provided in this case, the public interest includes the rights of the community. It requires that release considerations not be so tipped in favor of the accused that the citizens, in wonder and bewilderment, feel that the application of the bail aspects of the criminal law is either a mockery or not being done realistically or in the public interest. It involves the public image of the *Criminal Code*, the *Bail Reform Act*, the apprehension and conviction of criminals, the attempt to deter crime, and the protection of citizens.[128] The community under this view has a right, not only to remain safe and secure, but to feel safe and secure. Public confidence in, and regard for, the administration of justice deserves protection.[129]

Where a magistrate orders an accused detained in any situation covered by the qualified right to bail, the reasons for doing so must be recorded. Conversely, since the 1985 amendment, where a magistrate orders an accused released in cases not covered by the right, reasons must also be recorded.[130]

In addition to the two criteria for detention specified in the law, the statute governing bail in Canada lists several factors to be considered in determining where the criteria for detention are met. As case law makes clear, these factors do not constitute separate reasons for denying bail, but come into play only as aids for assessing the basic criteria.[131] Although any matter concerning the accused that the magistrate considers desirable to inquire into may be considered, four are specifically stated. These are previous criminal convictions of the accused, other charges pending against the accused, previous convictions for bail violations of the accused, and the circumstances of the offense presently alleged, particularly as they bear upon the probability of conviction.[132] Under the last, factors considered in addition to the probability of conviction are both the objective and "effective" gravity of the offense and the probability of incarceration as a punishment.[133] A major factor considered in assessing the criteria, although not specified in the statute, is what might broadly be called community ties. This includes family, relationships, home ownership, and business commitments.[134] Although these factors may contribute to proof of one of the criteria for denying bail, the mere presence or lack of one of them cannot be used by itself as grounds for denial.[135]

Procedural Considerations

A limited number of the most important procedural points of contrast between Canada and England require consideration. With regard to the handling of absconders, three variations are particularly salient. First is the possibility in Canada of trial being on indictment for absconding or other bail violation. Second, Canada makes no provision in the higher courts for the violation to be handled as if it were a contempt of court. Third, in trials for summary offenses where the defendant was released on an undertaking to appear, Canada permits a defendant to appear by counsel rather than in person unless the court specifically requires a personal appearance. The Saskatchewan Court of Appeal has held that where a defendant appears by counsel in such matters, no failure to appear occurs and consequently the accused cannot be convicted of absconding.[136]

Regarding the procedural implementation of the right to bail, there are again some noticeable contrasts between the Canadian and the English approach within a basic similarity. Canadian law requires that a person arrested and not released by the police should be brought before a magistrate without unreasonable delay and in any event within twenty-four hours, unless a magistrate is not available. If no magistrate is available within that period, it must be done as soon as possible.[137] In contrast to England, no authority exists in Canada for ranking police officers to extend this period.

The most striking difference between the two countries regarding delay in bringing an unreleased defendant before a magistrate is that in Canada it has been held to be a constitutional rights violation under Section 9 of the *Charter*. (This section protects against arbitrary detention or imprisonment.) In several cases the rights of defendants have been found to have been violated when they were detained by police for less than twenty-four hours but for longer than required for administrative purposes justifying their detention. Moreover, the defendants in these cases were held entitled to a just and appropriate remedy under Section 24(1) of the *Charter*. The specific remedy applied has varied, ranging from dismissal of the charges to a reduction to *nil* of a fine. Exclusion of evidence obtained as a result of the detention, where relevant, has also been suggested.[138] Moreover, the British Columbia Court of Appeal has pointed out that the remedy fashioned need not be one that is granted at the trial.[139] One clearly pertinent consideration in determining a remedy is the flagrancy of the police misconduct creating the violation.[140]

Once a defendant is before the magistrate—except in cases of guilty pleas—bail must be considered for all but those few serious offenses reserved for a judge. Although some earlier cases held otherwise,[141] the weight of recent judicial opinion is that even a defendant who must be detained in custody on another matter must be brought before a magistrate and is entitled to have release considered. Terms of release on the present matter should be set where appropriate, subject to detention on the other matter.[142] The magistrate may adjourn a release hearing, but without the accused's consent a three-day maximum delay is imposed.[143] This has been interpreted restrictively, moreover, to mean that the hearing must be resumed within the three days rather than on the fourth.[144]

If an accused is detained in custody by the magistrate at a release hearing and trial is delayed more than thirty days for a summary offense or ninety days for an indictable offense, one review of detention by a judge is required. The responsibility for seeking review is placed on whoever has custody of the accused. The judge conducting such reviews may consider the responsibility of both prosecution and defense for any unreasonable delays of the trial in making a decision about the defendant's release.[145] This review of any prolonged denial of bail, automatic from the defendant's perspective, is in addition to reviews by a judge that might be applied for by the accused in the normal pattern. Such a review may be reapplied for after thirty days.[146] It is also in addition to the possibility of a new order being substituted upon a showing of cause by the trial judge or magistrate, the magistrate conducting the preliminary hearing, or with the consent of prosecution and defense by the magistrate who made the original order or another magistrate.[147] Roughly comparable provisions exist for those whose offenses are only bailable by a judge except for the absence of the automatic review.[148]

In addition to the review alternative provided by the bail statute, limited use of extraordinary remedies has been permitted the accused in particular circumstances. These include *habeas corpus* when a detention following revocation of bail is claimed to be unlawful and *certiorari* where conditions are beyond the jurisdiction of a court to impose.[149] Where no statutory or inherent jurisdiction exists to remedy an unreasonable bail order, Section 24(1) of the *Charter* (which provides broadly for judicially fashioned remedies for rights infringements) may serve as a jurisdictional base. This does not apply, however, where other courts have a statutory jurisdiction.[150]

Canada thus provides extensive mechanisms to cause the appearance of the accused before a magistrate and the consideration of bail once this is done. Extensive opportunity for review is provided. The prosecution, it should be noted, also has the opportunity to seek review of bail orders.[151]

Procedures in Canada regarding recognizances, sureties, and deposits are generally as observed in England and the recognizance-based countries[152] and do not require elaboration. Because of the different constitutional situation in Canada from that of England, several procedural aspects of the bail hearing itself are noteworthy. A Saskatchewan Court of Queen's Bench opinion has found a right to have bail hearings conducted in the official language—English or French—of one's choice, at least in courts where providing it is practicable.[153]

A provision of the bail law requires the justice, upon the accused's application, to ban publication or broadcast of evidence taken, information given, or reasons specified when the prosecution shows cause to deny bail. This has been upheld as constitutional. According to the Ontario Court of Appeal, it is a reasonable limitation on the constitutional right of free press in the interest of the competing right to receive a fair trial.[154] The same court found that no appeal is provided from such a publications ban, but also that it does not extend to reporting the fact of denial of bail itself.[155] At least in purpose this provision is similar to ones found in several Australian states.

The bail legislation also protects the accused from examinations or cross-examinations by a magistrate or any other person about the offense, again much as in the Australian states.[156] Statements produced by such questioning have been held to be inadmissible and incapable of being used in any way adverse to the accused. However, neither do they warrant dismissing charges.[157] A problem nevertheless arises when in a reverse onus situation the defense wishes to employ such testimony. A Quebec Superior Court opinion has held that to forbid it deprives the accused of the right to present his case contrary to the *Charter of Rights and Freedoms* Section 7.[158]

Summary

Canada, like England, possesses a bail system whose chief sanction motivating compliance with bail requirements is the threat of criminal punishment for absconding. Nevertheless, the Canadian system has several major differences from the English. Canada has retained the possibility of the accused's recognizance being demanded as a term of release. Based upon the reported bail cases that specify the terms imposed, it is clearly employed in most serious or difficult matters.[159] The punishments for bail violations in Canada also differ from those in England in that they extend to breaches of bail conditions rather than being limited to absconding itself. Canada provides a written notice of the threat of punishment in the undertaking signed by the accused. Also under the Canadian legislation, proceedings against a bail violator can be tried on indictment—an alternative to the approach in England where it is always a summary offense but may be committed to a court of general trial jurisdiction for sentencing. Both countries' systems create a statutory right to bail, but Canada backs this with a constitutional right. Conversely, however, the number of offenses for which bail cannot be granted by a magistrate is larger in Canada and the use of reverse onus is imposed.

OTHER CRIMINAL PENALTIES SYSTEMS

Australia: New South Wales

All six of the Australian states have a criminal provision against absconding as at least an alternative or secondary sanction with which to enforce bail. However, only in New South Wales—the country's most populous jurisdiction—does the imposition of criminal penalties amount to a primary sanction employed to secure the accused's appearance for trial.

As with England and Canada, New South Wales conducted a study of its bail system prior to its alteration in the 1970s. The Bail Review Committee (N.S.W.) recommended decreasing reliance on financial bail and instead relying on nonfinancial conditions of bail to control defendants. It did, however, think that to encourage full use of these, a sanction in the form of a penalty for a newly created criminal offense should be created. The committee considered but rejected the possibility of extending the offense to cover breach of the nonfinancial bail conditions—as in Canada, South Australia, and Tasmania—on the grounds that it would in effect give magistrates the power to create too many new individual offenses by imposing conditions of bail.

Arrest and withdrawal of bail were deemed sufficient. A presumption of bail for all offenses and a right to bail for minor ones were recommended. Further proposals included specified criteria to guide bail decisions.[160] Most of the Committee's recommendations were incorporated in the *Bail Act 1978*.

The bail system created by the New South Wales *Bail Act* is in general much like that of Canada. The statute provides that bail is to be unconditional unless the court believes that conditions should be imposed to promote effective law enforcement or the protection and welfare of the community. No more onerous conditions are to be imposed than the nature of the offense and the circumstances of the accused warrant. Conditions are listed in order of their burdensomeness, and any given condition may not be imposed unless no prior condition or combination of conditions is likely to secure the objective sought. Upon an accused's request, however, any condition can be imposed.[161] Conditions available begin at the least burdensome level with specified nonfinancial requirements as to the accused's conduct while on bail. They then escalate to providing one or more acceptable acquaintances who will state that the accused is a responsible person likely to comply with the terms of bail. Financial conditions then follow. These begin with the accused's own recognizance at the least burdensome level. They can then progress through one or more sureties by recognizance, the accused's deposit of security, and the sureties' deposit of security. At the most burdensome end of the schedule come the accused's cash deposit and finally the sureties' cash deposit. The clear effect is to force preference to be given to nonfinancial over financial considerations.[162]

In New South Wales, as in Canada, however, behind these various bail term alternatives lies the creation of an offense of absconding. As established in the *Bail Act*, an accused who fails to appear without reasonable excuse is guilty of the offense. The burden of proving the reasonable excuse rests on the accused. Absconding is punishable by up to the same as the primary offense with, however, a maximum of three years' imprisonment or a $3,000 fine.[163] In line with the Bail Review Committee's recommendation, other breaches of bail are not covered, making the offense in New South Wales more comparable to that in England than that in Canada. However, the accused may be arrested for breach of a condition and bail may be withdrawn, or its terms made more severe.[164] Moreover, the New South Wales Court of Criminal Appeal has held that offenses committed while on bail should receive severely deterrent sentences including cumulative sentences for the subsequent offenses.[165]

The limited statistical information available tends to confirm that New South Wales functions as a criminalization system in practice. A study of combined police and court bail was conducted in 1980 during the act's first year of operation. It indicates that bail is granted unconditionally in about 65 percent of cases where a bail determination is made, and is refused in about 7 percent of the cases. Conditional bail accounts for 26 percent of the determinations and within that, financial conditions account for 72 percent, or about 17 percent of the total bail determinations. In contrast, nonfinancial conditions of conduct were employed in only about 5 percent of the conditional bails, or 1.3 percent of the total bail decisions. In an additional 23 percent of the conditional bails, nonfinancial acknowledgment of the accused's responsibility by an acceptable person was employed. This equals almost 6 percent of the overall bail decisions. Clearly, nonfinancial conditions, particularly nonfinancial conditions regarding conduct, cannot be said to be the principal control exhibited here, in spite of the prominent position they occupy in the statute.[166]

Correspondingly, that the criminal penalty for absconding is ultimately what is relied upon is suggested by the figures reported annually for persons appearing in the lower courts for the offense of failure to answer their bail. Figures are given for only the most serious offense charged. Therefore, bail violations would be underreported in cases where the main offense is relatively serious. Since these more-serious cases are likely to be the ones where financial conditions would have been imposed, an indication is provided of what is in fact relied upon to secure appearance in that large percentage of unconditional bails. Of 508 non-appearance cases in 1982, about 65 percent received fine or imprisonment. For 498 similar cases in 1983, about 71 percent received fine or imprisonment. Of the 631 cases reported for 1984, over 70 percent received fine or imprisonment. For 1985, of 817 reported, more than 73 percent received fine or imprisonment sentences. Of the 831 such cases in 1986, again over 73 percent received fine or imprisonment.[167] The low percentage of cases in which nonfinancial conditions are used confirms that, in spite of the fact that the law might seem to favor this category of control, the New South Wales bail system is not in practice a nonfinancial system. Conversely, the high percentage of unconditional bails combined with the indications of use of fines and imprisonment for absconding from trial on those less-serious offenses adequate to warrant bail suggests that in practice the criminalization of absconding is the operative part of the law. This being so, the New South Wales bail system, like the English and Canadian, functions as a criminalization system where bail is extensively granted without conditions, but the threat of criminal punishment is chiefly relied upon as the motive to prevent absconding.

One aspect of eligibility for bail in New South Wales is sufficiently different from the approach in England and Canada to require mention. New South Wales creates both a right to bail and a presumption of bail applicable to different situations. The right to bail applies to all offenses not punishable by imprisonment and any other summary offense specified by regulation. The only preconviction exceptions to this right pertain to individuals who have failed to appear when required or who have violated some other condition of bail, and to those who, whether by intoxication, drug use, injury, or otherwise, are in danger of injury or need of protection.[168] Moreover, not only must bail be granted, but the *Bail Act* requires that where this right applies it be granted either unconditionally or on terms that are reasonably and readily able to be met by the accused.[169]

Complementing this right to bail for minor offenses, New South Wales creates a presumption in favor of bail being granted for all other offenses except those of failing to appear to answer bail, robbery with violence or an offensive weapon, serious drug charges, and domestic violence charges. Even those failing to appear are granted the presumption in cases originally covered by this right. This presumption, unlike the right, is overcome where a court is satisfied that it is justified in refusing bail based on specified criteria. These criteria and the factors to be used to assess them are generally similar to those employed in England and Canada and are identical in all but a couple of particulars to those discussed in Chapter 6 under Australia's Northern Territory.[170]

The combination of right and presumption of bail in New South Wales has contributed to a fairly constant rate of release on bail over the three calendar years 1984–1986. Based on the bail status at final appearance in local courts for general offenses, about 7 percent of defendants remain in custody (7.1, 7.1, and 6.9 percent, respectively), just over 64 percent are released on bail (64.4, 64.9, and 64.4 percent, respectively) and about 28 percent are allowed at large without bail (28.5, 28.0, and 28.7 percent, respectively.)[171]

Scotland

Scotland's criminal procedure is separate from and in many respects quite different from that of England. Scotland possesses a mixed system, exhibiting elements of both Roman civil and English common law traditions. However, the bail component of its criminal procedure is in most respects one of its common law style elements. The *Bail (Scotland) Act 1980* replaced the former cash deposit system with a system combining criminal penalties and nonfinancial conditions roughly comparable in its principal characteristics to that found in New South Wales. Unlike New South Wales, data indicating which of these alternative sanctions predominates is not available for Scotland.

Under the Scottish bail law, bail may be granted subject to any nonfinancial conditions necessary to secure any of four specified objectives: that the accuseds appear as appointed, that the accuseds do not commit a crime while on bail, that they do not interfere with witnesses or otherwise obstruct the course of justice in relation either to themselves or to another, and that they make themselves available to enable inquiries or reports to be made.[172] Not only may specific conditions be fashioned to achieve these objectives, but the objectives themselves have been transformed into standard conditions mandatory in all bail cases. Thus, all bails are subject to the conditions of appearance, not committing offenses, not tampering with witnesses, and being available for the making of inquiries and reports. Courts have been held to have no discretion to dispense with these standard conditions.[173]

Breaking with the earlier bail system, the 1980 act makes unlawful granting bail under a pledge or deposit of money, or imposing a monetary pledge or deposit as a condition of bail, except where the court is satisfied that imposition of such a requirement is appropriate to the special circumstances of a case.[174] Thus, nonfinancial conditions of release are required, whereas financial conditions are restricted to cases where special circumstances justify them.

Like the other jurisdictions considered in this chapter, the chief sanction in Scotland when nonfinancial conditions fail to secure the accused's appearance is criminal punishment. Failure to appear when required without reasonable excuse is in most cases punishable by a £200 fine and imprisonment for up to 60 days. Up to three months' imprisonment may be imposed if conviction occurs in the High Court rather than in the district court. However, if the failure to appear is in relation to a solemn proceeding (implying a serious charge) and conviction for that failure is on indictment, the possible fine becomes unlimited and the imprisonment for up to two years. The bail violation punishment may be imposed cumulatively to the punishment for the underlying offense.[175]

Like Canada, but unlike England and New South Wales, Scotland makes breaches of other conditions of bail punishable offenses. The limits of punishment are the same as those ordinarily attaching to failure to appear.[176] To be subject to punishment, conditions must be specified and the specification must be included in the defendant's copy of the bail order.[177]

Bail may be granted in Scotland for any offense. However, bail in case of treason or murder is reserved to the High Court sitting with a quorum rather than with a single judge. Bail in murder cases is extremely rare, having been granted only once in this century.[178] For other charges the presumption is in favor of bail. Bail should be granted unless good grounds for refusal exist relating to the protection of the public interest or the administration of justice. Under these heads, bail may be refused in the following situations:

1. The accused has a significant record of repeating the offense with which he is charged, particularly a record including a recent prison release for it.
2. The offense charged was committed while on bail or in a similar position of trust.
3. Intimidation of a witness is alleged.
4. The accused has no fixed abode.
5. Reasonable grounds to suspect the accused will not appear are present.
6. The nature of the charge indicates very special circumstances.

In the presence of one of these circumstances, bail should be refused unless cogent reasons to allow it are found. Further police inquiries can justify bail denial after committal only if the prosecution can show that denial is in the public interest or in the interest of the administration of justice. Vague or unspecified claims based on further police inquiries are not adequate justification.[179] In Scotland as in the other jurisdictions procedural requirements act to force prompt consideration of bail matters.[180]

CONCLUSION

England, Canada and New South Wales are all jurisdictions in which commercial bail bonding has specifically been made illegal by statute. However, beyond these provisions the system of bail release common to them, as well as to Scotland, provides even less opportunity to commercial provision of bail than a recognizance system. The principal control on released defendants in this system is the threat of punishment for absconding. Therefore, in the great preponderance of cases no opportunity for a commercial bondsman to function is created. To the extent that each of the three jurisdictions resorts to cash or security deposits and third-party sureties, this immunity is compromised. However, as long as these are used in only a small percentage of cases, too little opportunity is provided to sustain a commercial business in bail bonding.

Even among those cases where a potential for commercialization exists, some factors can be identified that minimize or aggravate the possibility. Helpful are the English emphasis on closeness of sureties to defendants and the Canadian ability to specify sureties. Similarly serving to minimize the risk is the English principle against cash deposits by sureties and the Canadian cases distinguishing a lender of bail funds from a surety. Not desirable in this regard is the possibility of cash or security deposit being required of sureties in New South Wales, although the danger is mitigated by placing these options at the end of a long list of alternatives that must be preferred. England's very restrictive approach to the possibility of cash deposit, and New South Wales' listing of it after deposit of security in the list of alternatives (and preferring deposit by the defendant to deposit by the surety), all function to minimize the danger of commercial bail's development. Scotland's making unlawful financial conditions of bail in the absence of a finding of special circumstances justifying them similarly acts to minimize this danger.

In sum, the first three systems make commercial bail bonding illegal. Beyond this, however, by restricting the opportunity for it to function, all four render it impractical as an ongoing business.

NOTES

1. *Justice of the Peace*, 140 (1976), 174; *Justice of the Peace*, 138 (1974), 327; Home Office, *Criminal Statistics England and Wales, 1977* (London: HMSO, 1978), Tabs. 8.2, 8.5.
2. For example: A. Keith Bottomley, *Prison Before Trial*, Occasional Papers on Social Administration, No. 39 (London: G. Bell & Sons, 1970); Clive Davis, "Pre-Trial Imprisonment: A Liverpool Study," *British Journal of Criminology* 11, 1 (1971): 32–48; Brian Harris, "Bail—The Case for Reform," *New Law Journal* (1974): pp. 332–334; Michael King, *Bail or Custody* (London: The Cobden Trust, 1973); Michael Zander, "Bail: A Re-Appraisal," *Criminal Law Review* (1967): pp. 25–39, 100–111, 128–142.
3. Working Party on Bail Procedures in Magistrates' Courts, *Bail Procedures in Magistrates' Courts* (London: HMSO, 1974), pp. 32–35.
4. Ibid., pp. 27–29.
5. Ibid., pp. 35–37, 43.
6. *Bail Act 1976*, s. 6.
7. *R. v. Reader* (1986) [1987] 84 Cr App R 294 (C.A.).
8. *Bail Act 1976*, s. 7.
9. *R. v. Gateshead Justices, ex parte Usher* (1981) [1981] Crim LR 491 (Q.B.D.).
10. *R. v. Harbax Singh* (1978) [1979] 68 Cr App R 108 (Q.B.D.).
11. *D.P.P. v. Richards* (1988) [1989] 88 Cr App R 97 (Q.B.D.).
12. *R. v. Reader; R. v. Richards.*
13. *Laidlaw v. Atkinson* (1986) TLR (2 Aug), 26 (Q.B.D.).
14. *R. v. Neve* (1986) 8 Cr App R (S) 270 (C.A.).
15. *R. v. Tyson* (1979) 68 Cr App R 314 (C.A.).

16. *Bail Act 1976*, s. 8.

17. *R. v. Uxbridge Justices, ex parte Heward-Mills* (1982) 147 JP 225 (Q.B.D.); *R. v. York Crown Court, ex parte Coleman* (1987) [1988] 86 Cr App R 151 (Q.B.D.).

18. *R. v. Horseferry Road Magistrates' Court, ex parte Pearson* (1976) [1976] 2 All ER 264 (Q.B.D.); *R. v. Horseferry Road Magistrates' Court, ex parte Pearson.*

19. *Bail Act 1976*, s. 3(6).

20. *R. v. Mansfield Justices, ex parte Sharkey* (1984) 149 JP 129 (Q.B.D.).

21. *Bail Act 1976*, s. 3(8).

22. Ibid., s. 5.; Clifford Chatterton, *Bail: Law and Practice* (London: Butterworths, 1986), pp. 152–153.

23. *Bail Act 1976*, s. 7(3)(b); also see Home Office, *Remands in Custody*, Cmnd 9322 (London: HMSO, 1983), p. 5.

24. Chatterton, p. 149; A. P. Carr, ed., *Anthony and Berryman's Magistrates' Court Guide* (London: Butterworths, 1987), p. 415.

25. *Bail Act 1976*, s. 3(5), s. 5(7)–(9A).

26. *The Magistrate*, 93 (1987), 85.

27. "Baron Stands Surety in Fraud Case," *Daily Telegraph*, 14 Aug 1985, p. 3.

28. *R. v. Wells Street Magistrates' Court, ex parte Albanese* (1981) [1982] 84 Cr App R 180 (Q.B.D.).

29. *R. v. Crown Court at Warwick, ex parte Smalley* (1986) [1987] 84 Cr App R 51 (Q.B.D.).

30. "Money on Deposit," *Justice of the Peace*, 146 (1982): 555.

31. Home Office, *Criminal Statistics England and Wales 1985* (London: HMSO, 1986), Tab. 8.1. Figures are for the years 1980–1985 inclusive.

32. *Magistrates' Courts Act 1980*, s. 41.

33. *Bail Act 1976*, Sched. 1.

34. Ibid.

35. E. F. Jowitt, "Bail in Magistrates' Court," *The Magistrate* 93 (1987): 101–102; *In re Moles* (1980) [1981] Crim LR 170; *R. v. Mansfield Justices, ex parte Sharkey.*

36. *Bail Act 1976*, s. 5.

37. *Criminal Justice Act 1988*, s. 153.

38. *Ex parte Goswani* [1967] Crim LR 234 (Q.B.D.); *R. V. Governor of Pentonville Prison, ex parte Gilliland* [1984] Crim LR 229 (Q.B.D.).

39. *Bail Act 1976*, Sched. 1(9); Anthony and Berryman, pp. 414–415.

40. Anthony and Berryman, p. 419.

41. *Bail Act 1976*, s. 6; *R. v. Tyson.*

42. *Bail Act 1976*, s. 6; *Schiavo v. Anderton* (1986) 83 Cr App R 224 (Q.B.D.); *Practice Direction* (Q.B.D.); *Bail: Failure to Surrender* (1987) 1 WLR 79; *France v. Dewsbury Magistrates' Court* (1987) JP 301 (Q.B.D.).

43. *Bail Act 1976*, s. 6; *R. v. Tyson*; *R. v. Harbax Singh*; *R. v. Davis (Seaton Roy)* (1986) 8 Cr App R (S) 64 (C.A.).

44. *Magistrates' Courts Act 1980*, s. 43, s. 117; *Police and Criminal Evidence Act 1984*, s. 34, s. 41–47.

45. *Bail Act 1976*, s. 4; Barbra Brink and Christopher Stone, "Defendants Who Do Not Ask for Bail," *Criminal Law Review* (1988): pp. 152–162; Anthony and Berryman, pp. 418–419; "Practical Points #1," *Justice of the Peace* 142 (1978): 322.

46. *R. v. Nottingham Justices, ex parte Davis* (1980) 71 Cr App R 178 (Q.B.D.); Brink and Stone, pp. 54–62; P. W. H. Lydiate, "Bail Proceedings in Magistrates' Courts: Basic Procedures," *Justice of the Peace* 151 (1987): 164.

47. *R. v. Reading Crown Court, ex parte Malik* (1980) [1981] 72 Cr App R 146 (Q.B.D.).

48. *R. v. Tower Bridge Magistrates' Court, ex parte Gilbert* (1987) 152 JP 307 (Q.B.D.).

49. *R. v. Barking Justices, ex parte Shankshaft* (1982) 147 JP 399 (Q.B.D.).

50. *R. v. Tower Bridge Magistrates' Court, ex parte Gilbert.*

51. *R. v. Slough Justices, ex parte Duncan* (1982) 75 Cr App R 384 (Q.B.D.).

52. *Criminal Justice Act 1988*, s. 154.

53. *Criminal Justice Act 1982*, s. 60(2)(3); *Bail Act 1976*, s. 6A.

54. Brink and Stone, p. 158.

55. *Legal Aid Act 1988*, s. 19(1),(2),(4), s. 21(3),(5)-(7).

56. Brink and Stone, pp. 160–161.

57. *R. v. Reading Crown Court, ex parte Malik*; Practice Direction: Crown Court, Bail (1983) 77 Cr App R 69; *Supreme Court Act 1981*, s. 81; *Criminal Justice Act 1982*, s. 60; *Criminal Justice Act 1967* amend., s. 22; Chatterton, pp. 202–203.

58. *Legal Aid Act 1988*, s. 19, s. 21(2),(5)–(7).

59. *R. v. Guildhall Justices, ex parte Prushinowski* (1985) TLR (14 Dec.) 7 (Q.B.D.); *In re Herbage* (1985) TLR (25 Oct.) 28 (Q.B.D.); *R. v. Dacorum Justices, ex parte Darker* (1983) TLR (14 Aug.) 10 (Q.B.D.).

60. *Waltham Forest Justices, ex parte Parfrey* (1980) 2 Cr App R (S) 208 (Q.B.D.); *R. v. Central Criminal Court, ex parte Naraghi and Binji* (1980) 2 Cr App R (S) 104 (Q.B.D.); Chatterton, pp. 116–117.

61. *R. v. Southampton Justices, ex parte Green; R. v. Horseferry Road Magistrates' Court, ex parte Pearson; R. v. Knightsbridge Crown Court, ex parte Newton* [1980] Crim L R 715 (Q.B.D.); *R. v. Waltham Justices, ex parte Parfrey; R. v. Central Criminal Court, ex parte Naraghi and Binji; R. v. Gateshead Justices, ex parte Usher; R. v. Wells Street Magistrates' Court, ex parte Reddington* [1981] Crim L R 618; *R. v. Uxbridge Justices, ex parte Hewart-Mills; In re Smalley* (1985) 149 JP 319 (H.L.); *R. v. Inner London Crown Court, ex parte Springall; R. v. York Crown Court, ex parte Coleman.*

62. Home Office, *Criminal Statistics 1985*, Tab. 8.5.

63. Ibid., Tab. 8.8.

64. Ibid., Tabs. 8.9, 8.13.

65. Ibid., Tab. 8.12.

66. M. J. Doherty and R. East, "Bail Decisions in Magistrates' Courts," *British Journal of Criminology* 25 (1985): 258; L. M. Cutts, "Has the Bail Act Made Any Difference?" *New Law Journal* (1982): 1089–1090.

67. Michael Zander, "Operation of the Bail Act in London Magistrates' Courts," *New Law Journal* (1979): 109.

68. *Canadian Criminal Code 1953–54*, s. 451, s. 463.

69. *Canadian Bill of Rights 1960*, Pt. I, s. 2(a)(f); *Canadian Charter of Rights and Freedoms 1982*, s. 9, s. 11(e).

70. *Criminal Code*, 457(1) [now s. 515(1)].

71. Ibid., s. 457(2),(3) [now s. 515(2),(3).

72. *R. v. Cichanski* (1976) 25 CCC 2d 84 (Ont. H.C,), at 86; *Fraser v. The Queen* (1982) 38 OR 2d 172 (Ont. D.C.).

73. *Criminal Code*, s. 133(2) [now s. 145(2)].

74. Ibid,., Form 9.

75. Ibid., s. 458 [now s. 524].

76. *R. v. Bowman* (1972) 8 CCC 2d 237 (Ont. Co. Ct.).

77. *R. v. Stuart* (1981) 58 CCC 2d 203 (B.C. S.C. in Chambers).

78. *R. v. Neal* (1982) 67 CCC 2d 92 (Ont. Co. Ct.).

79. *R. v. Prenshaw, et al.* (1976) 31 CCC 2d 458 (Ont. Prov. Ct.), at 463–464.

80. Ibid., at 465.

81. Ibid., at 464–466.

82. *Criminal Code*, s. 457 (2),(3) [now s. 515(2),(3)].

83. *R. v. Pellerin* (1981) 62 CCC 2d 411 (B.C. Prov. Ct.); *R. v. Mackie* (1977) 38 CCC 2d 385 (Man. Q. B.); *R. v. Sandhu* (1984) 38 CR 3d 57 (Que. Sup. Ct.).

84. *Criminal Code*, s. 457(2),(3) [now s. 515(2),(3)].

85. *R. v. Cichanski; Frasier v. The Queen.*

86. *Criminal Code*, s. 457(2.1) [now s. 515(2.1)]; *R. v. Cichanski*, at 86; *R. v. Dubois (2)* (1983) 8 CCC 3d 344 (Que. Sup. Ct.), at 350.

87. *Criminal Code*, s. 457(2)(c), (C.1),(d) [now s. 515(2)(c),(c.1),(d)].

88. *R. v. Mackie.*

89. *R. v. Martin (2)* (1980) 57 CCC 2d 31 (Ont. C.A. in Chambers).

90. *R. v. Sandhu; R. v. Leclair* (1978) 39 CCC 2d 461 (Ont. Prov. Ct.); *R. v. Whalen* (1980) 57 CCC 2d 10.

91. *Criminal Code*, s. 457(2)(d) [now s. 515(2)(d)].

92. Ibid., s. 457(2)(c.1) [now s. 515(2)(c.1)].

93. Clay M. Powell, *Arrest and Bail in Canada*, 2nd ed. (Toronto: Butterworths, 1976), p. 29.

94. *Criminal Code*, s. 457(2)(c.1) [now s. 515(2)(c.1)]; for example: *Fraser v. The Queen; R. v. Cichanski; R. v. Wolf* (1982) 65 CCC 2d 331 (Alta. Q.B.)

95. *Fraser v. The Queen.*

96. *Criminal Code*, s. 457(2)(c),(c.1),(d) [now s. 515(2)(c),(c.1)(d)].

97. *R. v. Frenette* (1982) 30 CR 3d 123 (B.C. Co. Ct.); *R. v. Cochrane* (1981) 60 CCC 2d 329 (Sask. D.C.).

98. *Collins v. R.* (1982) 34 CR 3d 283 (Ont. Co. Ct.).

99. *Re Keenan and The Queen* (1979) 57 CCC 2d 267 (Que. C.A.) at 276–279.

100. *Collins v. R.*, at 286.

101. *Criminal Code*, s. 133(3) [now s. 145(3)]; for example see: *R. v. Gillespie* (1984) 16 CCC 3d 140; 42 CR 3d 391 (Ont. C.A.); *Ex Parte Clarke (2)* (1978) 42 CCC 2d 23 (Nfld. S.C.).

102. *Criminal Code*, s. 133(7).

103. Ibid., Form 9.

104. Ibid., s. 704, s. 705 [now s. 770, s. 771].

105. *Criminal Code*, s. 458 [now s. 524]; for example see: *R. v. Clarke* (1978) 41 CCC 2d 390 (Nfld. Prov. Ct.).

106. *Criminal Code*, s. 133, s. 449, s. 450–453, s. 453.1–453.4, s. 455.3–455.6 [now s. 145, s. 494, s. 495–498, s. 499–502, s. 507–510].

107. *Wigglesworth v. The Queen* (1987) 32 CRR 219 (S.C.).

108. *Criminal Code*, s. 457(1),(2),(3),(5),(5.1) [now s. 515(1),(2),(3),(5),(6)].

109. *Criminal Code*, s. 457(1) [now s. 515(1)]; *R. v. Brooks Thompson et al.* (1982) 2 CRR 246 (Ont. H.C.).

110. *Criminal Code*, s. 427, s. 457(1), s. 457(5.1)(d) [now s. 469, s. 515(1), s. 515(6)(d)].

111. Ibid., s. 457(5.1), s. 457.7(1),(2) [now s. 515(6), s. 522(1),(2)].

112. Ibid., s. 457(5.1) [now s. 515(6)].

113. *R. v. Desormeaux* (1979) 48 CCC 2d 396 (Ont. D.C.).

114. *R. v. Pugsley* (1982) 2 CCC 3d 266 (N.S. S.C.).

115. *R. v. Bray* (1983) 2 CCC 3d 325 (Ont. C.A.).

116. *R. v. Dubois (2); R. v. Gervais* (1988) 42 CCC 3d 352 (Que. Sup. Ct.); *Ibrahim v. Attorney General of Canada* (1982) 1 CRR 244 (Que. Sup. Ct.).

117. *R. v. Frankforth* (1982) 70 CCC 2d 448 (B.C. Co. Ct.); *R. v. Lundrigan* (1982) 67 CCC 2d 37 (Man. Prov. J. Ct.).

118. Ibid., at 450–451.

119. Ibid., at 451.

120. *Criminal Code*, s. 457(7) [now s. 515(10)].

121. *R. v. Bray*, at 328–329; *R. v. Lundrigan*, at 40–41.

122. *R. v. Quinn* (1977) 34 CCC 2d 473 (N.S. Co. Ct.).

123. *R. v. Bradley and Bickerdike* (1977) 38 CCC 2d 283 (Que. Sup. Ct.), at 287; *R. v. Dubois (2); R. v. Lundrigan.*

124. *R. v. Bray; R. v. Gervais; R. v. Sparks* (1982) unreported (N.S. Prov. Ct.), at 19, 22; *R. v. Dhindsa* (1986) 30 CCC 3d 268 (B.C. S.C.); *R. v. Bradley and Bickerdike.*

125. *R. v. Bradley and Bickerdike*, at 289.

126. See, for example, *R. v. Gervais; R. v. Dhindsa; Ibrahim v. A.-G.; R. v. Fortin et al* (1982) 2 CRR 67 (Ont. Co. Ct.), at 69–71; *R. v. Bradley and Bickerdike*, at 290–291.

127. (1972) 9 CCC 2d 533.

128. Ibid.

129. *R. v. Dhindsa*, at 379; *R. v. Spek* (1983) 4 CRR 67 (B.C. C.A.).

130. *Criminal Code*, s. 457(5),(5.1) [now s. 515(5),(6)].

131. *R. v. Bradley and Bickerdike*, at 289.

132. 132. *Criminal Code*, s. 457.3(1)(a),(c),(d),(e) [now s. 518(1)(a),(c),(d),(e)].

133. *R. v. Gervais*, at 367, 377.

134. *R. v. Dubois (2)*, at 349.

135. *R. v. Bradley and Bickerdike*, at 288–289; *R. v. Cichanski*, at 85–86.

136. *R. v. Okanee* (1981) 59 CCC 2d 149 (Sask. C.A.); *Criminal Code*, s. 735.

137. *Criminal Code*, s. 454 [now s. 503].

138. *R. v. Hay* (1986) 30 CRR 96 (Alta. Q.B.); *R. v. Kime* (1985) 16 CRR 31 (Sask. Prov. Ct.); *R. v. Erickson* (1984) 12 CRR 193 (B.C. C.A.); *R. v. Farncombe* (1984) 34 Sask. R 161 (Sask. Q.B.).

139. *R. v. Erickson*, at 199–200.

140. *R. v. Hay*, at 103–105; *R. v. Erickson.*

141. For example, *Re R. and Tabish* (1977) 37 CCC 2d 363 (B.C. S.C.).

142. *R. v. Erickson; R. v. Bazoni* (1983) 33 CR 3d 272 (Ont. C.A.); *Re R. and Kennedy* (1982) 1 CCC 3d 90 (Alta. C.A.); *Re MacDonald and The Queen* 3 CCC 3d 458 (Ont. H.C.).

143. *Criminal Code*, s. 457(1), s. 457.1 [now s. 515(1), s. 516].

144. *R. v. Khabra* (1978) 39 CCC 2d 475 (B.C. S.C.).

145. *Criminal Code*, s. 459(1) [now s. 525(1)]; *R. v. Gouveia* (1982) 1 CCC 3d 143 (Ont. H.C.).

146. *Criminal Code*, s. 457.5 [now s. 520]; *R. v. English* (1983) 8 CCC 3d 487 (Ont. Co. Ct.); *R. v. Saswirski* (1984) 17 CCC 3d 341 (Ont. H.C.); *R. v. Gouveia.*

147. *Criminal Code*, s. 457.8(2) [now s. 523(2)]; *R. v. Johnson* (1984) 13 CCC 3d 441 (N.T. S.C.); *R. v. Lee* (1982) 1 CRR 241 (B.C. S.C.).

148. *Criminal Code*, s. 457.7(2.2), s. 457.8(2)(c)(ii)-(iii) [now s. 522(4), s. 523(2)(c)(ii)-(iii)]; *R. v. Patterson* (1985) 19 CCC 3d 149 (Alta. C.A.); *R. v. Cook* (1986) 26 CCC 3d 188 (Ont. C.A.); *R. v. Martin (2); R. v. Yanover* (1982) 37 OR 2d 647 (H.C.).

149. *Ex parte Clarke (2); Re Keenan and The Queen; Re Kot and The Queen* (1983) 10 CCC 3d 297 (Ont. H.C.).

150. *R. v. Lee; R. v. Brooks Thompson, et al.*

151. *Criminal Code*, s. 457.6 [now s. 521]; *R. v. Bradley and Bickerdike; R. v. Morgan* (1978) 43 CCC 2d 550 (Que. Sup. Ct.); *R. v. Gouvia; R. v. Dhindsa.*

152. *Criminal Code*, s. 696–707 [now s. 762–773]; *R. v. Whalen; R. v. Leclaire; R. v. Coles* (1982) 2 CCC 3d 65 (B.C. C.A.); *R. v. Clarke (1); R. v. Pellerin; R. v. Cochrain; R. v. Frenette; R. v. Wolf; R. v. Sandu.*

153. *Tremblay v. R.* (1985) 17 CRR 309 (Sask. Q.B.).

154. *Criminal Code*, s. 457.2 [now s. 517]; *Re Smith* (1984) 38 CR 3d 209 at 221–228 (Ont. C.A.).

155. *R. v. Forget and The Queen* (1982) 65 CCC 2d 373 (Ont. C.A.).

156. *Criminal Code*, s. 457.3(1)(b) [now s. 518(1)(b)].

157. *Re Deom, et al. and The Queen* (1981) 64 CCC 2d 222 (B.C. S.C.); *R. v. Paonessa and Paquette* (1982) 66 CCC 2d 300 (Ont. C.A.).

158. *Millar v. R.* (1984) 36 CR 3d 102 (Que. Sup. Ct.).

159. For example, in twenty-four of the cases between 1976 and 1988 used here for their legal points, the terms of bail, either as originally granted or as resulting from the proceeding reported, are unequivocally stated. Of these, seventeen involved recognizances without cash deposit (twelve of these are with sureties and conditions, four are with sureties but no conditions, one is with conditions but no sureties). Six cases involve a cash deposit. In one, release was on a simple undertaking.

160. Parliament of New South Wales, *Report of the Bail Review Committee* (Sydney: 1976), pp. 14–21.

161. *Bail Act 1978* (N.S.W.), s. 37.

162. 162. Ibid., s. 36.

163. Ibid., s. 51.

164. Ibid., s. 50.

165. *R. v. Richards* [1981] 2 NSWLR 464 (Ct. C.A.).

166. New South Wales Bureau of Crime Statistics and Research, *Bail Reform in New South Wales* (Sydney: Bureau of Crime Statistics, 1984), Tabs. 20, 21. See also, F. E. Devine, *Bail in Australia* (Phillip, A.C.T.: Australian Institute of Criminology, 1989), pp. 14–18.

167. New South Wales Bureau of Crime Statistics and Research, *Court Statistics 1982–1986* (Sydney: Bureau of Crime Statistics, 1983–1987), Tab. 15.

168. *Bail Act 1978* (N.S.W., s. 8, s. 51.

169. Ibid., s. 8(2)(b).

170. Ibid., s. 9(1)–(2), s. 32. See also Devine, *Bail in Australia*, pp. 3, 7–8.

171. New South Wales Bureau of Crime Statistics and Research, *Court Statistics 1984, 1985, 1986* (Sydney: 1985, 1986, 1987), Tab. 2.9.

172. *Bail (Scotland) Act 1980*, s. 2.

173. *MacNeill v. Milne* (1984) 1984 SCCR 427 (H.C.J.).

174. *Bail (Scotland) Act 1980*, s. 1(a), s. 3, s. 4.

175. Ibid., s. 3, s. 5.

176. Ibid., s. 3(1)(b)–3(2).

177. *H.M. Advocate v. Crawford* (1984) 1985 SLT 242 (H.C.J.); *MacNeill v. Milne*, at 429 (comment); *MacNeill v. Smith* (1982) 1984 SLT 63 (S.C.).

178. *Criminal Procedure (Scotland) Act 1975*, s. 28, s. 35; J. B. Stewart, "Bail on Murder Charges," *Scots Law Times* (5 Feb. 1988): 45–57.

179. *Smith v. McC* (1982) 1982 SCCR 115 (H.C.J.), 185.

180. *Criminal Procedure (Scotland) Act*, s. 26(2), s. 28; *Gibbons, Petitioner* (1988) 1988 SLT 657 (H.C.J.); *Tin Fan Lau, Petitioner* (1986) 1986 SLT 535, 1986 SCCR 140 (H.C.J.); *H.M. Advocate v. Keegan* (1980) 1981 SLT 35 (H.C.J.).

6

The Nonfinancial Conditions Alternative

A third alternative to commercial bail bonding substitutes the use of nonfinancial bail conditions for financial liability as its principal method of securing appearance. By controlling the behavior of the accused pending trial, this approach aims at making absconding difficult or impossible. Other objectives such as the protection of witnesses or evidence or the prevention of repeat crimes may also be sought. If financially oriented bail systems are analogous to a deterrent theory of punishment, this approach is analogous to an incapacitation theory. The non-financial conditions approach is often combined with a criminal penalties element, so that if the conditions do not succeed some sanction remains. Where this occurs, although the principles of the systems are quite distinct, which element is primary can be extremely difficult to discern. More elaborate statistics than are usually kept would be required on both conditions imposed and prosecution for absconding. In spite of this difficulty, however, two jurisdictions—the Northern Territory of Australia and the lower courts of New Zealand—provide good examples of bail laws structured to rely principally upon this form of bail. In addition to these, many jurisdictions regardless of their principal bail form use nonfinancial conditions of bail as a secondary or supplementary means of enforcing bail obligations.

AUSTRALIA: NORTHERN TERRITORY

Background

Of all bail laws rooted in the common law traditions, the *Bail Act 1982* of the Northern Territory of Australia provides the clearest example of a statute giving primacy to nonfinancial conditions in the bail system it establishes. Illustrative of the connection between the two types of bail, this law was based on the New South Wales law discussed under the criminal penalty systems in Chapter 5. One major difference between the two laws accounts for their different classification. The Northern Territory's law does not make absconding a criminal offense. The original reasons for this deviation from the New South Wales pattern are obscure and may even have been inadvertent. However, when in 1987 a proposal was made by the police to introduce criminal penalties, it was opposed by aboriginal groups on the grounds that it unfairly imposed white time concepts on them. At this point—if not previously—an approach to bail that excluded criminal punishments became deliberate policy.[1]

Terms of Bail

The Northern Territory's *Bail Act 1982*, like that of New South Wales *Bail Act 1978*, provides that bail conditions can be imposed only if the court considering bail is of the opinion that they serve the purpose of promoting effective law enforcement and the protection and welfare of the community. Where conditions do not aid these interests, bail should be unconditional. Where the accused's undertaking to appear is to be enforced by some sanction, the law provides a list of the alternatives which are authorized. Only these may be imposed. The list is hierarchichally arranged from the least to the most onerous.[2]

Two provisions of the law establish the priority it places on nonfinancial over financial conditions. The first such clause establishes a principle of minimal burdensomeness in bail conditions. Conditions may not be imposed that are more onerous for the accused than are warranted by the nature of the offense and the circumstances of the accused. The second such clause explicitly gives preference to the employment of nonfinancial conditions. If the goals of effective law enforcement and the protection and welfare of the community can be secured by any combination of specified requirements regarding the accused's conduct while on bail, conduct constraint alone may be imposed. Only where a court is of the opinion that these cannot secure the goals can resort be had to other conditions. Financial requirements, whether in the form of giving security or depositing money, are specifically singled out for this limitation. The accused and any other party involved securing the bail are entitled to a copy of the conditions or a notice giving them. This applies also to variation of conditions.

Even the first supplementary option available to courts is nonfinancial in nature. They may require one or more acceptable third parties acquainted with the defendant who are willing to state that he is responsible and likely to comply with the undertaking to appear as required. Which individuals or classes of persons are acceptable for this purpose and the number required is placed at the discretion of the court.[3] Willfully making a statement under this provision knowing it to be false in any material particular is made an offense. Punishment is fixed at two years' imprisonment or a $2,000 fine. The court receiving this statement has the duty of warning the person making it of the offense. However, its failure to so warn is not a defense for having made the statement.[4]

If the court remains of the opinion that no combination of these nonfinancial conditions can secure the two goals, financial conditions can be employed. As with the nonfinancial conditions, none may be progressed to unless prior ones are deemed inadequate. The burden imposed on the accused must be minimized. Financial conditions in order of their onerousness—and consequent availability—are the following:

1. The accused's recognizance
2. The accused's recognizance with one or more sureties
3. The accused's security deposit
4. One or more sureties' security deposits
5. The accused's cash deposit
6. One or more sureties' cash deposits[5]

The nature and sufficiency of security deposited under the options for deposit of other than cash (i.e., numbers 3 and 4) are at the court's discretion.[6] As discussed previously, indemnifying or agreeing to indemnify a surety is an offense according to the *Bail Act*.[7] In general, where financial conditions are imposed they are enforced as in recognizance and financial security deposit systems.

Given the *Bail Act*'s emphasis on nonfinancial conditions, arrest for absconding or breach of conditions takes on particular importance. Arrest is aided by the geography and population patterns of the jurisdiction.[8] It may be made by a member of the police force who believes on reasonable grounds that a person released on bail has failed or is about to fail to appear as required or to comply with a condition of bail. The accused must be brought before the court as soon as is practicable. Arrest with a warrant is also authorized. A warrant or a summons may be issued by a magistrate on the same grounds.[9]

Once before the court, several options exist for dealing with the bail violator. Bail may be continued on its original terms or it may be revoked. Once revoked, new bail may be granted on any terms permitted by the act. Alternatively, further bail may be refused and the violator committed to prison, regardless of what his initial rights regarding bail might have been. The law does not, however, limit the right of a bail violator once in custody to again apply for bail.[10]

Eligibility for Bail

Eligibility for bail is a major area of difference between the Northern Territory's bail law and its New South Wales model. The law in the former jurisdiction contains no right to bail for minor offenses as does the latter. However, it too creates a broad presumption of bail. All offenses except murder and treason are covered by this presumption. A pretrial defendant on any other charge is entitled to be granted bail unless the court is satisfied that a consideration specified in the law justifies the denial of bail. Bail must be granted to anyone accused of offenses which qualify for it, even if he is in custody awaiting trial on another matter for which he is not entitled to bail.[11]

An accused not entitled to bail may still be granted it at the court's discretion. However, if the evidence in a murder case is such that the accused might be convicted on it, bail is rarely granted. It will be refused unless the accused can show special or unusual circumstances justifying granting it. The onus is on the accused to establish the exceptional situation.[12]

Considerations for Denying Bail

The Northern Territory's *Bail Act* specifies four considerations which are to be assessed, in so far as they can reasonably be ascertained, in the decision to grant or deny bail. They are, moreover, the only matters to be considered. A negative evaluation of one of the four suffices to defeat a presumption of bail that would otherwise exist. Moreover, under each consideration an exclusive list of the factors to be taken into account in its assessment is detailed.

The first of the bail considerations is the probability of the accused's appearing in court if released on bail. The factors indicative of this begin with that person's background and community ties. These are evidenced, in turn, by the individual's history and specifics regarding residence, employment, and family situations, and—if known—by his criminal record. Another such factor is any previous failure to appear in court as required by bail. A further indicator are the circumstances of the offense. These include its nature and seriousness, the strength of the prosecution's evidence, and the severity of the probable penalties. Finally, any specific evidence indicating the probability of the accused's appearance may be considered.[13]

Second among the bail considerations is the interest of the accused. The permissible factors here begin with the length of period of custody that would result from refusing bail and the conditions under which the detention would be experienced. The accused's need to be free to prepare for court or obtain legal advice and the need to be free for any other lawful purpose may be considered. Lastly, the consideration of whether the accused is incapacitated by intoxication, injury, or drugs, or is otherwise in danger of physical injury or in need of protection, may enter the evaluation of the accused's interests.

The third consideration in the bail decision is the protection and welfare of the community. The factors allowed to be considered here are any previous failure or arrest for an anticipated failure to observe a bail condition in the present case; the likelihood of the accused interfering with evidence, witnesses, or jurors; and the likelihood that if released the accused will commit another offense. A final factor included in the Northern Territory's law which differs from that of New South Wales' law arises where an offense is committed against or in respect of a child. In offenses where this element appears, the likelihood of injury or danger to the child if bail is granted may be considered.[14]

In assessing these considerations the court may consider any evidence that it believes to be credible or trustworthy, including hearsay. The test under the statute for this, and all decisions regarding bail, is the balance of probabilities.[15]

Procedural Considerations

Since a bail system relying principally on nonfinancial conditions does not require any unique procedures, the only procedural considerations under the Northern Territory's system requiring mention are those implementing the presumption of bail. When the matter of court bail is not avoided altogether by the use of summons or bail by the police, a member of the police force who arrests or charges an individual must, if practicable, bring that person before a magistrate forthwith. Deliberate delay in bringing a person arrested before a court is an offense punishable by up to two years' imprisonment. The court is required to deal with bail applications made by the accused as soon as is reasonably practicable. The number of bail applications that may be made is not limited; however, a court may refuse to entertain those that are frivolous or vexatious.[16]

Bail application may also be made to the Supreme Court, and provision is made for either prosecution or defense to seek review of bail decisions by the Supreme Court. One magistrate may not review another bail decision. Review is by way of rehearing. Additional evidence may be used. The bail decision may be affirmed, altered, or varied, including changing of conditions.[17]

Summary

Australia's Northern Territory, then, provides in its *Bail Act 1982* an archetypical example of a bail law giving primacy to nonfinancial conditions. Unlike its exemplar in New South Wales, it does not provide a criminal punishment fallback. Nevertheless, courts addressing bail are required by the law to consider two levels of nonfinancial conditions before resorting to financial ones. With the first of these the accused's appearance is secured by conditions of conduct imposed to incapacitate escape; with the second a person acceptable to the court who knows the accused must be brought forward. This person must be willing to assert under the threat of criminal penalties that the accused is reliable and will appear. Violation of bail conditions, or even the presence of reasonable grounds to believe they will be violated, can lead to rearrest. This in turn precipitates the possibility of bail being refused or granted only under more severe conditions either of conduct or of financial liability. Bail statistics are unfortunately not kept for the Northern Territory. Moreover, the cases on bail reported from the jurisdiction are too few to support even tentative conclusions about the results produced by the law in practice.

NEW ZEALAND

Background

New Zealand law creates a bail system in its lower courts that is in some respects an even stricter version of a nonfinancial conditions system than in the Australian Northern Territory. Although this system does not apply to bail granted by the country's superior courts, since the lower courts handle most bails, it constitutes also the dominant bail system for the country as a whole. In terms of statutory structure also the New Zealand approach to nonfinancial conditions differs considerably from the Australian jurisdiction discussed.

Prior to a 1987 amendment to the *Summary Proceedings Act*, New Zealand's bail system in all levels of courts was of a traditional recognizance type.[18] Courts had been held to have no authority under either statutory or common law to require cash deposits.[19] Indemnification of sureties was illegal.[20] The only nonfinancial condition authorized in the statute governing the lower courts was periodic reporting to the police by the accused; the superior courts occasionally imposed other nonfinancial conditions. Arrest warrants could be issued for those who absconded, were about to abscond, or failed to report to the police or appear in court as required.[21] A 1974 study in Wellington indicated that 60.7 percent of those remanded on bail in a magistrates' court were released on their own recognizance only. Reporting to the police was required in addition in 21.6 percent of the 664 cases studied. Securities were added to the recognizance in 10.2 percent of cases. All three sanctions were employed in 7.5 percent.[22]

The 1987 alteration in the New Zealand bail law took the deceptively simple form of an amendment replacing several sections of the *Summary Proceedings Act*. The result, however, was a bail system restructured on new principles. In many important respects—although not all—the amendments followed the recommendation of the Criminal Reform Committee's 1982 *Report on Bail.*

Terms of Bail

The *Summary Proceedings Amendment Act (2) 1987* makes fundamental changes in four areas that completely revamped the orientation of the New Zealand bail system then existing in the lower courts (District Courts). The first such area of change is the enlargement of the courts' powers to subject bail to conditions of conduct. Beyond conditioning bail on appearance in court as required, reporting to the police is retained as the one condition singled out for specific authorization. However, in addition to reporting, broad powers are created to impose any other conditions that the court considers reasonably necessary to ensure that the accused meets specified objectives of bail. Three of these are designated—the same three encountered in most jurisdictions worldwide. Conditions must be reasonably necessary to ensure that the defendant does appear in court on the date specified, does not interfere with witnesses or evidence, and does not commit any offense while on bail. Power to vary conditions is also conferred.[23] The form specified in the regulations pursuant to the act for certifying the grant of bail reinforces the emphasis placed by the law on nonfinancial conditions. The new form facilitates and encourages the imposition of conditions by certifying that bail is granted subject to certain conditions. Space is provided on the form for specifying conditions.[24]

The second area of change created by the amendment is the removal from the lower courts of their previous authority to impose financial terms of bail. This is accomplished by restriction on their newly created power to impose further bail conditions. The restriction simply states that courts shall not require as a condition of release any deposit, recognizance, guarantee, or surety from either a defendant or a third party.[25] Complementing and corresponding to the withdrawal of the power to require financial conditions of bail, the previous authorization of the lower courts to forfeit recognizances is abolished also.[26] Since financial conditions are unavailable in the lower courts, they obviously cannot be used to enforce nonfinancial conditions. Moreover, even in drug-dealing cases bailable only in the superior courts (High Court), requiring of sureties for conditions of conduct is forbidden by statute, although forfeiture of the accused's recognizance for countervening them is not. Thus, in the lower courts and to this extent in these drug cases, arrest and change of bail terms including outright denial is the sanction provided to enforce conditions.

The third major alteration of the New Zealand bail law regards the arrest of bail violators. The previously existing power of the lower courts to issue warrants for the arrest of absconders, those about to abscond, and those failing to appear in court as required is retained.[27] A further authorization is added by the amendment. Under the new provision, police are empowered to arrest without a warrant anyone absconding or about to abscond. The standard is reasonable grounds to believe that either of these situations is present. In addition—reflecting the new emphasis on nonfinancial conditions—they may arrest without a warrant anyone who they have reasonable grounds to believe contravened or failed to comply with bail conditions. They are then required to bring the individual before a judge as soon as possible. Reconsideration of bail is then mandated if the judge is satisfied that this defendant has absconded or was about to abscond or has contravened or failed to comply with bail conditions. Granting of bail under these circumstances is completely discretionary, regardless of what rights might previously have pertained.[28]

The final major change affected by the 1987 legislation was the creation of a criminal penalties sanction against absconders. An accused who fails without reasonable excuse to appear in court as required commits an offense. This is subject to summary conviction only. The penalty provided is up to a year's imprisonment or a fine not exceeding $2,000.[29]

Putting together these elements of the reformed New Zealand bail law results in an approach to bail in the lower courts quite altered from the earlier recognizance system. All forms of financially secured bail are eliminated. This includes the recognizance alternative with or without sureties traditional in that country, as well as the already forbidden financial deposit approach. Instead, the availability of nonfinancial conditions is enhanced and their use encouraged. At the same time, the primacy among these of reporting to police is to some degree suggested. Arrest is made more readily available as a recourse not only for absconding or its threat but also for violating nonfinancial conditions. Linked to arrest is the threat of possible loss of bail by the accused. Backing up this structure, the threat of criminal punishment has been added for absconders.

Under this system financially secured bail is only available to the superior courts and therefore available exclusively for a small number of the most serious crimes where only these courts can grant bail, or in cases of appeal or reapplication to these courts. The last of these presupposes bail has been denied or granted on unacceptable conditions by a lower court. This mechanism therefore acts to compel evaluation of the special necessity for financial conditions mandated by those systems—such as the Northern Territory, New South Wales, and Canada—that provide a hierarchical list of alternative conditions. The mechanism also limits the number of cases in which financial bail terms can even be considered.

Where superior courts do employ financial conditions, they are limited to recognizance with or without sureties. Their powers to forfeit these remain intact. The previously existing bans on cash deposits and on indemnified sureties remain. These courts also retain their power to impose nonfinancial conditions of bail.[30]

Eligibility for Bail

Under New Zealand law no offense is, in itself, totally precluded from bail, although a few are reserved for bail by a superior court judge only. Those accused of treason, communicating governmental secrets, or drug dealing (Class A and B drugs) may not be granted bail in a lower court.[31]

An extensive right to be granted bail before trial is created by statute. The basic criterion governing this right to bail is that anyone charged with an offense not punishable by death or by the maximum possible imprisonment of three years or more is bailable as of right.[32] Exceptions to this basic criterion exist in both directions. Anyone previously convicted of an offense punishable by death or imprisonment loses the right to bail. Likewise, anyone arrested for absconding or being about to abscond or for failing to comply with a bail condition, upon the court's being satisfied that one of these has been established, loses the right to bail.[33] Offenses involving assault on a child or on a female by a male are not covered by the bail right even if the punishment is less than three years. Conversely, about a dozen offenses are bailable of right even though the maximum penalty exceeds three years. None of these are offenses of violence or of theft and several are offenses of omission (e.g., failure to provide necessaries of life). Probably the most common of them is making false statements or declarations.[34]

The law makes explicit that any offense not bailable of right is bailable at the court's discretion.[35] Case law in New Zealand adds to the statutory right to bail a presumption of, or *prima facie* right to, bail for discretionary cases. This is based upon the courts' interest in protecting the presumption of innocence and the right to liberty. In the absence of evidence of a recognized consideration justifying the denial of bail, these principles entitle an accused to be released on bail. The onus of defeating the presumption is on the prosecution by establishing a contrary consideration.[36]

Considerations for Denying Bail

Considerations that constitute an appropriate reason for denying bail when it is discretionary are dictated by common law in New Zealand. The three principal considerations justifying denial of bail in that country are the three commonly observed in other bail systems: if the accused is unlikely to appear for trial, if the accused is likely to offend while on bail, or if the accused is likely to interfere with the course of justice.[37] (A fourth factor, not yet generally listed by authorities, has received some recent recognition in the courts. This is unjustified substantial delay while an accused remains in custody. In *James v. Police* (1986) a defendant was bailed after over three months' custody in spite of a serious charge and risk to the community from his assaultive behavior. The court commented that delay in excess of six weeks without evidence of guilt being taken was intolerable in normal circumstances. It noted that occasionally investigation of a complicated crime might justify such delay. The same considerations apply to drug cases evaluated for bail in the superior courts as to other bails in the lower courts.[38])

Some debate exists not over the existence of the second consideration but over its exact nature. The likelihood of a further offense as a grounds for denial is suggested by some authorities to be limited to the same offense.[39] By some it is construed to have a public interest or public safety component that might limit it to certain types of offenses (e.g., incest, brutal domestic assault, other serious assaults, drug dealing, criminal combinations, housebreaking).[40] In fact, an alternative classification of considerations makes the public interest or safety the essence of the exception and threats of repeated crimes merely the prime instance of its jeopardy.[41] On this grounds a recent case has indicated that on rare occasions release of the accused can be contrary to the public safety other than by the accused's repeating of the crime.[42]

The third consideration, the interests of justice, is constituted principally of two familiar components, tampering with evidence and subverting witnesses.[43] The mere fact that police investigation will be more unfettered if the accused is kept in custody can have no weight in considering bail.[44]

Factors to be taken into account in assessing these considerations have also been expounded to some degree by case law in New Zealand. Greatest attention has been paid to the factors relating to probability of appearance, which in their basics are much as in other countries. Three such factors are regularly cited as the principal ones: the nature of the offense, the strength of the evidence, and the severity of the punishment likely to be imposed in event of conviction.[45] Two authorities give as a fourth factor the extent of the danger that sureties may have been indemnified.[46] This, of course, now is only pertinent in the superior courts. Nevertheless, its listing among factors indicating a risk of absconding tells against commercial provision of bail. A further consideration, rarely listed probably because of its obvious nature, is something in the circumstances providing direct evidence to show that the accused will not appear.[47]

Factors bearing upon the interests of justice and the public safety or danger of a repeated crime have been much less systematically developed. Nevertheless, some can be identified. Among these are the nature of the crime or of the evidence pertinent to it. Some crimes will very probably be repeated if the accused is released; others are unlikely to be.[48] Evidence of some crimes may be retrieved to conceal or used to repeat the crime.[49] Other factors include the accused's record. This might indicate repeated commission of the same crime suggesting further repetitions; alternatively, it might suggest a threat to the public interest or safety.[50] Although the accused's character or particular behavior has been said not to be a factor to be used in considerations of absconding, it may be pertinent to considerations of public interest or safety.[51]

Procedural Considerations

A variety of procedural changes were required to adapt the mechanism of bail to the altered terms of bail in the 1987 amendment. Procedures for the forfeiture of bail recognizances in the lower courts are abolished, reflecting the elimination of recognizances themselves in the lower courts.[52] Reflecting the emphasis on nonfinancial conditions, provision is made for judges of these courts to vary them. If the variation entails only the time and place of reporting to the police, specific other court officers are authorized to make it. Application for variation under this provision is authorized only for the defendant.[53]

Similarly, the legislation altering the bail law creates an appeal for defendants against unacceptable conditions. This appeal is to the High Court against conditions imposed by a District Court. The procedures followed for appeals against summary conviction are applied. Creation of this appeal against conditions does not affect the High Court's already existing power to hear bail applications from those denied bail in the District Court; this remains intact. The newly created appeal complements it so as to provide a remedy in the area of the now possible nonfinancial condition.[54] In contrast, for the drug-dealing cases reserved for bail by the High Court, not only is the defense given an appeal to the Court of Appeal against conditions imposed, but the prosecution is given one against failure or refusal to impose a given condition. The condition, however, will be altered only if in the original decision about conditions discretion was wrongly exercised. Under the provision both parties may also appeal an adverse decision on the granting or refusal of bail.[55] The Court of Appeal in at least two recent cases called attention to its own lack of jurisdiction, except for drug cases, to hear appeals of bail cases reserved for the High Court. In both it suggested that legislation to create jurisdiction be considered.[56]

One procedure bearing upon the right to bail requires comment. A defendant bailable of right who makes no application and is therefore remanded in custody is to be brought before the court upon request to apply. The right to bail is preserved as if it were being made at the time of the original remand.[57]

Results of the System

Statistics demonstrating the results of the New Zealand bail system are not available. Moreover, bail cases where terms can be identified reported since the new law became effective are too few to support conclusions about results.

My own informal observation in Auckland District Court in mid-December 1988 supports the conclusion that the system functions in line with the provisions of the law described here. Bail was granted subject to conditions considerably more often than unconditionally. Reporting to the police was the most common condition; however, other conditions were occasionally imposed. Remand in custody was relatively rare and arrest warrants were invariably issued for those not appearing. One defendant had been bailed by the High Court on a drug-dealing charge and was continued on bail. One defendant who had been arrested after not appearing had the warrant canceled and was granted bail on new terms after providing a satisfactory explanation. Some indirect support for this emphasis on nonfinancial conditions in the New Zealand system is also provided by the study done under the prior bail law. Even under that recognizance-based system 29.1 percent of defendants were given reporting conditions.[58] This indicates the acceptability of that form of condition to the courts. With the law's change of orientation from recognizance to nonfinancial conditions, the conclusion that a substantial part of the almost 71 percent who formerly were bailed by recognizance would now be bailed on conditions of conduct is at the very least plausible.

New Zealand, then, seems to function in fact as a system relying on nonfinancial bail conditions much as its laws indicate it should. Conditions governing the accused's conduct pending trial are, by a clear margin, imposed more often than omitted on bails. Arrest and reconsideration of bail is imposed on violators, and criminal penalties are available as a sanction reinforcing bail appearance where required. Unlike New South Wales, where fairly strong evidence suggests that under a roughly similar law bail is typically granted unconditionally and the threat of punishment is the regular sanction, New Zealand typically relies on imposing nonfinancial conditions and resorts to punishments as further recourse in case they fail.

Summary

New Zealand's bail law is generally similar to the Australian Northern Territory's in that both emphasize nonfinancial conditions as the principal way of compelling appearance in court. Beyond this, however, important variations between the two exist.

New Zealand completely removed the possibility of imposing financial conditions from the lower courts, which handle most bails, so they can only impose nonfinancial conditions, release without conditions, or deny bail completely. This contrasts with the possibility of lower courts in the Australian territory imposing financial bail terms so long as they have first determined the inadequacy of nonfinancial ones. In New Zealand the power of lower courts to deny bail is limited by an extensive statutory right to bail and a common law presumption of it. Nevertheless, if bail is denied it can still be sought from superior courts. In these, recognizances and sureties are available options, although cash deposits are not. Thus, in its bail law New Zealand creates a structural impediment to financial conditions. This compels adherence to the statutory preference emphasizing nonfinancial over financial bail terms in a way that merely listing priorities among bail terms cannot.

New Zealand reinforces its use of nonfinancial conditions with criminal penalties for absconding. In this respect its statute is more like that of New South Wales than that of the Northern Territory. However, with New Zealand the available indications are that the system does predominantly employ the condition of conduct, especially reporting to police, as its first defense against bail violation. This contrasts with criminal penalty systems like New South Wales', where nonfinancial conditions are less frequently imposed and threat of penalties become the main protection against contravention of bail.

OTHER RELATED BAIL SYSTEMS

No other jurisdictions exhibit bail systems functioning principally through nonfinancial conditions; however, most authorize their use in some degree as a secondary bail-enforcing sanction. Probably significantly, of the three countries whose laws are most resistant to imposing nonfinancial conditions of conduct on bail (Philippines, Bangladesh, and Liberia), two are of the American cash deposit heritage. The other is a particularly strict version of the restraints placed on bail conditions under the legal heritage stemming from India.

Among the broad scope of countries employing nonfinancial bail conditions in a secondary capacity, some stand out by the emphasis their laws place on them. These provide the best available supplementary examples of varieties possible to nonfinancial conditions systems. Some of these—England, Canada, New South Wales, and Scotland—have already been discussed. Bail law and practice in two other jurisdictions—the Australian states of Tasmania and South Australia—similarly contribute to an understanding of conditions systems although they themselves are not predominantly of this sort.

Australia: Tasmania

The law governing bail in the lower courts of Tasmania places virtually all alternative bail forms on an equal footing without establishing any statutory preferences. Magistrates, therefore, may impose recognizances, sureties, cash deposits by defendants, and nonfinancial conditions at their discretion. A criminal penalty for bail violation is also created. Of all bail forms, only cash deposits by sureties are not authorized.[59]

In practice, almost two thirds (65 percent) of lower court bails in Tasmania for 1986 were without any conditions.[60] Thus, a system functioning principally by criminal penalties is indicated. Unfortunately, no figures for prosecutions or convictions for bail violations are available, but such prosecutions or convictions are encountered frequently enough to confirm that they are pursued. Of the third of bails in which conditions were imposed, no breakdown into financial and nonfinancial is made. A great majority probably are nonfinancial. As a judge of the Tasmanian Supreme Court observed privately, referring to the island state's geography, if conditions keep defendants away from airports and seaports, where can they go?

The wording of the clause authorizing nonfinancial conditions in the Tasmanian law provides in itself an interesting variation. The authority to impose conditions includes but is not limited to orders controlling the conduct of defendants, requiring them to report at specified times and places, and limiting their movements and social intercourse.[61] The criminal penalties provision is worded so as to allow its use to enforce nonfinancial bail conditions as well as court appearance. Failure to comply with any part of the bail order is punishable by up to three months' imprisonment or a $500 fine.[62] The generality of the wording on conditions has led to some creative conditions, including not entering an airport or seaport. In a drunk driving case, a condition of bail was not driving after consuming alcohol, while in a burglary case an 8:00 P.M. to 7:00 A.M. curfew was imposed. The breadth of wording of the provision has resulted in cases exploring dimensions of the use of conditions frequently not as thoroughly litigated elsewhere.

In considering what conditions may be imposed, the Tasmanian Supreme Court has started from two premises. The permissible conditions are not limited only to those calculated to ensure the accused's appearance in court. Nevertheless, limits must be implied that establish the ambit of restrictions permissibly placed upon defendants' conduct, movements, or social interactions.[63] Conditions should not be imposed for the purpose of restricting the accused's lifestyle while awaiting trial, although a condition is not necessarily impermissible in every case merely because it causes a restriction on the accused's lifestyle.[64] Consequently, conditions may properly be imposed to advance at least all the considerations accepted at common law as grounds pertinent to denying bail.[65] These include the safety and security of the public.[66]

The two elements of public safety mentioned in most jurisdictions as grounds for conditions are also included under Tasmanian law. Conditions designed to ensure noninterference with witnesses and to prevent repetition of the alleged offense or a similar one have been described by the Tasmanian Supreme court as within the ambit and purpose of the law, but these are only examples of many possible conditions contemplated by it.[67] In the attempt to prevent further offenses, the specific conduct prohibited need not in itself constitute an offense, providing the objective in imposing the condition can be inferred to be preventing the offense. Thus, in drink-related driving cases, a condition of not driving with any alcohol in the blood can be within the magistrate's power, providing other standards for imposing the condition are met.[68]

Within this rather general framework, the Tasmanian courts have approached the limitation of bail conditions by stressing the need for attention to the circumstances in the particular case in the exercise of discretion to impose conditions. Conditions must never be allowed to become standard, and should not be imposed as a matter of course unless a given defendant can persuade the court to allow an exemption. Rather, conditions should be imposed only for a reason that leads the court to apprehend a danger to the public interest. The judicial officer should be satisfied of the need or desirability on an individual case basis for imposing any particular condition. Since some considerations have general application and many cases have comparable features, similar conditions may often result. Moreover, a large number of smaller offenses or the need to devote substantial police resources to an area to maintain order may constitute factors in the individual's case appropriate for consideration. This should not obscure, however, magistrates' primary duty to exercise a judicial discretion based on the facts of a given case.[69] Therefore, with zero blood-alcohol conditions, for example, magistrates must direct their minds to the particular circumstances of the defendant's case and find some reason in it for concern about public danger from the defendant's driving irresponsibility.[70]

The result of the requirements for a demonstrable reason to impose bail conditions is that the prosecution must satisfy the court of their desirability. This does not, however, have to be done by a trial-like determination involving formal taking of evidence. The magistrate then has to balance the perceived need for the conditons against any disadvantages they cause the defendant.[71]

A quite different aspect of bail conditions that has been considered in Tasmania's courts arose because of the interaction of two aspects of the law: the use of conditions to prevent repeated offenses and the applicability of the criminal penalties provision to contravention of bail conditions governing conduct. A defendant charged with criminal trespass received bail conditioned on not repeating the trespass. He objected in part on the grounds that this would subject him to double jeopardy: he could be punished both for any further trespass in itself and as a breach of bail conditions. Therefore, by causing this situation, the condition was harsh and oppressive. Stated abstractly, would punishment for the offense to be prevented by a condition both in itself and as a breach of bail constitute double jeopardy so as to render the condition itself harsh and oppressive? The Tasmanian Supreme Court agreed that an accused in such a situation would be liable to double punishment. However, the court noted that in many situations one act could involve the commission of more than one offense, attracting additional punishments. It reasoned that in some circumstances punishing a person twice, once for committing an offense and again for a breach of some independent obligation occasioned by the offense, might be just. In circumstances where double punishment was inappropriate, proper exercise of sentencing discretion could alleviate any injustice. Therefore, the court concluded, the mere fact that the defendant could be prosecuted twice under different laws for violating the condition did not in itself make the condition harsh and oppressive. All the circumstances would have to be considered, however, if he were ultimately to receive double punishment.[72]

Although Tasmania does not rely predominantly upon nonfinancial conditions to prevent absconding, the state bail system does exhibit some interesting facets of that approach. Since the wording of the statute does not specify the permissible limits of conduct to be subject to conditions, this has been done by the courts. Except for setting broad parameters for bail conditions, Tasmanian cases have established limits by stressing the proper use of discretion in evaluating individual cases rather than the more usual emphasis on *a priori* concepts of the proper goals of bail conditions. The reasons for a given condition in the particular case become focal. Perhaps because of this, comparatively unusual conditions, but ones well tailored to exigencies of the cases, seem to be tried.

Since the jurisdiction is one of the minority that uses its criminal punishment provision to enforce violations of conditions other than appearance, it has also had a leading role in considering the relationship between the bail violation punishment and the punishment for a crime which constitutes the violation of bail. Again, so long as discretion is properly applied to the individual facts in sentencing, this double punishment need not be harsh or oppressive.

Australia: South Australia

The State of South Australia also requires consideration of the contribution it makes to understanding nonfinancial bail conditions, although its bail system does not principally rest upon these. The South Australian *Bail Act 1985* itself combines a variety of bail sanctions. Nonfinancial conditions are given preference, but financial ones are available. A criminal penalties clause is included as well. Thus, the law itself could support a system relying principally on either nonfinancial conditions or on criminal penalties. In actuality, strong evidence demonstrates that its early functioning remains as a recognizance system.

The chief published data directly indicating the present reliance on recognizance in South Australia relate to bail status after the final committal hearing (preliminary examination) on offenses to be forwarded for trial in the District Court or the Supreme Court. These are the more serious offenses. Consequently, matters appropriate for handling by nonfinancial conditions would be under-represented. Nevertheless, of the 438 defendants on bail in this context during the second half of 1985, 96 percent were released on recognizance without a cash deposit. Of the 4 percent in other categories, some may have been released on nonfinancial conditions but their release on cash or security deposits or with guarantors (sureties) is much more likely. For the first half of 1986, of 467 individuals bailed in this context, the comparable figures are 97 percent by recognizance without cash deposit and 3 percent on other terms.[73] A study of bail results for all bails in magistrates' courts during 1986 found 48 percent released on recognizance. However, in addition, of those released on bail by police prior to appearing before a magistrate, a recognizance by the accused or a surety was required of 76 percent.[74] Thus, the predominance of recognizance in the jurisdiction is clear. My own informal observations in Adelaide Magistrates' Court in September 1988 confirm the persistence of emphasis on recognizance.

In 1986 the South Australian Office of Crime Statistics concluded that although the legislation provided the framework of a fair and efficient system, administrative problems were undermining the *Bail Act*'s effectiveness for reforming the system. The problem identified as foremost was simply the continuing preference for imposing financial conditions among those administering the law. The office suggested changes in the law's administration that would encourage the use of nonfinancial conditions, discourage the use of financial ones, and emphasize prosecutions for absconding when nonfinancial conditions failed to achieve results.[75] The product of these reforms, if successful, could be a system which relies primarily on nonfinancial conditions and employs criminal punishments as the major secondary sanctions where necessary, much like the New Zealand system.

Since the statute in South Australia could support a principally nonfinancial system, its many innovative features in that regard suggest much about the possible use of nonfinancial conditions. Two provisions of the *Bail Act* emphasize the reliance on nonfinancial conditions. One of these provides that no condition other than one regarding the conduct of the accused while on bail shall be imposed unless necessary to insure compliance with the bail agreement. The other is that no financial conditions shall be imposed unless compliance cannot be secured by one or a combination of nonfinancial conditions.[76]

An anomalous definition of nonfinancial conditions in the act's interpretation section has been used by supporters of recognizance bail to justify the prevalence of bail on the accused's recognizance.[77] This definition includes only security deposits and guarantors (sureties) within the meaning of financial conditions. Whether intentionally or not, the accused's recognizance is omitted from its scope. However, even if this is an intentional omission, the former of the two conditions militates against a prevalence of recognizance bails.

A condition of all bails under the act is not leaving the state without permission for any reason. Permission may be given by a judge, magistrate, ranking member of the police, or person authorized by the Department of Correctional Services if it is charged with the accused's supervision.[78] Although a broad grant of discretionary power to impose conditions on bail is included, several possible conditions are specifically authorized. These begin with residence at a specified address. A stricter alternative requires not leaving the specified address except for paid employment, necessary medical or dental treatment, averting or minimizing a serious risk of death or injury to the accused or another, or other purpose approved by an officer of the Department of Correctional Services.[79] Where a residence requirement is imposed, a power to search to ascertain compliance is created. A fine is imposed for hindering such a search.[80]

Other specifically authorized conditions of conduct are reporting to the police at specified times and places, surrendering passports, and conditions for the physical protection of the victim. The accused, as a condition of conduct, may also be required to place himself under the supervision of an officer of the Department of Correctional Services and obey the directions of that officer.[81] The correctional officer is authorized to give reasonable directions about reporting, notification of any change of residence or employment, and any other matter stipulated by the court (or police officer) granting bail.[82] In selecting conditions, courts are enjoined to give special consideration to any submissions made by the prosecution on behalf of victims.[83]

Only after exhausting these conditions of conduct can other conditions including financial ones be considered. Thus, a wide range of nonfinancial conditions are given priority. Two further provisions of the law have, however, nearly nullified use of the home detention and supervision alternatives in the lower courts.[84] These are a requirement for prosecution consent and another for a Department of Correctional Services report (which may be oral) before the imposition of these conditions.[85] Although advocates for prosecution and defense agree that these requirements render the conditions practically unusable in the lower courts, they disagree over why this is so. Those who are prosecution oriented claim that the delay necessary to obtain the report is opposed by the defense. The defense-oriented claim that police prosecutors in the lower courts who have already opposed bail are unwilling to consent to the alternatives.[86]

Complementing this wide range of alternative conditions to control conduct, one other nonfinancial condition of bail comparable to one observed in the Northern Territory is specifically provided by the law. A bail applicant in South Australia can be required to provide a stipulated number of persons acceptable to the court who will provide written assurances that they are acquainted with the accused and that they are confident that he will comply with the terms and conditions of bail.[87] This is rarely done, apparently because of the perception that there are no procedures available in event of noncompliance.[88] A penalty for making false statements in this capacity, as in the Northern Territory, might help to ameliorate this problem. This might be done by extending to these persons the present penalty for false statements by the accused on the bail application. Also helpful might be extending to these individuals the existing South Australian criminal punishment—a fine of up to $1,000—for financial guarantors who knowing, or having reasonable suspicion, that their accused has failed to comply with bail conditions do not notify the police.[89]

Beyond the nonfinancial conditions, four levels of financial conditions are created by the South Australian bail law. Forfeiture can be incurred both by absconding and by contravening conditions. As in most jurisdictions, these begin with the accused's recognizance and escalate through a cash security deposit to one or more guarantors, or sureties. The state's is among those systems that also allow at the upper end of the scale a security deposit to be required of sureties. All deposits may be in money or valuables.[90]

As a final recourse, a criminal offense is created for contravening or failing to comply with a term or condition of bail without reasonable excuse. This wording places South Australia among the jurisdictions where violation of bail conditions as well as absconding can be punished. Several facets of this aspect of the law are unique and informative. The punishment is placed at a period of imprisonment equal to that for the principal offense upon which bail was granted. However, a maximum limit of three years is imposed on potential punishments under the clause. If more than one offense is charged, the single offense carrying the highest penalty determines the limit. A cumulative calculation of sentences is not used. However, the law explicitly provides that the punishment is in addition to any pecuniary forfeiture incurred by the violation of bail. The statute provides that these bail offenses should not be heard until after the proceedings for the main offense unless the offender elects or a court orders an earlier determination. The usual authority for arrest of bail violators with and without a warrant is applied.[91]

In reality, bail violators are rarely prosecuted. A practice is in place against both charging violators and seeking forfeiture.[92] Consequently, since recognizances are being used, prosecutions are not. For the nine months beginning in July 1985 only thirty-five prosecutions were reported.[93] Thirty prosecutions occurred during the second half of 1986. In 1987 prosecutions on bail violations dropped to twenty for the entire year.[94] This sparseness of prosecutions reflects the continued preference for monetary over nonfinancial bail conditions.

The problem of the definition of nonfinancial conditions and the practical difficulties of imposing the two most restrictive conditions in lower courts are the chief legislative impediment to South Australia's bail system functioning principally by nonfinancial conditions. However, neither absolutely precludes it. Much of the attention of bail-reform advocates in the state is, therefore, devoted to problems not with the law itself but with its administration. Particular attention is focused on the innovations in the 1985 act and its 1987 amendment which are underutilized. Some of the changes in usage recommended are encouragement of prosecutions for bail violations to diminish reliance on recognizance or security forfeitures, making courts more aware of the option of supervised bail in order to strengthen administrative procedure to implement it, and changing police standing orders to emphasize that financial bail conditions should be used only in exceptional circumstances.

One area of apparent success for reform is that of alteration of the bail forms. The old forms were in essence forms for recognizance with sureties. Nonfinancial alternatives were listed last, appearing to be a supplement to financial considerations. Bail decisions were obviously structured accordingly. The new form (at least in the proposed draft version) warns of liability to arrest and of conviction for an offense along with forfeiture. A checklist of nonfinancial conditions is provided, and only then does the range of financial terms begin.[95] The new forms are thus clearly more suitable for the altered emphasis. Should the proposed changes take place, this South Australian bail system could well be converted from what is in practice a recognizance system to a nonfinancial conditions system backed by criminal penalties.

A few salient points about eligibility for bail under South Australian law deserve comment. The jurisdiction starts from a presumption of bail from which no offense is specifically exempted. Under this presumption, bail should be granted unless in the light of a set of listed conditions the court considers that the individual should not be bailed. The only consideration included that is unusual is any need a victim of the offense may have, whether real or perceived, for physical protection from the bail applicant.[96]

In implementing this presumption, police are obliged to take reasonable steps to ensure that arrested persons understand their right to apply for bail. A written statement in a prescribed form explaining how and to whom a bail application may be made must also be provided, along with application forms. If bail is not granted by police, the accused must be brought before a magistrate as soon as possible on the next working day and in any event before noon. The magistrate then is to inquire if the person wishes to apply for bail.[97] A procedure is also provided for a magistrate to review by telephone an unsatisfactory bail decision by police where no magistrate in the vicinity is immediately available.[98]

South Australia might well be viewed as a jurisdiction whose law has been changed to emphasize nonfinancial bail conditions but whose practices in administering the law have not caught up to the change. The situation is instructive of the needs for various administrative changes if such an approach to bail is to exist. The need for a range of restrictions on conduct include—with proper safeguards to establish necessity—some viable, highly restrictive ones. The difficulties in imposing the more restrictive conditions of the South Australian law seem likely to encourage the substitution of financial conditions. A mild irony appears in the push of bail reformers in the jurisdiction for more prosecutions for bail violations. However, the perception that this is necessary to reduce dependence on financial forfeiture is well founded. Finally, this law's application of the criminal punishments to violations of bail conditions short of absconding could well serve as an early defense against that eventuality, but prosecution of them would have to be pursued with regularity.

CONCLUSION

The bail systems that place a predominant reliance for preventing absconding upon nonfinancial conditions are among the best insulated of all bail formats against the possibility of commercial bail bonding. Related systems, to whatever degree they employ the alternative, participate in this protection. Not only does the approach preclude commercial bail by eliminating the need to secure financial resources for bail, but it focuses attention in the bail decision on the hindrances to absconding or other objectionable conduct that could be effective in the particular case.

However preponderantly a jurisdiction relies on nonfinancial conditions, all such systems nonetheless introduce some alternative bail form for dubious cases or criminal penalties, for instance where the nonfinancial conditions fail in their objectives. Re-arrest and reconsideration of bail is never left as the only further sanction, although it is universally available in this type of bail. Use of criminal penalties as the further sanction rather than resort to financial bail better protects against commercial provision of bail. Where both of these are available the South Australian experience demonstrates two points. Prosecutions must be reliably pursued or financial bails will receive preference. The more restrictive conditions of conduct should not depend upon prosecutorial consent or financial bail, or denial of bail will be substituted.

Certain variations of detail enhance the use of conditions of conduct in bails. By in effect reserving financial bail to the superior courts, the New Zealand system has several advantages over the alternative approach of listing priorities in favor of nonfinancial bail but permitting lower courts to resort to financial bail. Since the nonfinancial conditions are the principal variable for a range of offenses among bail terms, they receive serious attention. Nevertheless, in cases where bail is acceptable only on financial terms, the mechanism is available to have them considered in the higher courts where often more information is available and a fuller hearing is possible.

Subjecting violations of nonfinancial conditions to criminal penalties also is a variation enhancing their usefulness. This possibility is created in South Australia and Tasmania. It provides both an early defense against absconding and a deterrent against other misconduct during the bail period. It thus has obvious potential to increase the usefulness of, and therefore the reliance upon, nonfinancial conditions of conduct in bail.

NOTES

1. Telephone interview with Simon Wells, Office of the Director of Public Prosecutions (Darwin), 12 November 1988.
2. *Bail Act 1982*, s. 25, s. 27, s. 28.
3. Ibid., s. 27(2)(a)(b), s. 27(3), s. 28, s. 42.
4. Ibid., s. 44.
5. Ibid., s. 27(2)(c)-(h).

6. Ibid., s. 27(3)(b).
7. Ibid., s. 45.
8. Wells.
9. *Bail Act*, s. 38.
10. Ibid.
11. Ibid., s. 8
12. Ibid., s. 12; *McKinlay v. Young*, 68 FLR 66 (S.C. N.T., 1983), at 67, 69.
13. *Bail Act*, s. 1(a).
14. Ibid., s. 24(1).
15. Ibid., s. 24(2), s. 46.
16. *Bail Act*, s. 16(1), s. 19; *Criminal Code 1983*, s. 106.
17. *Bail Act*, s. 23, s. 34, s. 35 s. 36. Also see *Green v. Lynch*, 70 FLR 206 (S.C. N.T., 1983).
18. *Summary Proceedings Act, 1957*, s. 49, s. 49A, s. 50, s. 58. See also *R. v. Murdoch*, 1981 (1) NZLR 249 (S.C., W., 1481); *Barratt v. Registrar, Magistrates' Court*, 1980 (1) NZLR 736 (H.C., A, 1980); *Yelash v. The Queen*, 1971 NZLR 447 (S.C., A, 1970).
19. *Nesbitt v. Patterson*, 1976 (1) NZLR 735 (S.C., C, 1976).
20. *Jones v. Kirby*, 1897 NZLR 48 (S.C., W, 1896); *Ware v. Attorney General*, 1961 NZLR 694 (S.C., H, 1960); *Crimes Act 1961*, s. 116; Francis B. Adams, *Criminal Law and Practice in New Zealand*, 2nd ed. (Wellington: Sweet and Maxwell [N.Z.], 1971), para. 2541; J.M.E. Garrow & R. A. Caldwell, *Criminal Law in New Zealand* (Wellington: Butterworths, 1981), s. 319; Criminal Law Reform Committee, *Report on Bail* (Wellington: 1982) para. 171; Prue Oxley, *Remand and Bail Decisions in a Magistrates' Court* (Wellington: Department of Justice, 1979), p. 115.
21. *Summary Proceeding Act*, 1957, ss. 53–55.
22. Oxley, p. 19.
23. *Summary Proceedings Act 1957–1987*, s. 49(1)(2), s. 50A.
24. *Summary Proceedings Regulations, 1958, Amendment No. 15 (1987)*, p. 2.
25. *Summary Proceedings Act*, s. 49(3).
26. *Summary Proceedings Amendment (2) 1987*, s. 4, s. 6; *Misuse of Drugs Amendment 1978*, s. 31(2), s. 33. Also see *R. v. Emery*, 27 June 1988, CL 775 (C.A., 1988).
27. *Crimes Act 1961*, s. 320; *Summary Proceedings Act*, s. 55.
28. *Summary Proceedings Act*, s. 53.
29. Ibid., s. 54.
30. *R. v. Emery; James v. Police*, 1986(2) CRNZ 54 (H.C., C, 1986); *Police v. Adams*, 11 Aug. 81, CL 647 (H.C., W, 1981); *Henry v. Police Department* 8 July 80 CL 633 (H.C., N, 1980); *Lunn v. Police* 5 Dec 78 CL 1061 (C.A., W, 1978); *In re R.*, 1944 NZLR 19 (S.C., W, 1943); *Crown Proceedings Act*, s. 21, s. 23; *Muasika and Rae v. Justice Department*, 19 July 83 CL 527 (H.C., D, 1983); *Waihape v. Police*, 8 July 80 CL 582 (H.C., N, 1980); *The Queen v. Hopewell, in re Langford*, 1958 NZLR 523 (S.C., W, 1958); *In re Fox and Fox*, 1949 NZLR 722 (S.C., W, 1949); Criminal Law Reform Committee, s. 21, s. 24, s. 203.
31. *Crimes Act*, s. 73, s. 76, s. 78, s. 318; *Misuse of Drugs Amendment Act 1978*, s. 30; *R. v. Benfield*, 1980(2) NZLR 754 (C.A., W, 1978), at 754.
32. *Crimes Act*, s. 319(1),(2).
33. Ibid., s. 319(4), s. 320; *Summary Proceedings Act*, s. 53(3).

34. *Crimes Act*, s. 319(2),(3).

35. Ibid., s. 319(5).

36. *In re R.; James v. Police.*

37. *In re Wynne*, 10 May 83 CL 297 (H.C., W, 83).

38. *R. v. Benfield; Lynn v. Police.*

39. *The King v. Vincent and Spring*, 1950 NZLR 653 (S.C., W, 1947), at 656; Oxley, p. 12. Also see *R. v. Benfield*, at 758:13.

40. Garrow and Caldwell, s. 319; Oxley, p. 12.

41. Garrow and Caldwell, s. 319; Oxley, p. 12. See also *James v. Police*, especially at 55:34.

42. *Eade v. Police*, 24 May 88 CL 679 (H.C., I, 1988).

43. Oxley, p. 12; *Carter v. Police*, 18 Nov. 75 CL 1351 (S.C. P.N., 1975).

44. *In re R.*, at 20:10–15.

45. *Henry v. Police Department; R. v. Benfield*, at 755–756; *The King v. Vincent*, at 655–656; Oxley, p. 12; Garrow & Caldwell, s. 319; Adams, para. 2541.

46. Garrow and Caldwell, s. 319; Adams, para. 2541.

47. *In re R.*, at 20:32–38.

48. *The King v. Vincent*, at 656:2–6; *R. v. Benfield*, at 758:12–16.

49. *Re Ritchie*, 26 Nov. 1985 CL 1958 (H.C., A, 1985).

50. *James v. Police; The King v. Vincent*, at 656:5–7.

51. Contrast *James v. Police*, at 54:45–50 with *The King v. Vincent*, at 655:35–36.

52. *Summary Proceedings Act*, s. 58; *Summary Proceedings Amendment*, s. 4, s. 6.

53. *Summary Proceedings Act*, s. 50A.

54. Ibid., s. 115D.

55. *Misuse of Drugs Amendment*, ss. 35–37; *R. v. Benfield*, especially at 754–755, 757.

56. *Re Translateur*, 5 Oct 82 CL 923 (C.A., 1982); *R. v. Clarke*, 1985 (2) NZLR 212 (C.A., 1985).

57. *Summary Proceedings Amendment*, s. 48.

58. Oxley, p. 19.

59. *Justices Act* (Amendments 1974, 1986) s. 35(2),(3),(7); F. E. Devine, *Bail in Australia* (Canberra: Australian Institute of Criminology, 1989), pp. 18–20.

60. *Australian Bureau of Statistics* (Tas.), 1988, unpublished data provided by Chris Sweeney. Data are for the lower courts only for all of 1986 by bail status at the appearance at which the most serious offense was finalized.

61. *Brown v. Lowe*, 1984 Tas. R 103 (S.C. Tas., 1984) at 104, 105.

62. *Justices Act 1959*, Amend., s. 35(2)(3)(7).

63. *Brown v. Lowe*, at 104.

64. *Levy v. Strickland*, 8 A Crim R 236 (S.C. Tas., 1983) at 245.

65. *Brown v. Lowe*, at 105; *Levy v. Strickland*, at 242, 244–245.

66. *R. v. Fisher*, S.C. Tas. unreported 46/1964, at 5; *Brown v. Lowe*, at 105.

67. *Levy v. Strickland* at 244, 245, 246.

68. *Brown v. Lowe*, at 105.

69. *Levy v. Strickland*, at 244–245, 246; *Brown v. Lowe*, at 105.

70. *Brown v. Lowe*, at 105–106.

71. *Levy v. Strickland*, at 243–244.

72. Ibid., at 244.

73. South Australia Office of Crime Statistics, *Crime and Justice in South Australia,* Series A, 18, 20, 22 (Adelaide: 1986–1987), Tab. 3.24.

74. Julie Gardner, South Australia Office of Crime Statistics, "Bail Research in South Australia." Paper presented before Australian Institute of Criminology: Seminar on Bail or Remand (Adelaide: 29 November–1 December 1988), pp. 7, 8.

75. South Australia Office of Crime Statistics, *Bail Reform in South Australia,* Research Bulletin #3 (Adelaide: 1986), pp. ii, 13.

76. *Bail Act* 1985, s. 4, s. 5.

77. Frank MacAvaney (Sr. Sargeant), South Australia Police, "The Prosecution Perspective on Bail." Paper presented before Australian Institute of Criminology: Seminar on Bail or Remand (Adelaide: 29 November–1 December 1988), p. 7.

78. *Bail Act* (Amend. 1987), s. 11(6).

79. Ibid., s. 11(2)(a)(i), (ia), (vi).

80. Ibid., s. 11(7)(a).

81. Ibid., s. 11(2)(a)(ii), (iii), (iv).

82. Ibid., s. 11(8).

83. Ibid., s. 11(2)(a).

84. MacAvaney, pp. 5–6; Russell Jamison, South Australian Council for Civil Liberties, "Bail or Remand—The Civil Libertarian Perspective." Paper presented before Australian Institute of Criminology: Seminar on Bail or Remand (Adelaide: 29 November–1 December 1988), pp. 3–4; South Australia Office of Crime Statistics, *Bail Reform in South Australia*, p. 12.

85. *Bail Act,* (Amend. 1987), s. 11(37),(3a).

86. MacAvaney, p. 6; Jamison, pp. 3–4.

87. *Bail Act,* s. 11(2)(b), s. 22.

88. MacAvaney, p. 7.

89. *Bail Act* (Amend. 1987), s. 17(a).

90. Ibid., s. 7(1), s. 11(2)(c)(d)(e)(f); *Gray v. Sweatman,* 26 A Crim R 157 (S.C. S.A., 1987).

91. *Bail Act* (Amend. 1987), s. 17, s. 18.

92. MacAvaney, p. 7.

93. South Australia Office of Crime Statistics, *Bail Reform in South Australia,* pp. 7, 11.

94. Unpublished data provided by Adam Sutton, South Australia Office of Crime Statistics, 1988.

95. South Australia Office of Crime Statistics, *Bail Reform in South Australia,* pp. ii, 9, 11–12, 13–14, 16–18; Gardner, pp. 5, 12–13.

96. *Bail Act,* s. 10(1)(c).

97. Ibid., s. 13.

98. Ibid., s. 14.

7

The Noncommercial Financial Security Deposit Alternative

A fourth and final alternative to commercial bail bonding is the one closest to it in form. Under this approach, either the accused or a third-party surety or both deposit cash or other valuables with the court to secure the accused's presence at trial. If the accused fails to appear as required the deposit is forfeited. Unlike with commercial bail bonding, however, in a noncommercial system the third party providing the deposit will be a relative, friend, or other personal associate of the accused. Providing bail for payment in these noncommercial systems is either illegal or at least obstructed from developing by the legal arrangements.

Even purged of commercialism, most countries avoid a bail system based chiefly on financial security deposits. A degree of connection between such systems and the repugnant commercial bail bonding is well perceived abroad.[1] Nevertheless, a system of pretrial release based upon financial security deposits can function without reliance upon commercial provision of bail. Such a system, therefore, does constitute an alternative to commercial bail bonding. Two countries, South Africa and Liberia, employ varieties of a noncommercial financial security deposit system as their principal sanction in pretrial release matters. Unfortunately, Liberian legal materials more recent than the mid-1970s are unobtainable. This undermines any confidence that an attempt to present that system would be accurate. In addition to these two jurisdictions, Scotland—while not basing its system principally upon such deposits—employs them in cases where nonfinancial conditions are thought inadequate. Going beyond this, Papua New Guinea makes this bail form equally available with others under its law. In practice it emerges as the predominant approach at least in those cases of sufficient seriousness or complexity to have resulted in a reported bail issue case. Statutory provision in Kenya and Hong Kong produces a similar discretion to impose deposits. Many jurisdictions, moreover, regardless of which bail form they principally employ, have noncommercial financial security deposits available in varying degrees as an alternative or a supplement to their basic sanction at least for some cases. In some of these, deposits acquire a notable importance.

SOUTH AFRICA

Background

South Africa's criminal procedure, including bail, is based on common law, although its substantive law is not. In spite of the vitiation of South African law regarding pretrial detention by special provisions for political offenses in recent years, that country's bail system provides the clearest available example of the workings of a noncommercial financial security deposit approach. As applied to what have been termed ordinary common law offenses[2]—"the usual thefts and assaults"[3]—the terms of bail in South Africa typify a system of this type. Such distortions as are created in the bail law applicable to nonpolitical crime affect principally the question of eligibility for bail rather than its terms where granted.

Prior to 1977, South African law placed its emphasis as to the form of bail on recognizance. However, in practice the system of bail in that country normally functioned by means of cash deposits. The 1971 *Report of the Commission of Inquiry into Criminal Procedure and Evidence* (the Botha Commission) recommended a cash deposit system be adopted in law to reflect the realities of practice. Following this aspect of the commission's recommendation, the 1977 *Criminal Procedure Act* conformed the law to the practice and established a statutory system in which clear preference is given to cash deposit.[4]

Terms of Bail

The South African bail system very clearly establishes cash deposit as the primary form of bail. The law gives primacy to the provision that courts may release the accused on condition of depositing money in the amount required by the court.[5] The discretion of the court in fixing this amount is limited, however, in that bail may not be excessive. An excessive amount is subject to appeal.[6] Several principal considerations bear on whether a given amount is excessive. The first is the likelihood that the accused will abscond. In assessing this, factors such as the seriousness of the charge, the nature of the offense (e.g., violent or political), and the potential punishment are pertinent. The second is the means of the accused. The sum required should not amount to an indirect refusal of bail; hence, evidence of the accused's means should be considered in determining excessiveness. Generally, the amount set should be within the reach of the accused, considering all alternative sources available to that individual, unless this is overridden by the seriousness of the offense.[7] A third consideration is that defendants on a similar footing should be treated equally.[8]

The South African bail statute explicitly specifies that a third party may provide the bail money on behalf of the accused.[9] However, even when the bail money is provided by another, the accused "is the person effecting the process of providing bail."[10] Provision of bail money by a third party might be thought to invite commercial provision of bail, but as previously discussed, courts are to refuse deposits by anyone who they have reason to believe has been or will be indemnified or given any financial benefit for the deposit.[11] Conversely, provision of the bail money by relatives, friends, or associates is valued by the courts as creating an additional constraint on the accused. Thus, not only is commercial provision of bail precluded, but courts are "pleased to see" a strong personal tie between the accused and the person providing bail money.[12]

If the defendant fails to appear as required by his bail, or appears but fails to remain for the proceedings, bail is provisionally canceled, the bail money is provisionally forfeited, and an arrest warrant is issued. An accused who then appears before the court within fourteen days may undertake to satisfy the court that the failure to appear or remain was not due to fault on his part. Where this attempt succeeds, the provisional forfeiture lapses; otherwise, it is confirmed. After fourteen days without an appearance by the accused the provisional forfeiture becomes final unless the court has extended the period for good cause.[13] This provision gave rise to the rather extreme situation that where a defendant committed suicide the court was found to have no discretion to remit bail money to the third party who provided it.[14]

After a final forfeiture only the Minister of Justice or an officer acting on his authority has discretion to remit forfeited money in whole or in part.[15] Courts have disagreed over whether an appeal on the merits of a forfeiture is permissible, but the more recent cases are against allowing it. However, review is available based upon such grounds as lack of jurisdiction; bias, malice, or corruption; gross procedural irregularity; or erroneous admission or rejection of evidence.[16]

South African bail law provides for an alternate form of bail to cash deposit. Courts may permit release upon the accused's entering into a recognizance with or without sureties. To qualify for this alternative the accused must show good cause for resorting to it.[17] Forfeiture for nonappearance is governed substantially and procedurally by the same legal provisions as with cash deposit.[18]

When sureties are required, as explained earlier, they may not under common law be indemnified.[19] In addition, individuals become ineligible to be accepted by the courts as sureties if with reasonable cause they are suspected of being indemnified or compensated.[20] Generally, the law governing sureties is as in the recognizance systems. However, since surety forfeitures are governed by the same law as those of cash deposits, South Africa—unlike most countries—makes no provision for a surety to defend against forfeiture by arguing a lack of culpability for the accused's failure to appear. This leaves remission by the Minister of Justice the only possible recourse for a surety in this situation.[21]

As is the case in most other forms of bail system, supplementary nonfinancial terms of bail may be added to the financial requirements imposed. South African law specifies five types of nonfinancial conditions as permissible—those that require reporting, forbid entry into specified places, prohibit or control communication with prosecution witnesses, specify the place documents may be served, or ensure against jeopardy to the proper administration of justice.[22] Typical examples of this final type are surrender of one's passport or not leaving the jurisdictional district.[23]

How narrowly courts understand themselves to be limited by these categories appears to vary, especially in cases with political overtones. One court has moved in the direction of constraint to the point of questioning the propriety of conditions that do not aim either at the accused's appearance or at preventing his prejudicing the preparation or prosecution of the case against him. On this view, if conditions to prevent the commission of further crimes are proper at all, they must aim narrowly at preventing a repetition of the particular offense for which the defendant awaits trial.[24] In a similar vein, conditions were struck down in another case from the same court because they prevented the accused from protesting and from attending gatherings. Conditions, the court said, may only be imposed to constrain protesting unlawfully or attending gatherings with the intention of persisting in unlawful conduct or persuading others to act unlawfully.[25] Nevertheless, in an internal security case before another court, conditions were imposed—albeit with consent of defendants who might otherwise have been denied bail—that extended to not taking part in any manner in any activity of an organization named in their indictment. This prohibition included also any group affiliated with an organization named. Attending or addressing any gathering under the auspices of such bodies was also specificallyforbidden.[26]

Conditions may not, by reason of being too vague or too broad, impose an excessive burden on an accused to determine whether an action might violate bail terms. They must also be capable of achieving an appropriate result. They may not be imposed to prevent lawful conduct. If under the circumstances a condition is not needed and thereby constitutes an unnecessary curtailment of (or threat to) the freedom of the defendant, it should not be imposed.[27] Conditions once established may be altered by the court before which a charge is pending upon application of either prosecution or defense. An accused aggrieved by conditions imposed also may appeal them to the superior court having jurisdiction.[28]

South Africa is among those countries enforcing bail conditions violations with possible cancelation of bail and forfeiture of bail monies. A prosecutor who believes bail conditions have been violated may apply to the courts to offer evidence to prove this. Proof that the specific violation of conditions endangered the interest of justice is not required nor is proof that it reflects an intent to abscond. Thus, bail was held to have been properly revoked where a defendant was chronically ten to twenty minutes late in reporting.[29] If the defendant is present, the prosecutor offers evidence of the breach. The accused in turn can offer evidence that he did not fail to comply or that the failure was not due to fault on his part. If the accused is not present, the court may issue an arrest warrant and when he does appear hear evidence from prosecution and defense.[30] The prosecution bears the burden of establishing on the balance of probabilities that the accused breached the condition due to his own fault.[31]

Unlike a failure to appear, once a culpable violation of nonfinancial conditions has been established the court has discretion whether or not to cancel bail and forfeit bail monies. The onus at that point shifts to the defendant to show why these steps should not be taken. The issues of cancelation and forfeiture have been held to require separate consideration; specifically, forfeiture does not automatically follow from cancelation. Different considerations may be relevant to determining each of the two. For example, a breach of conditions might be sufficient to warrant cancelation to protect the interest of justice, but not be serious enough to require forfeiture. Alternatively, if bail money was provided by a third party who had no part in the breach, cancelation but not forfeiture might be appropriate.[32]

A further dimension of bail terms in South Africa's system aims at preventing absconding by arrest. As under other bail forms, the court before which a charge is pending, upon a sworn information that a defendant is about to evade justice or to abscond, may issue an arrest warrant and cancel bail. If action by that court is not practicable, any magistrate can issue the warrant and cancel bail upon application by a police officer supported by a sworn written statement that he has reason to believe one of the required circumstances.[33]

In interpreting the similar predecessor to the present provision, withdrawal of the accused's liberty once bailed was said to require convincing facts. A magistrate must exercise proper discretion in the matter and not cancel bail simply because that is requested by the prosecutor. Cursory and unsubstantiated information attributed to an undisclosed informer is entirely unsatisfactory as grounds to cancel bail.[34] Nevertheless, where the Attorney General with a full sense of responsibility declares that an accused is about to abscond, but refuses in the interest of justice to give details or name informants, his statement must be given due weight. Conversely, allowance must also be made for the difficulties created for the defendant by such a lack of particulars in refuting the claim. On balance, bail can be revoked when the Attorney General's claim is made in a context where the inducement to flee is great, others connected with the case have fled, extradition would be impossible, the accused has been collecting money, and the accused intends to leave the country after trial.[35]

South Africa's *Criminal Procedure Act* provides in a separate chapter an alternative to the main bail system described to this point. Known as "release on warning," it amounts to a separate and discrete criminal penalties alternative. South African law views this not merely as an alternative form of bail but as an alternative to bail itself.

Under this provision an accused is released with a warning to appear at the court specified at a particular time.[36] Unlike regular bail, release on a warning does not require an application from the defendant.[37] Release on warning may be unconditional or subject to the same nonfinancial conditions applicable to normal bail. Failure to appear or to adhere to conditions are offenses. Upon a conviction following a summary enquiry, both types of breach are punishable by a fine of up to R300 or by up to three months' imprisonment unless the defendant satisfies the court that the infringement was not due to fault on his part. An arrest warrant may be issued once a court is satisfied that an accused has either failed to appear as required or failed to comply with a condition.[38]

In contrast to a number of countries that make criminal penalties available as a secondary sanction supplementary to their principal bail form in all cases, the South African offense and attached penalties pertain only to those released under this independent provision. Those released under the main bail provision with a deposit or sureties are not subject to sentencing under this section.[39]

South Africa's approach to bail for those accused of ordinary common law type crime presents a clear example of a system that relies upon cash deposit as its principal sanction to enforce the defendant's appearance. At the same time, this system takes precautions against accused's resorting to commercially provided sureties. It thereby demonstrates that a noncommercial system employing financial security deposit for the accused's appearance is possible and can be workable. Nonfinancial conditions to control conduct can be added to the financial ones to achieve specified objectives including appearance. These, too, can be enforced by the financial deposit sanction. Arrest is also available to prevent absconding. Alternatively, upon a showing of cause for its use, a recognizance with or without third-party sureties, can be substituted for the cash deposit. Finally, although it is not strictly considered a form of bail, the separate criminal penalties option can be substituted.

Eligibility for Bail

The *Criminal Procedure Act* has been held to create a "substantive right" to apply to the courts for bail for any offense.[40] Consideration of bail does, however, require such an application.[41] As a consequence of the right to apply, courts are obliged to hear and decide bail applications outside of normal court hours and on noncourt days.[42] In furtherance of this right, where a summons has not been used or police bail has not been granted, detention for more than forty-eight hours without being brought before a court is unlawful. Failure to meet this requirement precludes consideration of judicially authorized further detention available under this provision.[43]

No constitutional or statutory right to be granted—as opposed to applying for—bail exists. This leaves the granting of bail to the discretion of the courts. In exercising this discretion the courts have recognized a *prima facie* entitlement, or right, to be granted bail in the absence of one of a group of recognized considerations for denying bail.[44] Thus, under normal circumstances bail will be granted in response to this common law right.[45]

Clearly the most controversial provision of South African bail law permits the Attorney General to preempt the court's discretion to grant bail for a number of the most serious offenses specified. These include such major common law crimes as murder, arson, kidnapping, robbery, and burglary.[46] In addition, political offenses such as treason, sedition, sabotage, terrorism, and some internal security offenses come under a provision whereby the discretion of the courts to grant bail can be more permanently excluded.[47] To invoke the provision for a serious crime, the Attorney General needs only to inform the court in person or in writing that he has information which in his opinion shows that the accused's release is likely to affect adversely the administration of justice or to constitute a threat to the safety of the public or to the maintenance of public order. Thereafter, although the accused may still apply for bail, the court is required to deny the bail application. The Attorney General is also authorized to state that in his opinion his information cannot be disclosed without prejudice to the public interest or to the administration of justice. The effect of such a statement is to require the court to issue its mandatory denial of bail blindly.[48]

Furthermore, to facilitate the Attorney General's exercising this power, any prosecutor can delay consideration of bail for fourteen days in cases involving these serious crimes while the matter of bail is referred to the Attorney General for his possible intervention. Failure to intervene within that period has been held to preclude exercise of the power and to restore discretion to the courts.[49] When bail is denied under this provision, if no evidence is led against the accused within ninety days from arrest, the court regains its discretion regarding bail.[50] This ninety-day limit does not pertain to the provision governing political offenses, which is in various respects more restrictive of the courts.

The removal of bail decisions from judicial control has been criticized both in and outside of the courts. The Botha Commission report recommended eliminating the possibility of invoking it in the interests of justice, observing that depriving the courts of jurisdiction to consider bail could never be in the interest of justice.[51] The Natal Provincial Division of the Supreme Court called the Attorney General's deciding bail issues a "complete anathema."[52]

In spite of the apparently considerable judicial dislike of this provision, the courts view themselves as being bound to acquiesce in it. South Africa has a flexible constitution and adheres to the British tradition of parliamentary supremacy. Consequently, a law passed by a majority of the legislature cannot be voided by the courts on the grounds of unconstitutionality. Thus, when a law such as this one regarding bail restricts an individual liberty or the powers of the courts, the judiciary has at most the recourse of interpreting it strictly so as to limit its effects as much as the statutory language reasonably permits.[53]

The result of this legal perspective has been that the courts hold themselves deprived of discretion to release on bail in the face of an Attorney General's order that it be denied.[54] Surprisingly, whereas in political cases the courts do on occasion review the jurisdictional bases of an Attorney General's order for whether the statutory conditions giving rise to authority to issue it exist, this does not appear to occur with serious ordinary crimes.[55] This may be in part due to the statutory ability of the Attorney General to withhold his reasons for opposing bail without explanation or justification under the provision for serious ordinary crimes.

Overall, with regard to the law on eligibility for bail for ordinary crimes, South Africa presents a complicated mixed picture. No constitutional or statutory right to bail exists. However, a statutory right to apply for bail has been created. Granting of bail is discretionary, but discretion is guided by a common law *prima facie* right to have bail granted unless certain recognized conditions are present. An overriding negative component of the system is the ability of the Attorney General to preempt the discretion of the courts to grant bail for ninety days, without revealing reasons, in matters involving ordinary serious crimes. The courts' jurisdiction can be preempted completely for political crimes, although courts do at times examine jurisdictional questions regarding the preemptive order.

Considerations for Denying Bail

The South African bail statute creates a broad discretion in the courts regarding bail.[56] The exercise of this is normally guided by considerations established by case law. The preservation of the liberty of the accused—who is presumed innocent—is to be balanced against the due administration of justice.[57] If no considerations affecting the administration of justice are present, the accused has a *prima facie* right to bail. Normally, in the absence of such considerations bail will be granted.[58]

The usual considerations affecting the administration of justice—and therefore the usual reasons for denying bail—are those indicating that accuseds will avoid standing trial if released on bail, that they will interfere with witnesses or hamper the investigation of the offense, or that they will otherwise hinder the proper course of justice.[59] Tampering with a witness includes tampering either by threat or by inducement.[60] Other hindrances to the investigation or the administration of justice include warning other possible co-defendants.[61] The onus of establishing on a balance of probabilities that considerations affecting the administration of justice are not present is borne by the accused.[62]

These usual grounds for denying bail, however, have been held not to constitute the only proper reasons for doing so. Even where they are not present, bail may be denied based upon indications that an accused, if released, might constitute a threat to the security of the state, to the public safety, or to the maintenance of law and order.[63] Bail may also be refused in at least some circumstances and for some crimes on the grounds that the accused has a propensity to commit the type of offense with which he is charged.[64] It should not, however, be denied simply because the accused may commit some crime if released.[65]

Factors that South African courts rely upon in deciding whether or not an accused may attempt to abscond are fairly typical. All relevant facts may be considered, whether or not they would be admissible as evidence at the trial.[66] Whereas due weight should be given to the accused's statement under oath that he does not intend to abscond, implicit reliance should not be placed upon it. It should be evaluated in the light of the circumstances, which include previous history regarding absconding, seriousness of the offense, and severity of the probable punishment. Among other matters considered are intention regarding plea, personal or property ties in South Africa or elsewhere, citizenship and fixed abode in that country or abroad, and irregularities regarding the defendant's passport.[67]

Different factors pertain to denial of bail to protect the interest of justice. Important among these are indications of past threatening behavior toward witnesses. Such vindications might be provided by former convictions—particularly if recent—for defeating the ends of justice, or by evidence that threatening behavior has occurred in the present case. Other factors are the seriousness of the charge, the opinion of the investigating officer regarding the threat, and the ease with which the accused could gain access to the witness to interfere.[68]

In general, then, the considerations employed by the South African courts in considering the denial of bail—and in turn the factors used to assess these—are similar to those used elsewhere. The risk of absconding and the risk of interference with the processes of justice are the principal focus of this decision. Preventing the potential commission of crime as a reason to deny bail has a more tenuous status and a more limited application than in many other countries. The major exception to this is crime involving state security. The emphasis placed in case law on state security as a reason to deny bail is notable, particularly considering that the Attorney General can preempt even the consideration of bail in many such cases.

Procedural Considerations

Procedural considerations relating to the terms of bail have already been dealt with in that context. Procedures implementing the right to apply for bail remain for consideration. Defendants who are not released by the police under other alternatives must be brought before the courts within forty-eight hours. This includes even those defendants for whom the Attorney General will preempt the granting of bail.[69] Bail application may be made prior to this if the accused appears in court or at any stage after this point.[70] A defendant to be tried before a superior court may make a bail application before the lower court at his first appearance. If no application is made to the lower court, it may be made to the superior court with jurisdiction over the case. If, however, application is made and denied before the lower court, it may be renewed before the superior court only on the basis of new facts. Preemption of a bail decision by the Attorney General has been held not to constitute a denial for these purposes. Therefore, application could be made again to the superior court.[71]

Where bail has been refused by a lower court, or terms objectionable to the accused have been imposed, an appeal lies to the superior court.[72] This is an appeal strictly understood and not a reapplication.[73] Therefore, it is conditioned by procedural requirements similar to those of an ordinary criminal appeal, which are likely to consume a substantial amount of time and entail considerable expense.[74]

Two other remedies are available for limited purposes. Where only the terms or amount of bail are at issue, the court before which a case is pending may alter these upon application by either defense or prosecution. Finally, if the accused believes that an error subject to the process of review was committed, that may be taken before the Supreme Court.[75]

Once bail is granted, it may be canceled only for a violation of its terms or based on convincing facts indicating that the accused is about to abscond or evade justice. Since by granting bail a court provides official recognition of the defendant's right to be at liberty, the discretion to retract bail under the latter provision must be narrowly construed.[76] Courts have disagreed as to whether when bail has been canceled it may again be sought. The stronger view is that a new application is not precluded, although the cancelation is a consideration in whether it should again be granted.[77]

The right of the accused in South Africa to apply for bail initially is accommodated by procedural requirements that provide the opportunity to make application. However, where an application has been denied, the possibility of reapplication appears more constricted than in many other countries. Appeal is available, but subject to procedural constraints comparable to appeal of a final judgment.

Results of the System

Clear indications are discernible that South African practice follows its law in giving emphasis to bail by cash deposit over the recognizance or recognizance with sureties alternatives. Even before the 1977 *Criminal Procedure Act* created the legal preference for cash deposit, practice favored it. The act conformed the law to the practice.[78] The Botha Commission commented that sureties were hardly ever accepted in practice.[79] Although not necessarily representative, some indication of this can be gained also from the cases considered here for points of law. Of forty-two defendants in twenty-one cases where the terms of bail can be determined, only two cases involving three defendants employ a recognizance with a surety. Moreover, even in these cases substantial cash deposits were also made. The recognizance with a surety was supplementary to the deposit. Thus, in all cases including these, a cash deposit was employed.

In addition to the cash deposit, in virtually every case nonfinancial conditions were imposed as well. In one case with a single defendant who was given permission to leave the country, no conditions appear to have been imposed. In two others with four defendants, three had no conditions imposed on their initial bail but conditions were added later on an appeal of bail terms. The fourth defendant had conditions imposed from the start. In four cases with five defendants the status regarding conditions cannot be discerned.

Some use of warning with the criminal penalties sanction is indicated, even though no case subsequent to the 1977 statute, among those consulted here, involved the alternative. Again, this provision was introduced to bring the law into conformity with an established practice.[80] Its use seems to be confined to minor matters.

Summary

South Africa provides a clear example of a system in which bail functions principally by cash deposit. It does so, however, without resorting to commercially provided bail. Not only is the common law against such bail applied, but courts considering bail are instructed to reject any sureties who may have been paid. Complementing this, courts are pleased to have sureties or providers of bail monies who have personal ties of kinship or friendship to the accused. The means of the accused, including all such sources, are to be considered in setting bail amounts. Various aspects of eligibility for bail under South African law exhibit problems of restrictiveness, which are magnified where offenses have political overtones. Nevertheless, South Africa demonstrates that a cash deposit bail system can function without commercial bail bonding. Moreover, neither the use of the cash deposits nor the avoidance of commercial bail relates to the problem areas.

LIBERIA

Although the Liberian criminal bail system cannot be discussed with confidence due to the age of the available legal material, one point uniquely well exemplified by that system is necessary for an overall understanding of bail systems based principallly upon noncommercially provided financial security deposits. This is the fact that the financial security tendered need not take the form of cash as in South Africa. Such systems may include deposits of the deeds to real property or of negotiable securities.

The Liberian Supreme Court has consistently rejected a cash-only view of security deposits. In a 1975 case, that court overturned a statute that required bail to be secured by cash only for a particular type of offense. The accused had attempted to secure bail with real property. The court held that the cash-only bail requirement amounted to excessive bail contrary to the constitution (long since suspended). It reasoned that the statute unconstitutionally resulted in the practical denial of bail by arbitrarily restricting the means of providing bail security.[81]

The Supreme Court similarly held in a 1971 case that judges or magistrates have no discretion to insist upon cash bail in a given case. Here the defendant offered security in the form of two sureties willing to secure their suretyship with real property. The court maintained that no discretion exists to reject sufficient surety in any legally authorized form and demand cash. If the sureties were willing to accept the risk, the judge must.[82]

Demonstrably, then, financial surety deposits need not be limited to cash.

OTHER RELATED BAIL SYSTEMS

Although few countries statutorily establish deposit of noncommercially provided financial security as their principal bail sanction, most permit them to some degree. In some of these the deposits attain particular importance. Not all jurisdictions whose statutes permit courts to accept deposits take the usual restrictive interpretation of the courts' role. A 1979 opinion of the Swaziland High Court takes the view that bail implies a monetary deposit. That court, therefore, doubts that authority exists there for courts to release defendants on recognizance without a cash deposit.[83] The consequences of this view would place that country firmly in the noncommercial financial security category, in spite of the similarity of its statute to those of the traditional recognizance systems.[84] Short of this, in Tanzania, although recognizance is the most common form of release in the reported bail cases (as the statute suggests it should be), several instances of demands for cash deposit by the High Court in difficult cases are reported.[85] Isolated cases of the same sort appear as well in a few other countries with provision for accepting deposits.

Scotland requires particular mention, since under the Scottish system security deposits provide the statutory alternative to the principal bail form where release under it is not acceptable to the court. In Scotland, if release on nonfinancial conditions subject to criminal penalties for absconding is thought inappropriate, cash deposit is the alternative established by the *Bail Act*. The traditional form of bail in Scotland prior to this 1980 law was by cash deposit.[86] Under the present system, if a court is satisfied that special circumstances of the case require more than the threat of punishment it has—reflecting the traditional bail form—the option of imposing a cash deposit. The deposit may be by the accused or by a cautioner (surety) on his behalf.[87]

Three jurisdictions—Papua New Guinea, Hong Kong, and Kenya—go beyond Scotland in the direction of a security deposit bail system avoiding commercialism. Although none of these establishes security deposits as having legal priority over other alternatives, they do make them equally eligible for imposition. In Papua New Guinea, as a result, deposits are the usual form of release, at least in the reported cases where a bail matter has been appealed. Although information to determine whether security deposits predominate over all in that country is not available, Papua New Guinea provides the best available supplement to South Africa and Liberia in demonstrating alternatives within noncommercial financial security systems.

Papua New Guinea

Like so many other countries, Papua New Guinea reformulated its bail law in the mid-1970s. This was accomplished principally by the *Bail Act 1977*, which was supplemented in the revision process by parts of the related *Arrest Act* of the same year. As was frequently the case, the legal reform was preceded by a study of the existing system. This was conducted by the Law Reform Commission of Papua New

Guinea and was issued the year previous to the change as *The Report on Arrest, Search and Bail*. Under the earlier law the deposit of cash by the accused or by another was a common bail requirement in serious cases. A recognizance alternative was also available for either or both. Regardless of the alternative used, indemnification of the third party by the accused was forbidden.[88] The 1977 law generally preserved the options of the prior system with some modifications. The statutory impositions of up to two years' imprisonment for attempting to obstruct, prevent, pervert, or defeat the course of justice and of up to seven years' imprisonment for conspiring to do the same were not affected by the act.[89]

Section 18 of the *Bail Act* creates broad authority for courts to place conditions on their grants of bail. These conditions, the section stipulates, may include both those to be complied with before release as well as those for compliance afterward. Financial and nonfinancial conditions are not distinguished. The inclusion of financial conditions among those for prior compliance is immediately indicated by the requirement that courts satisfy themselves that the conditions imposed will not cause the accused financial hardship.[90]

Section 22 of the *Bail Act* proceeds to provide for the forfeiture of the accused's security for contravening or failing to comply with bail obligations. These obligations include both appearance and compliance with all conditions of the bail.[91] Therefore, nonfinancial conditions of conduct can be enforced by forfeiture as well as by appearance. Notably, forfeiture of either a cash deposit or a recognizance is equally and explicitly authorized.[92]

To regularize procedure among the courts, the National Court in 1986 held that a uniform sequence should be followed in bail forfeitures. When a breach of conditions—whether of appearance or conduct—occurs, the first step in response should be an application for an arrest warrant by the prosecutor. The question before the court at this point should be restricted to whether or not the warrant should be granted. Revocation of bail and forfeiture should not be considered. Only upon the accused's arrest and appearance before the court should revocation and forfeiture be considered. In this way the accused can be heard on these two points.[93]

A forfeiture, if ordered, may be of either all or part of the security. In addition, a person affected by a forfeiture order has fourteen days to apply to the courts to vary or revoke it. In a 1985 case, the Supreme Court held that no order varying or revoking a bail forfeiture could be made after this period had expired. On a two-to-one split, the limit was ruled constitutional. In doing so, however, members of the court called the limit unfortunate, uncalled for, unfair, inappropriate, and arbitrary as applied to defendants who are prevented by circumstances beyond their control from being present to seek relief.[94] The 1986 holding of the National Court just discussed, which delays the consideration of forfeiture, was in part an attempt to deal with this problem, which also was encountered in South Africa.

The *Bail Act* further provides that if after the imposition of financial and nonfinancial conditions the court remains unsatisfied that the accused will meet bail obligations, a maximum of two court-approved guarantors may be required. These individuals undertake to see that the defendant appears in court and meets other conditions of bail. Additionally, they may—but need not—be required to deposit an amount of money or enter into a recognizance in support of their undertaking. The statute requires that their financial means be considered in setting the amount.[95]

Contrasting these guarantors to commercial bail bondsman highlights informative differences. The fact that guarantors need not always incur financial liability demonstrates the reliance placed on the persuasive influence of a guarantor connected to an accused by personal ties. The role is primarily one of personal guarantor; it is only secondarily one of surety. The required consideration of means also reflects the importance of the personal connection to the individual vulnerable to loss over the mere amount of money subject to forfeiture.

The law in Papua New Guinea regarding nonfinancial conditions of bail is innovative in that, instead of the more usual statement of what conditions may be imposed, it grants broad powers to create conditions but specifies certain restrictions or limitations on these powers. Conditions imposed may not cause undue interference with the accused's domestic life, interfere with the accused's legitimate means of earning a living or being available for work, interfere with rights to political freedom of action or movement except as necessary to secure appearance in court, or cause financial hardship. They may not be unreasonable in the light of all of the circumstances.[96]

A bail condition to which Papua New Guinea devotes particular attention is that of not leaving the country. Individuals with foreign connections are required as a matter of practice to surrender passports as a bail condition.[97] The *Bail Act* makes special provision for those on bail who for urgent personal or occupational reasons wish to leave the country while awaiting trial. Permission to leave may be granted only by the National Court or the Supreme Court. The court must be satisfied by defendants on the balance of probabilities that they will return for trial. Conditions to help assure this may qualify the permission.[98]

In addition to the sanctions enforcing bail already discussed, a 1982 amendment to the act adds a further method of enforcing bail obligations. This amendment creates an offense of contravening or failing to comply with bail obligations. Conviction entails a punishment of up to twelve months' imprisonment.[99] Since, as noted, bail obligations include both appearance and observing conditions, these latter are enforceable by this provision as much as is court attendance.

Eligibility for bail in Papua New Guinea is guaranteed by Article 43(6) of the constitution for all crimes except treason or willful murder, unless the interests of justice require that it not be granted. The right to be brought before a court without delay is also constitutionally protected.[100] If bail is refused, further constitutional protections require, upon request, a statement of the reasons for refusal and provide for summary bail applications to the higher courts.[101] The *Bail Act* reinforces the constitutional right to and presumption of bail.[102]

The *Bail Act* provides a list of specific considerations that justify denial of bail. The three considerations employed worldwide are included: the accused is unlikely to appear, is likely to interfere with witnesses, is likely to commit an indictable offense.[103] *Likely* here means a tendency or real possibility. It does not mean "more likely than not," "probably," or "very likely."[104] If the present offense was committed while the accused was on bail, bail may also be refused. Offenses involving serious assault, the threat of violence, or possession of a firearm, imitation firearm, other offensive weapon, or explosive also negate the right to bail. In addition, offenses involving substantial unrecovered property that the accused might deal with if released, or offenses involving the possession, importation, or exportation of narcotic drugs, are exempted from the bail right.[105]

These considerations for denying bail affect murder and capital cases differently from other offenses. Bail in willful murder, murder, and treason cases is reserved for the National Court or the Supreme Court.[106] Moreover, in these matters a shift in the burden of proof occurs: the onus is upon the defense to show why bail should be granted. This must be done based on the listed considerations. Arguments that other considerations necessitate bail in the interests of justice are not available.[107]

In cases involving offenses other than those reserved for the higher courts—although some earlier cases indicated otherwise[108]—recent cases have found that the *Bail Act* list of considerations does not exhaust the reasons for denying bail. The constitutional provision allowing denial in the interests of justice is argued not to be limited by the statutory considerations in these cases. Courts nevertheless should generally be guided by the statutory considerations in exercising their discretion. Where the prosecution establishes that a statutory consideration is present, the bail applicant acquires the burden of showing why detention in custody is not justified. In this situation arguments resting on the interests of justice might be employed.[109]

Papua New Guinea's *Bail Act*, then, emphasizes conditions both financial and nonfinancial as the sanctions enforcing trial appearance. Cash deposit is prominent among these. The evidence, albeit scant, of actual practice provided by the cases considered for points of bail law is, at least, uniform. For these mostly serious or complex cases cash deposit by the accused combined with nonfinancial conditions is virtually invariably imposed. Reflecting the statutory requirements of additional necessity to require a guarantor, this is rarely encountered. The recognizance alternative, financial conditions alone, or exclusive reliance on the threat of criminal punishments also are rarely encountered in serious cases like these. In spite of this substantial reliance upon cash deposits, however, recourse to commercial bail bonding is avoided.

Hong Kong and Kenya

Like Papua New Guinea, Hong Kong puts cash deposit on a footing of equal availability with other bail forms. However, this result is produced in a different way in Hong Kong. Prior to 1976 Hong Kong had a traditional type of recognizance system. Third-party sureties could be required. Nonfinancial conditions aimed at appearance, the interest of justice, or the prevention of crime could be imposed.[110] In that year an amendment added to the existing alternative broad powers for the courts to order security deposits. Although this added authority encompasses deposit in the form of cash only, the courts are given an uncommon degree of control over who is to provide it. Courts may condition an accused's admission to bail on deposit of money by the accused, by a surety, or by both. Cash deposits may be ordered in addition to any recognizance with or without sureties that might be demanded.[111] Failure to appear as required but not breach of other bail conditions can result in forfeiture. Breach of either requirement can result in arrest.[112]

Kenya makes similar provision for courts to require security deposits in place of a recognizance. The Kenyan provision is broadly worded to permit property as well as cash to be deposited. The High Court has held that a cash bail must be returned upon appearance. Courts may not order fines to be deducted from it.[113]

CONCLUSION

Relatively few countries employ noncommercially provided financial security deposits as their principal bail sanction. In some instances the alternative is rejected in part because a connection between it and commercial bail bonding is perceived. The former is foregone to avoid the latter. Nevertheless, enough systems exist where security deposits of noncommercial origin are used as the principal bail sanction or at least as an important one in serious cases that the viability of such systems is evident. South Africa's bail system is the clearest example. Supplementary indications are provided by Liberia, Swaziland, Papua, New Guinea, Hong Kong, Kenya, and Scotland.

At the root of the defense against commercialism in all cases except Liberia is the common law provision against indemnified sureties or its statutory replacement. Added defense is provided by South Africa's statutory requirement mandating rejection of providers of bail deposits who are suspected of being indemnified for it or of profiting from it.

Accepting that a security deposit system is by its nature more vulnerable to commercialism than other bail forms, certain aspects of these noncommercial deposit systems stand out as useful protections. The required consideration of the accused's means of meeting bail taking all circumstances into account is clearly helpful. This is salient in the law in South Africa and Papua New Guinea. If defendants can usually raise the required bail money noncommercially, the need to resort to a commercial source for it is obviously curtailed. The encouragement of relatives or friends of the accused to serve as sureties, guarantors, providers of money and the like complements this. It alters the emphasis from the amount of money involved to the nature of the personal tie and its influence. Thus it further reinforces a nonmercantile approach.

Factors from Liberia, Kenya, and Hong Kong are also instructive. Although most deposit systems require cash, Liberia's acceptance of other forms of deposit seems beneficial. Kenya likewise permits the deposit of property as well as of cash. By accepting forms of security other than cash, convoluted arrangements to render the other property form into cash are avoided. This enhances the possibility of a noncommercial bail being realized. A further defense against commercial sources of bail is provided by the Hong Kong Law's provision giving the courts greater power to specify the exact source of cash deposits.

Thus, apart from direct steps to prohibit commercialism in bail, even security deposit systems have options available to help discourage commercial bail bonding.

NOTES

1. See for example The Law Reform Commission of Western Australia, *Review of Bail Procedures* (Perth: Law Reform Commission, 1977), pp. 147–148; Home Office, *Bail Procedures in Magistrates' Courts* (London: HMSO, 1974).

2. Albie Sachs, *Justice in South Africa* (Berkeley: University of California Press, 1973), pp. 232–233.

3. John D. Jackson, *Justice in South Africa* (Hamondsworth: Penguin Books, 1980), p. 142.

4. John Dugard, *South African Criminal Law and Procedure*, vol. IV (Capetown: Juta, 1977), p. 73; *Annual Survey of South African Law, 1977* (Capetown: Juta, 1978), p. 447; *Criminal Procedure Act 1977*, s. 60.

5. *Criminal Procedure Act*, s. 60.

6. *R. v. Vermeulen*, 1958(2), SA 326 (T.P.D.).

7. *S. v. Budlender*, 1973(1) SA 264 (C.P.D.), at 266–269; *S. v. Ho*, 1979(3) SA 734 (W.L.D.) at 738–739; *R. v. DuPlessis*, 1957(4) SA 463 (W.L.D.), at 463–465; *R. v. Vermeulen*, at 327–328; *S. v. Visser*, 1975(2) SA 342 (K.P.A.).

8. *S. v. Budlender*, at 273.

9. *Criminal Procedure Act*, s. 69(1).

10. *Mapumulu v. Pieterse, N.O.*, 1962(2) SA 198 (D. & C.L.D.), at 200.

11. *Criminal Procedure Act*, s. 69(3).

12. *S. v. De Abreu*, 1980(4) SA 94 (W.L.D.) at 98; *S. v. Budlender*, at 269.

13. *Criminal Procedure Act*, s. 67.

14. *S. v. Cronje*, 1983(3) SA 739 (W.P.A.).

15. *Criminal Procedure Act*, s. 70.

16. *Da Costa v. The Magistrate, Windhoek*, 1983(2) SA 732 (S.W.A. S.C.), esp at 738; *Sebe v. Magistrate, Zwelitsha*, 1984(3) SA 885 (C.S.C.), esp. at 888–889; *S. v. Casker*, 1971(4) SA 504 (N.P.D.), esp. at 509; *Jack v. Vermeulen N.O.*, 1979(1) SA 659 (C.P.D.), esp. at 660; *Pillay v. Regional Magistrate, Pretoria*, 1977(1) SA 533 (T.P.D.), esp. at 534–535.

17. *Criminal Procedure Act*, s. 60(2).

18. Ibid.; *Da Costa v. The Magistrate, Windhoek*, esp. at 742.

19. Alfred V. Lansdown, *South African Criminal Law and Procedure*, V (Capetown: Juta, 1982), 341; Dugard, p. 74.

20. *Criminal Procedure Act*, s. 69(3).

21. *Criminal Procedure Act*, s. 67, s. 70; *Da Costa v. The Magistrate, Windhoek*, at 746–748.

22. *Criminal Procedure Act*, s. 62.

23. *S. v. De Abreu*, at 101; *S. v. Ramgobin (2)*, 1985(4) SA 130 (N.P.D.), at 132.

24. *S. v. Russell*, 1978(1) SA 223 (C.P.D.).

25. *S. v. Budlender*, at. 271.

26. *S. v. Ramgobin (2)*, at 132.

27. *S. v. Budlender*, at 271.

28. *Criminal Procedure Act*, s. 63, s. 65.

29. *Jack v. Vermeulen*; *S. v. Casker*.

30. *Criminal Procedure Act*, s. 66(1)(2).

31. *Sebe v. Magistrate, Zwelitsha*, at 890.

32. Ibid., at 890–891.

33. *Criminal Procedure Act*, s. 68.

34. *Maqungu v. Assistant Magistrate, Whittlesea*, 1977(2) SA 359 (E.C.D.).

35. *S. v. Kantor*, 1964(3) SA 377 (W.L.D.).

36. *Criminal Procedure Act*, s. 72.

37. *Attorney General, Transkei v. Additional Magistrate, Umtata,* 1988(3) SA 229 (Tk. S.C.), at 234.

38. *Criminal Procedure Act,* s. 72.

39. *S. v. Sibuya,* 1979(3) SA 192 (T.P.A.); *Criminal Procedure Act,* s. 72.

40. *Keagile v. Attorney General, Transvaal,* 1984(2) SA 816 (T.P.D.), at 820–821.

41. *Attorney General, Transkei v. Additional Magistrate, Umtata,* at 234.

42. *Twayie v. Minister van Justisie,* 1986(2) SA 101 (O.P.A.).

43. *Criminal Procedure Act,* s. 50; *Attorney General, Transkei v. Additional Magistrate, Umtata,* at 233.

44. *S. v. Ramgobin (1),* 1985(3) SA 587 (N.P.D.), at 589; *S. v. De Abreu,* at 100; *S. v. Fourie,* 1973(1) SA 100 (D. & C.L.D.), at 101.

45. *S. v. Ramgobin (1),* at. 589; *S. v. Fourie,* at 101; *Keagile v. Attorney General, Transvaal,* at 821; *S. v. De Abreu,* at 100; *S. v. Baker* 1965(1) SA 821 (W.L.D.), at 822. Although no general constitutional right to bail exists, some of the so-called "homelands" have such a constitutional right under some circumstances. (See *Smith v. Attorney General, Bophuthatswana,* 1984(1) SA 196 (B.S.C.).)

46. *Criminal Procedure Act,* s. 61.

47. *Internal Security Act, 1982,* s. 30.

48. *Criminal Procedure Act,* s. 61(1).

49. Ibid., s. 61(4); *S. v. Chiloane,* 1988(2) SA 41 (T.D.P.).

50. *Criminal Procedure Act,* s. 61(3).

51. Dugard, p. 75.

52. *S. v. Ramgobin (2),* at 589.

53. Ibid., at 589–590. See also *S. v. Ramgobin (1),* at 131; *Bethelezi v. Attorney General, Natal,* 1986(4) SA 377 (D. & C.L.D.) at 379; *S. v. Baleka,* 1986(1) SA 361 (T.D.P.), per Preiss, J. at 392–395, but to the contrary Eloff, J. at 403–404; *S. v. Chiloane,* at 46; *S. v. Genu,* 1988(3) SA 974 (W.L.D.), at 976.

54. *Attorney General, Transkei v. Additional Magistrate, Umtata,* at 234; *Ramgobin (2),* at 589–590.

55. *Buthelezi v. Attorney General, Natal; Attorney General, Transkei v. Additional Magistrate, Umtata; S. v. Ramgobin (1); S. v. Ramgobin (2); S. v. Baleka; Keagile v. Attorney General, Transvaal.*

56. *S. v. Baker,* at 823.

57. *S. v. Mhlawli,* 1963(3) SA 795 (C.P.D.), at 796; *S. v. Ramgobin (2),* at 588.

58. *S. v. Fourie,* at 101; *Keagile v. Attorney General, Transvaal,* at 821; *S. v. Barker,* at 822.

59. *S. v. Fourie,* at 101; *S. v. Ramgobin (2),* at 588–589; *Maqungu v. Assistant Magistrate, Whittlesea,* at 360.

60. *S. v. Hlongwa,* 1979(4) SA 112 (D. & C.L.D.); *S. v. Maharaj,* 1976(3) SA 205 (D. & C.L.D.).

61. *S. v. Mhlawli,* at 796.

62. *S. v. Hlongwa,* at 113; *S. v. Maharaj,* at 208.

63. *S. v. Ramgobin (2),* at 588–589; *S. v. Fourie,* at 101; *S. v. Mhlawli; S. v. Barker; S. v. Nangutuuala,* 1973(4) SA 640 (S.W.A.).

64. *S. v. Fourie,* at 102–103; *S. v. Ho; S. v. Patel,* 1970(3) SA 565 (W.L.D.).

65. *S. v. Russell,* 226; *S. v. Fourie,* at 102–103.

66. *S. v. De Abreu,* at 99; *S. v. Maharaj,* at 208; *S. v. Hlongwa,* at 112; *S. v. Hudson.*

67. *S. v. Hudson; S. v. De Abreu*, at 97–99; *S. v. Maharaj*, at 208; *S. v. Mhlawli*, at 796.

68. *S. v. Maharaj*, at 208–209; *s. v. Hlongwa.*

69. *Criminal Procedure Act*, s. 50; *Attorney General, Transkei v. Additional Magistrate, Umtata*, at 232–234.

70. *Criminal Procedure Act*, s. 60; *Twayie v. Minister van Justisie.*

71. *Criminal Procedure Act*, s. 60; *S. v. Baleka*, 1986(1) SA 361 (T.P.D.), at 374–377, 397.

72. *Criminal Procedure Act*, s. 65; *S. v. Baleka*, at 374–376.

73. *S. v. Ho*, at 737.

74. *S. v. Maliwa*, 1986(3) SA 721 (W.L.D.); Jackson, pp. 137, 143, 145.

75. *Criminal Procedure Act*, s. 63; *S. v. Baleka*, at 376.

76. *Criminal Procedure Act*, s. 68; *Maqungu v. Assistant Magistrate, Whittlesea; Mngemane v. Attorney General, Transvaal*, 1958(2) SA 84 (W.L.D.); *S. v. Casker*, at 507.

77. *S. v. Nkosi*, 1987(1) SA 581 (T.P.A.); *S. v. Barnard*, 1985(4) SA 439 (W.P.A.).

78. *Annual Survey of South African Law, 1977*, p. 447.

79. Dugard, p. 73.

80. J. W. van Greunen, "Own Recognizance," *South African Law Journal* 86 (1969): 93; *S. v. O'Neill*, 1967(4) SA 84 (S.W.A.); Dugard, 76.

81. *Addo-Mills v. Thorpe*, 24 LLR 27 (S.C., 1975), esp. at 34.

82. *Hassen v. Krakue*, 20 LLR 653 (S.C., 1971).

83. *Ndlangamandala v. R.*, 1979–1981 SLR 7 (H.C., 1979).

84. *R. v. Dube (2)*, 1979–1981 SLR 269 (H.C., 1981); *R. v. Cassamo (2)*, 1979–1981 SLR 330 (H.C. 1981), at 334.

85. *Saidi Gurhl Shabel v. Republic*, 1976 LRT n.4. (H.C., 1974), esp. at 15, 16; *Jaffer v. Republic*, 1973 EA 39 (H.C., 1972); *Panju v. Republic*, 1973 EA 282 (H.C., 1972), also 1972 HCD 167, sub nom. *R. V. Panju.*

86. Robert W. Renton and Henry H. Brown, *Criminal Procedure According to the Law of Scotland*, 4th ed., Gerald H. Gordon, ed. (Edinburgh: W. Green & Son, 1972), pp. 47–52.

87. *Bail (Scotland) Act*, s. 1(3), s. 4.

88. D.R.C. Chambers and A.H. Palirvula, *An Introduction to the Law in Papua New Guinea* (Sydney: The Law Book Company Ltd., 1977), p. 104; John A. Griffin, *Criminal Procedure in Papua New Guinea* (Sydney: The Law Book Company Ltd., 1977), pp. 111–123.

89. *Criminal Code*, s. 131, s. 139.

90. *Bail Act*, s. 18(1)(d).

91. Ibid., s. 17, s. 22.

92. Ibid., s. 22(2)(a)(b).

93. *State v. Kaliloboa*, 1986 PNLR 143 (N.C., 1986) at 144. See also *Parakas v. State*, 1985 PNLR 224 (S.C., 1985), at 229–231.

94. *Parakis v. State*, esp. at 227–232, 233, 235, 237.

95. *Bail Act*, s. 19.

96. Ibid., s. 18(1).

97. *Ex parte Smedley*, 1978 PNGLR 156 (N.C., 1978), at 157.

98. *Bail Act*, s. 23; *Re McMillan*, 1980 PNGLR 138 (N.C., 1980); *Ex parte Smedley.*

99. *Bail Act*, s. 28.

100. *Constitution*, Article 43(3).

101. Ibid., Article 43(7).

102. *State v. Paul*, 1986 PNLR 96 (N.C., 1986), at 99.

103. *Bail Act*, s. 9.

104. *Kysely v. State*, 1980 PNGLR 36 (N.C., 1980), at 39.

105. *Bail Act*, s. 9.

106. Ibid., s. 4.

107. *Re Keating*, 1983 PNGLR 133 (S.C., 1983), at 139, 141; *Re Kou Dua*, 1984 PNGLR 22 (N.C., 1984).

108. *Re Diawo*, 1980 PNGLR 148 (S.C., 1980); *Re Awabtawi*, 1980 PNGLR 195 (N.C., 1980).

109. *Re Keating*, at 134, 135, 136, 139, 140; *State v. Paul*, esp. at 99.

110. *Criminal Procedure Ordinance*, s. 12A, s. 13A.

111. Ibid., s. 13AA.

112. Ibid., s. 13AA, s. 13B.

113. *Criminal Procedure Code, Rev. 1983*, s. 136; *Kinyanjui v. Republic*, 1980 Kenya LR 119 (H.C. App. S., 1980).

8

Commercial Bail and Its Alternatives

INTERNATIONAL ASSESSMENT OF COMMERCIAL BAIL

The rejection of commercial bail bonding in the rest of the common law world is both long established and widespread. Antipathy to indemnified bail sureties is discernible in a treatise on bail written in England over two hundred years ago. The crucial developments in the legal struggle against its development occurred in the second half of the nineteenth century. Ironically, the contemporary development of bail law in the United States was offering support to commercial bail. While the U.S. Supreme Court was holding that indemnification of sureties did not affect their rights, courts in three other countries acting independently of each other found the opposite. The fact that the initial anti-indemnification stances in England, India, and Ireland were each developed as cases of first impression mutually confirms their logic that something inherent in the concept of a bail surety is offended by converting the role to a commercial transaction.

The defenses mounted against commercialization of bail in other countries have three prongs. First, contracts or less formal agreements to indemnify sureties are treated as illegal contracts that are unenforceable at civil law. Second, bail sureties who are suspected of being indemnified are rejected, and if the circumstances indicate that all potential sureties might be indemnified bail may be refused completely. A variation on this places sureties believed to be indemnified in a disadvantageous position regarding mitigation of forfeitures. Third, agreements for the indemnification of sureties are regarded as criminal conspiracy subject to punishment.

The first of these defenses against compensated bail emerged in England between the 1850s and 1881. In an independent beginning, Indian courts initiated a similar response in 1878. Crucial holdings placing commercialized bail agreements squarely within the ambit of illegal, unenforceable contracts occurred over the following quarter century. Partial indemnifications were accepted as adequate to constitute the illegality, and fees paid over the amount of the bail were viewed as part of the evidence of indemnification. Third-party indemnifications were also held to be covered. Although the focal point of these refinements was in the English courts, those of India and New Zealand actively contributed to them as well. This civil law obstruction remains the principal defense against commercialism in India and other countries of the region.

Equally informative of the world view of compensated bail with the refusal to enforce contracts for it is the reason given for refusal. In the view of court after court, such agreements constitute a public mischief and therefore are contrary to public policy. Their mischief lies in their depriving the public of the security for an accused's appearance sought by requiring the surety. To the extent that a surety is indemnified, these courts perceive them to have lost their motivations to secure the accused's presence in court. Upon this perception, courts in India, Australia, and South Africa have supported disciplining lawyers for professional misconduct when they have abetted such arrangements.

The origin of the second defense, rejecting potentially indemnified sureties and denying bail, is in Irish cases of the mid-nineteenth century. Here, where any and all potential sureties were likely to be indemnified, grounds for denying bail was held to exist. The principle that a surety should be rejected when indemnification is suspected is perhaps the most widespread of all remedies against commercial bail. Nigeria, for example, which has not developed case law regarding the other preventative measures, has included surety indemnification among its reasons to deny bail. The reason given for it in the early Irish cases is also telling: not to deny bail in the face of a threat of indemnified sureties would aid in defeating the ends of justice.

A variation upon this defense treats possible indemnification as a consideration against mitigation of forfeiture where an accused has failed to appear. This is apparently the most actively used discouragement of compensated bail in Pakistan. It is also a significant consideration in Australian case law, particularly in that of the state of Victoria. A further variation upon the same basic principal is the finding in the legal opinions of several countries that corporate sureties are unacceptable. By their nature they are thought more immune to remedies against indemnification than personal sureties, and therefore they are not permitted.

The third defense against bail for compensation reveals most about the attitude toward commercial bail throughout the common law world. It constitutes a crime in many countries. Agreements to indemnify bail sureties have been punishable as a criminal conspiracy in English law since just after the turn of the twentieth century. The perceived nature of the illegality rendering it criminal is probably the aspect most informative of the view taken elsewhere of such activity. It is viewed as a public mischief in that it attempts to pervert and obstruct the course of justice. The view is expressed in cases from many jurisdictions worldwide including England, Australian states, New Zealand, Tanzania, and South Africa. It is accepted in many others.

The message to be derived from this extensive effort of courts worldwide to prevent an essential aspect of commercial bail—payments to a surety—is amplified in the legislative endorsement of the effort implicit in the statutory enactments on bail of the 1970s and 1980s. Many of these included statutory provisions making explicit that compensated bail activities are crimes and eliminating any ambiguities that might be created by too narrow an interpretation of the word *indemnify*. In numerous instances studies preparatory to the statutory change surveyed the alternatives presented worldwide and made very pointed pleas to prevent American-style commercial bail by this section of their legislation.

The Canadian example is the most informative of a number of well-taken lessons provided in this wave of legislation. Even prior to the 1970s legislation, Canada had taken the lead in declaring by statute that surety indemnification was a crime. Proximity to the negative U.S. examples seem likely to have influenced this. As formulated from the 1950s, compensated bail suretyship was included under the offense category of willful attempt to obstruct, pervert, or defeat the course of justice. Grouped with it under this class of crime was bribing witnesses or jurors. This classification provides as graphic an illustration as any of the view taken elsewhere of the commercial bail system.

The Canadian reform of this provision in the 1970s, given that compensated bail was already criminal, strengthened that provision. Concern that the word *indemnification* might be too narrowly interpreted had been expressed. The law was therefore modified to explicitly include within the crime any payment of a fee or agreement to pay a fee to a surety. No longer would this be illegal only under the construction that it constituted partial indemnification. Third-party indemnification was also specifically covered along with the already existing specifications of indemnfication in kind and partial indemnification. The result produced for Canada the most carefully comprehensive statute on compensated sureties yet devised.

In short, whereas only the Philippines has adopted a U.S.-style commercial bail system, the rest of the common law heritage countries not only reject it, but many take steps to defend against its emergence. Whether they employ criminal or only civil remedies to obstruct its development, the underlying view is the same. Bail that is compensated in whole or in part is seen as perverting the course of justice. As these jurisdictions understand the logic of bail suretyship, to be paid for its provision or to be protected against possible loss by forfeiture undermines its proper working.

ALTERNATIVE FORMS OF BAIL

Four methods of controlling the accused's appearance can be identified among those common law countries eschewing the commercial approach. These are recognizance, criminal penalties, nonfinancial control of conduct, and noncommercial financial security deposit. Depending upon which of these predominates in a given jurisdiction, its bail system can be placed into one of four categories. Nevertheless, since all bail systems are blends of more than one of these methods, on one hand subtypes can be distinguished within bail system categories, and on the other hand systems in one category may blend into those of another. Each bail category has its own strengths and weaknesses in defending against commercialization. Some are more vulnerable to it than others.

Very much the most common type of bail system is the recognizance system. The principal control exercised under this system is a pledge to pay money to the state if the accused defaults in appearing in court when required. At the core of this arrangement is a conditional debt entered into by the accused in favor of the state. The condition is the accused's appearance as required. Upon violation of that condition the debt is incurred. In traditional recognizance systems a similar undertaking by one or more sureties who agree to produce the accused is typically required. Under these recognizances no money is paid prior to a declaration of a default on appearance. Although in many jurisdictions sureties may be dispensed with, that is not commonly done. However, in England prior to 1976 and New Zealand prior to 1987 an accused's recognizance without sureties was the common form of release.

Various mixtures of other controls may be added to this core provision. Although traditionally deposit of cash or security is not required at the time of release under this approach, a common modification provides for this to be allowed at the initiative of the accused—not the court—in place of sureties. A few countries, moving in the direction of the modified recognizance system, permit courts to require deposits. Similarly, nonfinancial conditions can be added to bail terms in certain situations in many of these countries. These are widely limited to discretionary bails or to superior courts. Again, however, some jurisdictions tending toward modified recognizance systems permit these more widely. Criminal penalties can also be created for absconders, but this is less common and represents a partial modification of the traditional system.

Fully modified recognizance systems keep their recognizance core but provide by statute for all of these other controls to be employed as supplements when needed. They are marked by a hierarchical arrangement of the alternatives thus created. Upon a finding of necessity, courts can advance up the hierarchy to the level of burdensomeness of controls found necessary.

Recognizance systems of the traditional type are not particularly vulnerable to the development of commercially provided bail. Since no payment is required of either the accused or any sureties unless a default occurs, the impetus to seek bail from a commercial source is limited. Only in instances where an individual cannot find sureties or where bail is unusually large would a commercial option even be tempting. Courts counter this by looking for personal ties between accused and sureties. In addition, it is precisely when sureties are unavailable that a deposit is permitted as a lesser evil to a commercial surety. This small proportion of cases where commercially provided bail might be tempting is not likely to be capable of sustaining an ongoing commercial system. Moreover, these cases are likely to involve high risk defendants who would not be commercially attractive.

The second category of bail system is the criminal penalty system. This is a relatively recent form, the product of the 1970s reforms. Consequently, to date only a comparatively few jurisdictions, including England, Canada, and New South Wales, have instituted this form. Numerous countries in addition use these punishments as a supplement to their main bail form. Under this bail form the chief control imposed upon a released accused is the threat of criminal penalties for absconding. Not only is no deposit of money or securities required of the defendant but no financial pledge or conditional debt is exacted. Failure to appear is treated as any other crime and punished upon conviction by a fine or imprisonment.

As with the recognizance systems, other modes of control are able to be added to the central one. England does not use the accused's own recognizance, but it is still available in Canada and New South Wales. Sureties are generally a supplementary option. Cash deposit is most restricted in England and least restricted in New South Wales, providing less onerous terms are judged inadequate. Scotland, however, puts considerable emphasis upon deposit. Nonfinancial conditions are particularly compatible with a criminal penalties approach. The accused can be released with these behavioral controls and then punished if he fails to appear in court.

Under the criminal penalties form of bail even less opening is offered to commercial provision of bail than under the typical recognizance system. Since in most cases no deposit, pledge, or surety is required, obtaining bail is not a pertinent consideration. To the extent that deposits or even sureties are required, some opening is offered to potential commercialism. However, the use of these alternatives are placed under sufficiently concrete restrictions in all such systems so that the opportunity for sustaining ongoing commercial bail activity is not a substantial threat. Furthermore, among the jurisdictions with this bail form are to be found some of the best available criminal statutes against indemnification.

The third category of bail system is the nonfinancial conditions system. Under this approach the chief control exercised to secure the accused's appearance is the set of conditions placed upon the behavior of the accused when released. These may include, for example, periodic reporting to police or others and restrictions on travel and residence. Only two jurisdictions having particularly favorable geographical situations appear to rely principally upon this form. However, it is widely used as a supplement to other forms. As noticed, it has characteristics particularly complementary to the criminal penalties form.

As with other bail forms, methods of control may be borrowed from the other types and added to the principal one under this form. Australia's Northern Territory does this on a hierarchical scale of onerousness with advances requiring justification, but does not add criminal penalties. New Zealand, alternatively, makes available criminal penalties but moves all power to impose financial bail terms to the upper courts.

Under New Zealand's version of this category absolutely no room for commercial bail exists in the lower courts. The occasion for it simply cannot arise. Superior court bails are very unlikely to be numerous enough to support a commercial bail enterprise even if these could be gotten past the greater scrutiny to which bail matters can normally be subjected in the higher courts. To the extent that sureties and deposits are used in the Northern Territory a theoretical opening to commercialism exists. However, this remains less than in the recognizance systems. The law against indemnification, moreover, is quite plain in that jurisdiction.

The fourth alternative is the noncommercial financial security deposit system. This is not widely used in spite of the fact that enough instances of such systems can be found to demonstrate that emphasizing financial bail deposits in a system is perfectly possible without their being commercially provided. South Africa bases its bails upon such deposits and they are a major component of the bail systems in Papua New Guinea, Liberia, Hong Kong, Kenya, and Scotland. They are also available as a supplement to the principal bail form in most countries, although frequently their employment is significantly restricted. Under this type of bail an accused is released typically upon making a cash deposit. Whether and what other valuables may be substituted for cash in the security deposit varies from country to country. If the accused appears as required, the deposit is refunded. If not, it is forfeited. Typically the money or valuable may be provided by either the accused or another. Generally such systems make provision for a recognizance-only alternative where a case is thought suitable. Nonfinancial conditions may also be attached to bails in most of these jurisdictions. Criminal penalties have been created for bail defaults in some of these jurisdictions and take an important place under the Scottish law.

Security deposit systems are the most vulnerable to the potential development of commercialism. A defendant who must raise such a deposit prior to release obviously might be tempted to secure it by commercial means. Hence, jurisdictions making extensive use of such deposits have only their laws against compensated bail to defend against commercial development. Consequently, South Africa (as the clearest example of a bail system relying principally upon security deposit) has reinforced its adherence to the common law against surety indemnification with a specific statute created to preclude third parties from providing cash deposit where reason is present to believe that they have received a financial benefit for doing so.

In conclusion, certain points emerge. Virtually the entire body of countries sharing the common law heritage reject commercial bail bonding. They fight against its development with a range of legal provisions up to making it a crime. In many instances they do this with the example of the U.S. system as the archetype of what they wish to prevent. These countries view the commercial bail system found in the United States as an obstruction or perversion of justice rather than as an implementation of it. In the absence of commercially provided bail they are able to formulate workable bail systems of several types. Although some of these are preferable to others, all of them are more rationally constructed to secure the accused's presence at trial than a commercial system in which the accuseds equally lose their bail money whether or not they appear for trial.

CONCLUSION

The opening chapter of this book referred to complaints by a group of bail bondsmen that judges releasing more trustworthy defendants without a bail bond placed these bondsmen in an unfair dilemma. The group members, as a consequence, had to choose between reduced profits from accepting higher-risk clients or making the effort to bring bail violators before the courts. With the international perspective in mind, the truly preposterous nature of this argument is blatantly clear. Nowhere outside of American jurisdictions would such an argument be taken seriously. Elsewhere, excepting only the Philippines, no question would exist of the appropriateness of releasing low-risk defendants on, at most, their personal recognizance. Moreover, elsewhere, including the Philippines, no question would arise of the duty of sureties to make the effort to secure the appearance of the accused. That is their principal obligation. Forfeiture is a sanction for failure, not an alternative presented on a par for the surety's cost/benefit-motivated choice. Finally, elsewhere, the criminality or illegality of payments to sureties would settle the complaints based on their reduced profit margin. Even in those jurisdictions where surety payments are not illegal, the absurdity of basing decisions about bail terms on their maximization would be plain from their general disrepute.

Why, then, are such arguments seriously entertained in the United States? One answer is lack of awareness of the alternatives, or even that alternatives exist. A recent student, upon learning that compensated bail is a crime in some countries, exemplified this by responding, "What in the world do they do instead?" The commercial system is often seen as a necessary evil even by those who are aware of specific abuses. As the judge in *Stephens v. Bonding Association of Kentucky* remarked, it exists because no better system has been provided. The difficulty arises since, if commercialism is necessary, then any reform which lessens its viability by reducing its profitability is suspect. In reality it is not necessary; rather, it is an unscrutinized evil. The rest of the criminal law world does without it much better than American jurisdictions do with it.

Do commercial bail bondsmen ever perform a socially useful function? Intermittently they do. The point to be learned from the bail systems in other countries is that their systems accomplish these functions regularly and purposefully, without imposing the cost upon defendants of supporting bondsmen. In return for their support in commercial systems, the bondsmen in most cases perform no real service, and when they do perform one they do so no better, if as well, as in these alternative systems.

The commercial bail bonding system in most American jurisdictions is, in sum, an international embarrassment. For the price of its inherent ineffectiveness and tendency to corruption, only one advantage is obviously provided by it that could not more effectively be provided by other alternatives. As a sort of intellectual foreign aid it has served, and continues to serve, not only as a warning to other countries in the common law tradition to avoid it, but also as a laboratory demonstrating—given a modicum of study on their part—how to avoid it. Most have learned well.

Selected Bibliography

AUSTRALIA

Aronson, M. I., et al. *Litigation: Evidence and Procedure*. Sydney: Butterworths, 1982. Chapter 15.

Bishop, John. *Criminal Procedure*. Sydney: Butterworths, 1983. Chapter 4.

Bureau of Crime Statistics and Research (N.S.W.). *Bail Reform in N.S.W.* Sydney: B.C.S.R. Attorney General's Department, 1984.

Bureau of Crime Statistics and Research and Criminal Law Review Division, "Bail in N.S.W." *Crime and Justice Bulletin* June 1987.

Cook, Catriona, ed. *A.C.I. Supplement to the Law Handbook (N.S.W.)*, 3rd ed. Canberra: Faculty of Law, Australian National University, 1985. Part 3.

Devine, F. D. *Bail in Australia*. Canberra: Australian Institute of Criminology, 1989.

Director of Public Prosecutions' Working Party on Drug Legislation. *Bail in Drug Cases*. Melbourne: 1988.

Donovan, B. H. K. *The Law of Bail: Practice, Procedure and Principle*. Sydney: Legal Books, 1981. Chapter 3.

Gardiner, J. R., et al. *Legal Resources Book*. Melbourne: Fitzroy Legal Services (updated looseleaf service).

Herlihy, J. M., and R. G. Kenny. *An Introduction to Criminal Law in Queensland and Western Australia*, 2nd ed. Sydney: Butterworths, 1984, pp. 552–560.

Legal Services Commission of South Australia. Regina Graycar, et al., eds. *Legal Resources Book (S.A.)*. Allen & Unwin (Aust.), updated service. Chapter 3.

Lynch, John. "The Bail Act Ten Years on." *Law Institute Journal (Vic.)* 61 (Nov. 1987): 1125–1126.

McKelvey, Chris and Noel Nunan. *Legal Resource Book (Qld.)*. Brisbane: Caxton Street Legal Services, 1983. Chapter 3.

Mobbs, Michael, ed. *Legal Resources Book (N.S.W.)*. Sydney: Redfern Legal Centre, 1978–1982.

Nash, Gerald. *Magistrates' Courts*. North Ryde (N.S.W.): The Law Book Co., updated service. Part 2.

Office of Crime Statistics, South Australia. *Bail Reform in South Australia*. Adelaide: 1986.

Sikk, E., and I. R. Matterson. *Tasmanian Commentary to Ward and Kelly Summary Justice*. North Ryde: The Law Book Co., 1984. Chapter 4.

Stubbs, Julie, and John S. Andrews. "A Review of the Operation of the N.S.W. Bail Act 1978." In Mark Findlay et al., eds., *Issues in Criminal Justice Administration*. Sydney: Allen & Unwin, 1983, 83–95.

Ward, Michael, and P. M. St. L. Kelly. *Summary Justice*. North Ryde (N.S.W.): The Law Book Co., updated to 1988. Part 9.

Weatherburn, Don, et al. "Drug Charges, Bail Decisions and Absconding." *Australian and New Zealand Journal of Criminology* 20 (1987): 95–109.

BANGLADESH

Dacca Law Reports. *The Law on Bail*. Dacca: Dacca Law Reports Office, 1985.

Zahirul Huq. *Law and Practice of Criminal Procedure*. Chittagong: Ayesha Mahal (Pub.), 1980.

CANADA

Barton, P. G., and N. A. Peel. *Criminal Procedure in Practice*. Toronto: Butterworths, 1979, pp. 114–132.

Peltomaa, Arthur. "Bail Hearings and the Charter of Rights and Freedoms." *Criminal Law Quarterly* 24 (1981–1982): 427–429.

Powell, Clay M. *Arrest and Bail in Canada*. Toronto: Butterworths, 1976.

Scollin, John A. *Pre-Trial Release*. Toronto: Carswell, 1977.

ENGLAND

Anthony and Berryman's Magistrates' Court Guide. A. P. Carr, ed. London: Butterworths, 1987 pp. 411–419.

Brinks, Barbara, and Christopher Stone. "Defendants Who Do Not Ask for Bail." *Criminal Law Review* (1988): 154–162.

Chatterton, Clifford. *Bail: Law and Practice*. London: Butterworths, 1986.

Doherty, M. J., and R. East. "Bail Decisions in Magistrates' Courts. *British Journal of Criminology* 25 (1985): 251– 266.

Gibbs, Frances. "Variations in Bail at Magistrates Courts." *The Times*, 28 Nov. 1984, p. 5.

Holdham, Susan. "Nottingham Justices—Where Are We Now?" *New Law Journal* (1985): 471–472.

Lydiate, P. W. H. "Bail Proceedings in Magistrates' Courts." *Justice of the Peace* 151 (1987): 164–167, 181–183.

Raymond, Brian. *Bail: A Practical Guide*. London: Oyez, 1979.

INDIA

Battacharjee, A. M. "*Maneka Gandhi* and Law of Bail." *Criminal Law Journal* 89 (1983): 14–19.

Hatolkar, L. K. "Concept of 'Bail' and Some Conflicting Views." *Criminal Law Journal* 89 (1983): 37–40.

Mehrotra, K. C. *Law of Bails, Forfeiture of Bonds and Habeas Corpus*, 2nd ed. Revised A. N. Saha. Lucknow: Eastern Book Co., 1985.

Narula, R. K. *Jail or Bail*. Bombay: Himalaya Publishing House, 1979.

Pannalal Dhar. "Anticipatory Bail." *Criminal Law Journal* 89 (1983): 35–36.

Prasad, Vindeshwari. *The Law of Bails*, 3rd ed. Revised R. N. Misra. Allahabad: Hind Publishing House, 1985.

Shri Pradyot Kumar Sen Gupta. "Detention or Remand of the Accused Persons." *Criminal Law Journal* 89 (1983): 12–14.

Singh, K. K. *Law of Bails*. Allahabad: National Law Agency, 1986.

IRELAND

Ryan, Edward F., and Philip Magee. *The Irish Criminal Process*. Dublin: The Mercier Press, 1983. Chapter 7.

NEW ZEALAND

Criminal Law Reform Committee. *Report on Bail*. Wellington: Criminal Law Reform Committee, 1982.

Garrow, J. M. E., and R. A. Caldwell. *Criminal Law in New Zealand*. Wellington: Butterworths, 1981.

Tan, Jacintha Chai. "The Law Relating to Bail." Thesis, University of Auckland, 1985.

NIGERIA

Aguda, Takinola. *The Criminal Law and Procedure of the Southern States of Nigeria*. London: Sweet & Maxwell, 1982.

Jones, Jeffrey Richard. *Criminal Procedure in the Northern States of Nigeria*. Zairia: Gaskiya Corp., 1979.

PAKISTAN

Mahmood, Shaukat. *Law of Bail*. Lahore: Legal Research Centre, 1987.

PAPUA NEW GUINEA

O'Neill, N. K. F., and R. W. Desailly. *The Criminal Jurisdiction of Magistrates in Papua New Guinea*. Sydney: New South Wales Institute of Technology, 1982.

SOUTH AFRICA

Lansdown, Alfred V. *South African Criminal Law and Procedure*. Cape Town: Juta, 1982. Volume 5.

Index

ABOUT THE AUTHOR

F. E. DEVINE is Professor of Criminal Justice at the University of Southern Mississippi. Among his publications are several monographs and numerous articles on comparative criminal justice that have appeared in journals in England, Australia, and the United States. Some of the research for this book was conducted in Australia under a Fulbright Senior Scholar Award in Law.